TWO
TALES
OF A
CITY

TWO TALES OF A CITY

REBUILDING CHICAGO'S ARCHITECTURAL AND

SOCIAL LANDSCAPE, 1986–2005

Gail Satler

Foreword by Lee Bey

NORTHERN ILLINOIS UNIVERSITY PRESS / DeKalb

Published by the Northern Illinois University Press, DeKalb, Illinois   60115

Manufactured in the United States using acid-free paper

Design by Julia Fauci

Library of Congress Cataloging-in-Publication Data

Satler, Gail.

Two tales of a city: rebuilding Chicago's architectural and social landscape, 1986–2005 /

Gail Satler; foreword by Lee Bey.

    p.   cm.

Includes bibliographical references and index.

ISBN-13: 978-0-87580-357-9 (clothbound : alk. paper)

ISBN-10: 0-87580-357-1 (clothbound : alk. paper)

1. Urban renewal—Illinois—Chicago. 2. Inner cities—Illinois—Chicago.

3. Community development—Illinois—Chicago. 4. City planning—Illinois—Chicago.

I. Title.

HT177.C5S28 2006

307.3'4160977311—dc22

2005029768

For Chicago—its people and its places

CONTENTS

FOREWORD

Lee Bey

It's a warm afternoon in Chicago and people have nearly jammed a half-mile of Michigan Avenue sidewalk between Washington and Jackson. The crowd is made up of office workers and the typical downtown habitués. But they are outnumbered by tourists, souvenir hunters, young mothers with strollers, and young lovers strolling. Empty nesters are walking arm-in-arm, taking in the sights. An R&B- and jazz-flavored brass band performs an impromptu concert while selling CDs of their music to passersby.

That this eastern border of Chicago's downtown area is teeming with life is one of the most significant urban revival stories in America right now. A decade ago, Chicago's downtown was suffering. The commerce that had kept it going had slowly decamped for suburban office parks and the glitz of North Michigan Avenue—the famed Magnificent Mile—located across the Chicago River several blocks north.

Downtown's main stem, State Street, was then a shell of its former self. Turned into an ill-kempt pedestrian mall in 1979, the famed street had devolved into fast-food restaurants and discount clothing emporiums. The Carson Pirie Scott and Marshall Field's stores remained; the old swells who stuck around after the once grand neighborhood hit the skids.

The irrepressible city that rebuilt itself after the Great Fire of 1871 and created a modern downtown during the rise of suburbia following World War II was able to pull its central business district back from the brink of disaster in the late 1990s. How did it happen? And who were the people who made it happen? In this book, Gail Satler undertakes an important task, not only detailing how Chicago is rejuvenating its downtown—and make no mistake, the process is ongoing—but also interviewing the principals who are making it happen.

We learn, for instance, that Chicago embraced the universities that were converting former office buildings into classroom and dorm space. Instead of bemoaning the student population, the city welcomed students into the mix, as a stabilizing force downtown. Chicago officials also used special tax-increment financing to pump hundreds of millions of dollars into downtown redevelopment and streetscape improvements. With TIF financing, property tax increases are held within a TIF district for redevelopment purposes.

Chicago also pushed for residential development within the downtown area, laying odds that this would help. The downtown is no longer left empty at 5 p.m., when it is abandoned by office workers. Now it is a neighborhood with activity around the clock.

The most significant development is the superlative lakefront Millennium Park, a $550 million addition to Grant Park over a sunken, active railyard that for a century had blighted Michigan Avenue between Randolph and Adams. The city covered the cost of the park, while the stupendous amenities were funded by city corporations, millionaires, and billionaires. The park features a huge public fountain in which children and businesspeople alike wade on hot days. There are a visually stunning musical bandshell and a pedestrian bridge, both designed by Frank Gehry, and an ice-skating rink along Michigan that is destined to become a staple in any Chicago-based romance movie from this day forward. There is a Sea Grill–style restaurant, with landscaping and overlooks. The park drew 3 million visitors in its first full year of operation in 2005. This is partly why the sidewalks of Michigan Avenue are crowded with every kind of humanity on any given day. The pull of Millennium Park is just that strong.

Cities across the country are looking for ways to revamp their downtowns. This book provides a roadmap. Chicago is celebrated now. Mayor Richard M. Daley, who presided over this dramatic turnaround, was given a prophet's welcome when he visited Toronto to discuss urban redevelopment issues in 2005. But it was not that long ago that Chicago seemed an object lesson in the failure of big cities. In the closing decades of the twentieth century, Chicago no longer made steel, stacked wheat, butchered hogs, or performed any of the tasks that had made it such a city of legend. Sunbelt cities took the jobs, and the suburbs, with their growing populations and political power, were threatening to finish off the aged city for good.

The resurrection of Chicago's downtown happened with a plan, and this book underscores the importance of solid, visionary urban planning. To the outsider, Chicago may seem to be a plucky, shoot-for-the-stars type of a city—and it is. But since the Chicago Plan of 1909, the city almost never shoots successfully without a forecast followed by some type of plan. It is a lesson from which other cities can learn. The city developed plans for State Street, and it gave landmark status to the architecturally significant ensemble of Michigan Avenue buildings that now overlook Millennium Park.

The city's willingness to stand behind its downtown—and to put down the necessary money—gave developers the confidence to do the same. There are substantial new buildings on Dearborn, Wacker Drive, and other major streets downtown. A block west of Millennium Park, a namesake building is being erected. The fifty-seven-story Heritage at Millennium Park condominium tower (where the units sell for as high as $3.25 million) overlooks the park, each its own amenity. New York developer Donald Trump is building a ninety-story glass residential tower on the Chicago River, replacing the squat, coffin-shaped former confines of the *Chicago Sun-Times* newspaper headquarters. Trump International Hotel and Tower is the city's tallest building since the Sears Tower was completed in 1974.

And if other cities are taking note of the triumphs in this book, they would do well to mark the failures also. At this writing, Chicago has still failed to rebuild downtown's notorious Block 37, a three-acre site across State Street from the Marshall Field's flagship store. Once a tattered but functioning block of stores, aged office buildings, and single-screen movie theaters dating from the 1920s, the block was condemned and razed in 1989 by city officials, who crossed their fingers that a planned new Magnificent Mile–style retail-residential-hotel complex would save the block and the Loop. That nothing has been built at Block 37 after sixteen years is a warning to all cities not to hang their hats on a megaproject. Ironically, the Loop began to pick up, without the block's being developed, and the gaping hole remains a blight to downtown. But Chicago has never stopped trying to crack the mystery of Block 37. It has courted Macy's, Harrods, and any other big retailer it could dial up. At this point, the current proposal features a wealth of retail, but without a huge retail anchor, while hotel and residential aspects remain sketchy.

The current proposal also features a stroke of genius, which was missing from other plans and which may be the trick in getting the current proposal jumpstarted: an underground rail station with a straight, nonstop link to O'Hare International Airport. O'Hare-bound passengers could perform all their preboarding functions at the station, and then be whisked along the rails to the airport. If the link were to prove fast, convenient, and architecturally attractive, it might be the seed that grows the rest of what is undoubtedly a billion-dollar project.

That's Chicago. Pushing. Thinking. Planning. Building. Solving.

ACKNOWLEDGMENTS

While writing is a solitary and isolating experience, getting to and through it is, thankfully, a communal one. Many people extended assistance and support to me during this six-year endeavor. I thank them all. I would especially like to acknowledge those who have been truly heroic during the process. Funding for the project was generously provided through grants from the AIA College of Fellows, the Richard H. Driehaus Foundation, the Graham Foundation, and a Presidential Award from Hofstra University.

In New York my dean at Hofstra University, David Christman, facilitated additional monies, offered insightful observations and feedback on parts of my manuscript, and was always willing to provide an ear and a strong shoulder. Monica Yatsyla created order and beauty out of the chaos that thousands of photos produce. She did it with patience, skill, and a smile. Linda Merklin and her staff assisted me in typing the manuscript and its many revisions. Victor Scotto and Brooke Jamieson provided a hideaway during the initial stages of this project at the Chateau Briand, and Chef Carlo DeGaudenzi provided me with food for my soul as well as my stomach. Te amo.

In Chicago, Saskia Sassen opened her home to me so I could make all the trips I needed in order to interview and observe. She is also the finest mentor, muse, and role model one could have. The women of the photo department in East 55th Street Walgreens in Hyde Park—Patrice, Kimberly, Yolanda, Lakisha, and Lula—lovingly developed thousands of photos and cheered me on. To all the accommodating people at the City of Chicago Department of Planning and Development, Department of Aviation, Greater State Street Council, Art Institute, and at the Chicago Historical Society, and all the architectural firms working magic in the city who gave of their time, knowledge, interest, and encouragement, I would like to say I am humbled and most grateful. They reify and reaffirm the slogan given to Chicago as "The city that works"—and then some.

From California, Keith Mendenhall of Frank O. Gehry Partners provided access to all the materials I needed during the building of the Pritzker Music Pavilion as well as to Frank Gehry himself. Keith also provided invaluable feedback, encouragement, and (when needed) comic relief.

The enthusiastic and hardworking people at Northern Illinois University Press have transformed what was first in my head, and then on paper and film, into a coherent book. This is my second project with them and I hope not the last.

On a daily basis, my students, my friends, and especially my family—
Helen and Ignatz and Helen and Sol Satler—have always encouraged me
to do what I believe in. They never allowed me to give up; they are my
rock and my salvation. And when all else failed, I sought and received divine intervention from Bertrand Goldberg. I know he knows how much I
wanted to write this book about his Chicago . . . and now mine.

LIST OF ABBREVIATIONS

ATA	American Trans Air
BBB	Beyer Blinder Belle
CAP	*The City's Central Area Plan, 2000–2002.* City of Chicago DPD 2000a
CBD	Central Business District
CCFP	Cook County Forest Preserve
CDOE	Chicago Department of the Environment
CDOT	Chicago's Department of Transportation
CHA	Chicago Housing Authority
CLA	Chicago Loop Alliance
CRCD	*Chicago River Corridor Development* (1999) plan
CRCDGS	Chicago River Corridor Design Guidelines and Standards (1999)
CTA	Chicago Transit Authority
CZT	Concentric Zone Theory
DOA	Department of Aviation
DPD	Department of Planning and Development
EL	elevated trains that encircle the Loop area, also known as the "L"
FAA	Federal Aviation Administration
FHA	Federal Housing Authority
GFRC	Glass-reinforced concrete
GGN	Gustafson Guthrie Nichols, LLP
gsf	gross square feet

GSSC　　Greater State Street Council (now known as the Chicago Loop Alliance—CLA)

HWC　　Harold Washington College

IMM　　International Monetary Market

ISTEA　　(Federal) Intermodal Surface Transportation Efficiency Act of 1991

LAN　　Local Area Network

LED　　light-emitting diode

the Loop　term used to designate Chicago's CBD

the Merc　the Chicago Mercantile Exchange

MWRD　　Metropolitan Water Reclamation District of Greater Chicago

NBG　　National Budget Group

NEGSC　　*A New Economy Growth Strategy for Chicagoland* (2001)

OMP　　O'Hare Modernization Program

RFP　　Request for Proposals

SCB　　Solomon Cordwell Buenz & Associates

SOC　　Suburban O'Hare Commission

SOM　　Skidmore, Owings & Merrill

SRO　　Single Residence Occupancy

SSA　　State Street Special Service Area

SSC　　State Street Commission

TIF　　Tax Increment Financing

WAN　　Wide Area Network

TWO
TALES
OF A
CITY

THE QUESTION OF CENTRALITY

"Chicago," observed architect Laurence Booth, "is the middle surrounded by America" (Booth, in Zukowsky 1984, 78). Perhaps nowhere more than for Chicago has the notion of centrality been so essential to a city's internal and external definition and character. Yet, as Booth's description implies, centrality embodies a certain amount of duplicity. Initially the concept seems obvious but in fact is more complex. The presence afforded the city by its geography is fixed and clear, but its sense of place—achieved in relationship with what surrounds it—is more elusive. Which component provides Chicago with its meaning: the physical or the social? Both do, even though at times they stand in contradiction to each other.

Founded on the edge of the country's frontier in the early 1800s, the city soon came to serve as gateway between east and west sections of America, as well as heartland of the rest of America. By the late nineteenth century, Chicago had become the archetypal modern city, shaped by industrialization, powered by unprecedented physical and population growth. The world watched as Chicago took center stage for all that could go right and all that could go wrong for a city in the making.

The building designs pioneered here in the 1880s, 1890s, and early 1900s by a group of innovative architects, collectively known as the Chicago School of Architecture, were central to this new city type. Perhaps more a compilation of attitudes and approaches than any one style, the Chicago School was "bold, willing to break strongly with the past and show in its designs the technological innovation that makes such departures possible" (Portman, in Zukowsky 1984, 83). The buildings embodied a sense of openness, pragmatism, and experimentation. Their creators conceived them as resolutions to the challenges of urban growth, on a canvas that had effectively been wiped clean by the Fire of 1871. But architects and the entrepreneurs they primarily built for were not the only ones who gravitated to Chicago at this time.

As the first generation of Chicago architects were sculpting the city's center, a group of sociologists converged at the newly built University of Chicago in order to study and reframe the new cityscape into a decipherable whole. Using Chicago as their laboratory, they devised a variety of empirical techniques for studying urban life, marrying theory and practice, physical and social growth patterns. Although not officially affiliated with the architects, members of the Chicago School of Sociology understood the power of the city's physical image. Yet they also knew that the city was something more than its formal presence. One of the Chicago School's earliest and most prominent practitioners, sociologist Robert Ezra Park, wrote: "The city is not merely a physical mechanism and an artificial construction. It is involved in the vital processes of the people who compose it" (Park [1925] 1967, 1). Meticulously mapping, tallying, and documenting the life histories of Chicago's inhabitants as they underwent rapid and radical change, Park and his colleagues literally took social theory into the streets of the city. More specifically, they set out to investigate the reflexive relationship between human interaction and spatial form, the city's human ecology, neighborhood by neighborhood.

Along with his colleague Ernest Burgess, Park formalized physical and social changes that occurred as a result of the city's growth in the early twentieth century. Their theory, the Concentric Zone Theory, captured a sense of the city parallelling the dynamic current that lies beneath a seemingly placid body of water, as when a pebble is tossed into the water—ripples form, grow, and expand, the staid body comes to life and the source of its power is revealed, that is, the deeper and interconnected effects that local and ordinary events can have on the larger whole become visible. At the core of the Concentric Zone Theory was the zone known as the Central Business District (CBD), a term Park and Burgess coined to denote the space "where the economic, cultural and political life centers; where local and outside transportation converged" (Burgess, in Park 1967, 52). They envisioned the CBD as being as much a space defined by the mobility it afforded through transportation and communication networks moving in and out of it as a place for these networks and for people to converge.

GOLDBERG'S VISION—CREATING RIPPLES

During the 1950s and 1960s, cities across America including Chicago experienced a large outmigration to the newly built suburbs. In this movement, the CBD weakened and the center began to shift. A new sense of centrality and the role of the city emerged. Among the first visions for the city was the one created by Chicago architect Bertrand Goldberg (1913–1997). Born and raised in Chicago, he was passionate about cities, and about his own in particular. His clear strong sense of Chicago changed the city's physical and social landscape profoundly. Hoping to lure families, particularly middle-income families, to Chicago, Goldberg used the assets of the city's Central Area—the proximity to workplace and shopping and, no less important, the uplifting experience of living beside the water.

Goldberg viewed the Loop, Chicago's CBD, as the city's life force not only because it was the commercial hub but also because it was a place for people (including families) to live. In this, he sharply differed from many of his predecessors and contemporaries, who dismissed the Central Area (and, in some cases, anywhere within the city's boundaries) as a viable place to live and who, more recently, were even beginning to question the role of the city as a center for business. Goldberg also took exception to the commonly held assumption that Lake Michigan and Michigan Avenue were the city's defining couplet. He framed his center instead around the Chicago River and State Street. From these, he found his inspiration and context. On these, he built his most comprehensive statements about Chicago and urban living: Marina City (1962) and River City (1986). Both have become icons of their time and place. Today, they serve as lodestars from which to locate and navigate what is emerging as the new Central Area.

Marina City (1962)

Literally floating on the main branch of the river where it intersects with State and Dearborn streets, Marina City afforded residents an uncluttered view of the city and a tranquil counterpoint to the frantic energy of urban life. "I think," Goldberg recalled, "that the river as a scenic device for relieving the humdrum of urban density had not been recognized, and still hasn't been adequately recognized. . . . People still don't understand the wedding of earth and water" (Goldberg 1992, 192). The pie-shaped rooms of Marina City's two sixty-story cylindrical towers extend into rings of semicircular balconies that transform the smooth cylinders into lively repetitive patterns, further relieving the monotony of the urban landscape.

Following the tradition of the Chicago School, Goldberg used the newest building technologies available to create a structure of many firsts. When Marina City opened in 1962, it was the world's tallest apartment complex and tallest concrete building. It drew thermal energy from the river water. It was an all-electric building, without a central boiler room or chimneys. Its lighting system heated the office space while providing glare-free illumination at a brighter level than any other U.S. office building.

Goldberg clearly understood the ways in which Marina City's engineering would shape the social life of its residents. He intended to foster individuality and allow people to live the way they chose. Because Marina City had no central system for heating and cooling, for example, tenants could at all times control the temperature and ventilation in their own units. At the same time, Goldberg's architectural design encouraged a sense of community. Apartments unfolded like petals, while elevators and garbage rooms were located at the building's stem, so that, coming and going, or merely taking out the trash, tenants were given the opportunity to meet. So too, the laundry rooms dispersed throughout the residential portion offered spaces with spectacular views of the city for residents to interact with one another or to quietly soak in the cityscape. Goldberg's designs reflected his sensitivity concerning architecture's contribution to the quality of life in urban settings, literally elevating what would otherwise have been just another mundane domestic activity into a potentially extraordinary experience.

Marina City was the first mixed-use complex to be built in the United States. In addition to residential units and parking spaces for cars and boats, it housed offices and retail shops. At street level, amenities such as grocery stores and cleaners, and a post office, bowling alley, gym, pool, skating rink, theater, and restaurant allowed people to more easily interweave work and play. Whereas convenience encouraged residents to use facilities within the structure, they could also easily move out into the larger urban terrain and take advantage of what the city, more generally, offered—just as nonresidents could make use of some of Marina City's amenities. In this way, Marina City created a sense of community and security without being isolated from the larger cityscape. Through obvious and subtle design elements, Marina City emphasized connectivity and mobility within each apartment, throughout all parts of the buildings, and with the city more generally.

Marina City was an immediate success. No privately sponsored apartments attracted more attention or were more involved in urban ecology. Marina City changed people's view of where and how they could live in the city. But the city continued to change in other ways also. In the two decades that followed the opening of Marina City, the country's economy was shifting from manufacturing to service. New centers of commerce began to displace older ones as places to work and live. By the 1980s, Chicago found itself competing not just with suburban areas but with cities in other regions of the country that offered better economic and living options.

River City (1986)

In the face of new challenges, Goldberg continued to refine his ideas of urbanism and urban design. His response came in the form of River City. Sited on an abandoned railroad yard, River City anchors the southern branch of the river and the city's South Loop area in much the same way as Marina City anchors the heart of the Central Area. Like Marina City, River City was also located in an area considered by many to be a wasteland, a marginal space, but which Goldberg viewed as an urban frontier, rich with potential. He intended to expand the Loop beyond its traditional boundaries and to build a critical mass so that the amenities he envisioned as essential for a community's viability would have the necessary tax base.

Formally, River City's serpentine-shaped complex offered the possibility of expanding or shrinking apartment size to meet the changing needs of families over time. Goldberg included on-site educational, medical, and recreational facilities in addition to residential, commercial, and retail space. Staff from nearby hospitals were available on-site and through telematic links; a daycare and a preschool established for residents also welcomed children from the larger community. Landscaping was an important design element of River City. Here again, Goldberg fostered individuality and community simultaneously. Each resident could choose the flowers or foliage for the planters installed in front of their apartment, while neighbors decided collectively what to grow in the common planters lining the internal walkways. These plantings softened the rather massive concrete and glass structure to create a more human and natural environment.

As at Marina City, Goldberg aimed to connect his creation to the rest of Chicago. River City was designed to link the South Loop with the greater city by means of, in Goldberg's terms, real and virtual river roads. The street level and marina were designed with pathways connecting River City to the larger Central Area. Computers and cable access would virtually connect residents to various medical, educational, and cultural facilities. Goldberg believed that by enticing people to move beyond the limits of what was viewed as the city's traditional center, to areas perceived as marginal, the center could shift and expand south and west of its historic frame. Only the first stage of the project was built, with many modifications and concessions. Whereas River City did not enjoy the success of Marina City, it did set changes in motion. But it would take nearly two decades for Goldberg's initial efforts to take hold and come to fruition.

At the time of River City's opening in 1986, Chicago was experiencing what was probably its most critical point in recent history. No less significant than the Fire of 1871, this crisis was precipitated, in part, by the decline of manufacturing, the outmigration of jobs and residents to suburbia, and competition for economic and social viability with emerging cities in America and abroad. The city that had inspired Burgess and Park's Concentric Zone Theory and Goldberg's living and working complexes was again called upon to inspire a new generation of visionaries to react to new upheavals.

In the mid-1980s, the city of Chicago began to undertake such a reevaluation and produced a series of specific plans and projects whose purpose was to redefine Chicago in this new landscape. The city, in partnership with the private sector, responded to the challenge with a three-tiered revitalization campaign: citywide policies, plans for individual areas of the city, and detailed plans for specific improvement projects. The most notable of these were the *Vision for the Future of Greater State Street* (1987–1995) and the *Vision for a Greater State Street* (1997; hereafter cited as the Vision plan), *The Central Area Plan* (2000; hereafter cited as CAP), and *A New Economy Growth Strategy for Chicagoland* (2001; hereafter cited as NEGSC). Not since the Chicago Plan of 1909, prepared by Daniel H. Burnham and Edward H. Bennett, had there been such a systematic effort to rebuild Chicago, and especially but not exclusively its downtown area. The new Chicago, planners hoped, would grow organically, each part developing synchronically and symbiotically to complete the whole.

The New Central Area

In the process of revitalizing itself, the new Chicago would transform the very notion of the center by opening up the Central Area to embrace areas once considered marginal. At a time when many people were predicting their demise, this move would confirm the importance of cities and central business districts, not by marginalizing peripheries but by highlighting and encouraging the reflexive relationship that exists between them.

Drawing upon its architectural and sociological legacies, the city found new meanings for existing structures, many of which were built for the city's entry into the industrial era. State Street's revitalization relies on the preservation and landmarking of architectural gems, which now serve new functions. It is, as Manuel Castells defines it, a "space of place" while the riverfront, in contrast, is a "space of flows" (Castells 1993, 252, 254). With its undeveloped areas, the riverfront affords the opportunities and challenges associated with forging the new frontiers of open spaces, and spaces that facilitate new economics and a new urbanism. The riverfront lured the best and brightest to create new structures, which would facilitate Chicago's entry, this time, into the information age.

Bridging the spaces of place and flows, Millennium Park expands the sense of what a city must contain in order to be a viable place to work, live, and visit. The park's composition is guided by the original line of the city, its natural terrain and horizon, and by the larger urban terrain. And elements of the city that currently exist or once existed are integrated with new ones so that the resulting composition gives voice to all of the parts, rather than just the most dominant ones. By incorporating both built and natural forms in its reconsideration of leisure and recreation, the park also reflects a rethinking of what an urban landscape can be. It invites both built and unbuilt forms, framed by an even broader canvas—the environmental landscape. The park brings us back to the land and our relationship to it. Millennium Park has been instrumental in re-creating or shifting the Central Area, both literally and symbolically. More than any other new development, Millennium Park challenges traditional notions of what the Central Area can be, along with notions of centrality and marginality. It is contested space. This too is an essential component of the physical and social textures of the city.

READING THE CITY—A NOTE ON METHODOLOGY

In the pages that follow, I explore the creation of Chicago's New Central Area, from plans to buildings, between 1986 and 2004 (see Plate 1). Over these two decades, Chicago's Central Area has undergone a number of significant changes, many concentrated in three key sites: Greater State Street, the Riverfront, and Millennium Park. Planners confronted a particular set of problems at each site, as well as a particular configuration of resources for resolving those problems, out of which they crafted a specific strategy for change. Devoted to these three sites respectively, Parts 1, 2, and 3 of this book, in essence, are case studies, each designed to present the rhythm and character of the area it covers. Together, these sites provide a sense of how local and global processes are informing changes currently being played out in the new Central Area and in the city, more generally.

Change is one of Chicago's most essential characteristics. Current changes are already driving future ones; and because the peripheries are an essential feature of the new center it is important to look at how changes there are impacting the center. In Part 4, I discuss some of the works in progress that are located beyond the Central Area, but which flow from the city's new vision of centrality. Ultimately, this four-part exploration provides a feel for Chicago's new Central Area as well as a sense of where it is today, how it got there, and where it may be heading. The early Chicago sociologists believed it was impossible to understand social life without understanding the arrangements of particular social actors in particular social times and places. That is, no social fact makes sense if it is abstracted from its context in social (often geographic) space and social time. My exploration of the Central Area is framed by these tenets and by this approach. This story of Chicago's Central Area is then told in two ways: through the examination of its built forms and through observation and analysis of how these forms are used. The reader can thereby approach plans and designs, both in terms of how they concretely manifest in the specific site and also in terms of the larger urban landscape. The following case studies at once typify how any city can revive itself and also exemplify what is uniquely of and by Chicago, especially those traits exhibited through the architectural and sociological schools then and now.

The New Central Area should be understood as the city's center in much the same way Booth described the city itself: shaped by and shaper of the larger whole, gateway and heart for Chicago, but also for America and the world. The restructuring and transformation of the Central Area offers a way to examine in microcosm many of the local and global issues that the city has had to respond to, more generally, and a way to see the ripple effect of its architecture and social dynamics in the decisions and outcomes, as well as a way to see how the legacies of this city's earliest crafters and observers have remained and been transformed.

A DUAL PERSPECTIVE FOR A DUAL CITY

While Chicago is still the middle, surrounded by America, in 2005 Chicago and America are part of a very different socioeconomic and geopolitical landscape. Consequently, the meaning of being in the "middle"—the notion of centrality—compels a fresh investigation. Chicago has had to recenter itself in the face of local and global forces. The city's response has been to reimage itself as a dual city. On the one hand, it is place-centered, in the sense that it is embedded in a particular and strategic location. On the other hand, it is transterritorial, in the sense that it must provide networks for interaction among groups and individuals who are geographically distant. New information technologies and the new global economy must allow, paradoxically, for dispersal as well as for centralization (Sassen 1999). While there is no longer a simple, straightforward relation between centrality and such geographic entities as the downtown or the Central Business District, as was the case in the past, the CBD remains a key symbol and component of centrality.

As a dual city, a global city, Chicago requires examination so as to expose the complexity of forces contributing to its new morphology. A reflexive connection exists between architectural spaces and the human social interactions taking place within them, but now this connection also includes virtual networks via telematics allowing for flows of information in cyberspace. In order to evaluate plans and designs in terms of how they have materialized at any specific site or in the larger urban landscape, it is necessary to examine Chicago's built forms and also to go into the streets to observe them in use. And in particular, to do so in a way that shows how spaces of place interact with spaces of flows through their design and use to achieve this new place for the city.

The view of the city offered here moves spatially rather than temporally in the ethnographic traditions of the Chicago sociologists and oral historians. Ethnography is the written text that the researcher produces upon returning from the field. Ethnography, as opposed to historiography, is a narrative that recounts the present rather than the past, moving spatially rather than temporally as historiography does (Cappetti 1993, 50). The sketches offered here of the city's streets are framed by what is occurring in real time. I draw from the past when it is useful or necessary to put plans and designs into context. This means that the following order will also include a certain disorder—the messiness of the street, the happenstance and disjuncture. Readers should therefore be prepared for incongruities and sometimes startling juxtapositions. In the midst of a discussion of telecommunications and economic globalization, for example, I might introduce the reality of the office buildings that house these processes and then discuss how they are used by workers to find respite during their lunch break. Understanding abstract concepts through the concrete, visible changes completed or near completion in the Central Area renders the processes by which Chicago is becoming a global city more transparent and more accessible.

At the same time, particular designs and arrangements are shaping interactions among people. Stores, restaurants, theaters, parks, offices, and apartment buildings, all are spaces where people encounter one another and interact as they go about their daily lives. Do these spaces foster both individuality and community? As we move through a street engineered for retailers and consumers, we suddenly confront the homeless, so we must ask: For whom has Chicago built the Central Area? Who is included? Who is excluded? If architecture embodies ideology and social relationships, it also offers potential for reshaping the life of a city.

Each building or site I have chosen in the new Central Area contributes to and reifies the forms and functions of the new Central Area in real time. The Chicago Mercantile Exchange is a case in point (see Figure 1). Designed by Fujikawa, Johnson, Associates and built between 1983 and 1988 along the southern branch of the river, the Merc (as it is called) quietly houses a powerhouse of Chicago's economic past, present, and future. The Merc dates back to 1874, when the Chicago Produce Exchange was set up to trade butter, eggs, poultry, and other agricultural products. In the 1960s, when the Merc began trading futures in livestock and meat, these perishable products were traded on a major commodity exchange for the very first time. In 1972, the Merc opened the International Monetary Market (IMM) and eventually began trading financial futures (Edgerton and Heise 1982, 474). By 1991, thanks to the IMM, the Merc was supporting trade with an underlying value of approximately $50 trillion—almost forty times the value of all equities traded on the New York Stock Exchange. As structure and institution, the Merc has "helped Chicago bridge the ocean that separates a city from the status of important, even world class, to that of a global one" (Abu-Lughod 1999, 328). Workers represent all strata, that is, high-end to low-end positions. Many intersect at the base of the building where they eat, smoke, or just unwind by looking at the river or at the panhandlers who also inhabit this space.

The working image of the Central Area I have chosen to use here is a visual or verbal sketch rather than a description or snapshot. This is because sketches make visible the motive and inspiration behind the reality. A sketch begins with an intuitive gesture; it has an ambiguity that is fleshed out as it is modified over time by the influence of external sources, in much the same way a city comes to be built, used, and understood. If you can resist mere description and allow also

for impression, the city can come alive—
and parts of the city, once invisible, can
emerge in proper scale and significance. It
is this dynamic, interactive approach to
viewing Chicago that I hope to share with
readers, more than anything else.

I identify my research as following the
extended case method that investigates
how microlevel social situations are influenced by external forces. This is in order to
clarify the texture and consequences of
macrolevel processes through their outcomes in the local context. The works of
sociologists and political economists Saskia
Sassen, and Manuel Castells, and architect
and architectural critic Charles Jencks have
been invaluable. They provide a method to
articulate the local and global processes
found in structures and actions.

I have relied on the actual texts of the
plans, on the architectural renderings and
specs, and on other documents I secured
from the key organizations involved in the
transformation of the Central Area—in particular, the Office of the Mayor, the City of
Chicago Department of Planning and Development (DPD), the Chicago Loop Alliance
(CLA), and the architectural firms that were
building on the sites I chose in particular.
When possible, and in almost every case, I
conducted interviews with the men and
women directly involved in the plans and
projects. In many cases my contact was and

1—"The Merc"—the Chicago

Mercantile Exchange,

January 2003

is ongoing. These men and women provided information that served several purposes. They clarified and deepened the textual or visual information with additional factual and anecdotal input. Frequently, they would refer me to new contacts. Often they provided a historical context for what I was observing. I can say
without exception that there was no one I approached for help who turned me
away. On the contrary, they generously gave of their time and energy.

For additional historic information, and in addition to the organizations
mentioned above, I searched the archival materials at the Chicago Historical Society, the Art Institute of Chicago, and the University of Chicago. Marshall
Field's, the Hotel Burnham, the Merc, and many other individual buildings, large
and small, have their own archives. I used these materials and also interviewed
their archivists or employees to further deepen the connection between the site
and other buildings in the present as well as in the past.

As befits a study of a dual or informational city, I have used the World Wide Web for my research. Government agencies and other organizations are increasingly making available online statistics, census data, maps, speeches, and minutes of proceedings. In some cases, online databases have superseded hard copy documents, so the internet is the only place to obtain such information in a systematic way. I also referred to anthologies and readers. I selected those which collected articles, papers, or essays that appeared nowhere else, or those which efficiently collected definitive works in their area and focus.

All the archival research, personal interviews, and scholarly literature cannot substitute, however, for being on the street. Only there could I investigate the ways in which the city in form and the larger social and economic forces shape face-to-face interactions. Regular visits over the course of five years provided me with many opportunities to engage in informal conversations with the people who work in, live in, and use the area. Riding the buses and trains, stopping at a park, shopping, just strolling about, all provided many insights. In some cases, I became friendly with owners and workers in stores and restaurants I frequented regularly. Like the formal interviews, these interactions added dimension and depth to my awareness of the changes taking place, from the users' point of view. When I was away from the site, I relied on e-mails, phone calls, and local newspapers for hard facts and opinion. These enabled me to stay immersed in the mind-set of the city and its residents.

In my research as a participant observer, I make no claims to have attained the kind of objective stance intended by survey research. As noted, some of my research technique utilized active participation in addition to neutral observation. This active position offers what Michael Burawoy has identified as the hermeneutic dimension in social science, which seeks interpretation and understanding through a dialogue between the participant observer and the observed, rather than dialogue between theory and data (Burawoy et al. 1991, 3). It was my intention to get as many perspectives as possible, and to measure their validity and reliability against what other sources suggested, what documents stated, and ultimately what I observed for myself. In the end I feel my knowledge and sense of the city expanded and deepened in a natural way, that is, I came to know the city as ethnographers intend. This account is in no way meant to be comprehensive or complete. It is intended deliberately to be open-ended, and to leave to the readers the task of fleshing out my sketch, as their knowledge of and interest in the issues and sites I have explored will dictate.

Almost a century has passed since Burgess and Park proposed their theory of concentric circles, and Chicago, like the rest of America, has undergone many changes. For that matter, a great deal has changed since 1984, when Booth made his observation about Chicago and when Goldberg's River City joined Marina City. But the resonance of the first- and second-generation architects and sociologists can still be felt and seen in what may be defined as the best of the "Chicago way": the commitment to addressing difficult architectural and social issues by staying in the problem to find a resolution. The two schools also frame part of what is the new centrality—working with the notion of periphery in order to define the center. The problem is the center, yet the center is simultaneously at the periphery of change.

The Chicago that Goldberg built for was the Chicago of his childhood, the Chicago that shaped a career spanning over sixty years, and the Chicago he envisioned in the future. Goldberg's Chicago was about paradoxes and juxtapositions, about creating boundaries, blurring them, and moving beyond them. Most important, his Chicago was a living entity, formed and transformed by the people who, he believed, "come together in a very natural way" and inhabit its spaces. As he put it: "each building is a comment, a statement, a mirror, of the way each person in that building will reach out and either surround himself with that space or touch the space or remodel the space" (Goldberg 1992, 264, 322). This too is the Chicago way. It is this Chicago and this way of approaching its current issues that I have tried to uncover and explore.

PART

Reinstating State Street

To look at State Street today is to see a dynamic, diverse, and classic urban thoroughfare in the heart of Chicago's downtown area, colloquially known as the Loop. For nearly a century, State Street was the retail spine of the city's Central Area, but in the 1960s State Street went into a period of spiraling decline. As recently as the early 1990s, many were uncertain there would be a State Street at all, much less one deserving the nickname "the Great Street," given it in the 1922 song "Chicago." Greater State Street incorporates the thirty-four-block area between Dearborn and Wabash that stretches north from Congress Parkway to the Chicago River. In 1984 the Greater State Street Council (GSSC)—a nonprofit group (now known as the Chicago Loop Alliance, CLA) that was founded in 1929 representing businesses for Greater State Street—set about developing a long-range comprehensive plan to revitalize the struggling street. The plan was based on interviews with merchants, private- and public-sector officials, a variety of other experts, and users of the street. The GSSC's conclusions were encapsulated in *Vision for the Future of Greater State Street* (hereafter referred to as the Vision plan).

Drawing upon the unique role played by State Street in the city's history and economy, the plan proposed to weave the street back into the fabric of the downtown area. Whereas the plan focused on the one-mile stretch of State Street between Congress and the Chicago River, true to its title it encompassed the Greater State Street area with references to other redevelopment plans or, in some cases, actual provisions for specific projects at adjacent sites. The plans for Wabash and Dearborn avenues, for example, complement the larger plan but distinguish themselves from State Street proper.

Endorsed by the City of Chicago in 1987, the plan set in motion a series of discussions and collaborative efforts with numerous city departments and downtown civic groups including Chicago's Department of Transportation (CDOT), the Department of Planning and Development (DPD), the State Street Commission (SSC), and the GSSC, with the goal of initiating a program for the design and use of the streetscape. In 1993 the Chicago Plan Commission adopted a comprehensive set of guidelines for the renovation of State Street, the *State Street Development Plan and Urban Design Guidelines*. In 1994 the city initiated the final phase of the planning program, most of which (as of August 2005) has been completed and further expanded.

State Street's transformation verges on the miraculous, and for that reason alone, the story of its most recent comeback is worth telling. There are, however, additional reasons to examine State Street and the plans that revitalized it. The re-construction of State Street, in many ways, was a catalyst for the subsequent re-working of the entire Central Area and, more generally, for the city's shift from predominantly a site of manufacturing to one that now includes information and service sectors. This transition involves more than changing economic venues—it requires changes in the ways in which space is conceptualized and used. Space becomes more than a place; it serves as connector as well. One of the most visible ways State Street enacted its role as connector was through its architecture. Here, Chicago's rich architectural legacy serves both as a window into the city's past and as a door to its future. The Vision plan ensured that redevelopment would enhance the street's location and architectural character.

The plan also recognized the importance of the street as a social hub. Incorporating human activity and architecture into designs and plans draws not only from Chicago's architectural heritage but also from its sociological heritage—the methods and perspectives of the schools of architecture and sociology—in order to address current problems. By building from street life, the interplay of people and forms in microscopic and macroscopic ways, the planners demonstrated an understanding that people and their actions are what define the city and all its components.

State Street is once again significant in redefining Greater State Street and the new Central Area. However, the reasons for its decline and subsequent comeback, as those planning its revitalization understood, lie in a new meaning of the term *center*, one with more complexity and fluidity. Today State Street, acting as both a tentacle and a lightning rod for the larger hub, serves to draw together diverse activities and users, which generate diverse sources of energy and definition—some new and some renewed. As a result, State Street's growth is helping Chicago's CBD reach beyond its traditional physical, social, and economic boundaries to include much more of the city, the nation, and to some extent the world. As a result, State Street serves as a figurative as well as a literal bridge for rebuilding and understanding the city.

The Vision for the Future of Greater State Street forms the core for what became the *State Street Renovation Plan* and is therefore the primary document for exploring the theories and methods, the intentions for and the outcomes of urban planning and design that informed the renovation process and created the State Street we currently see. *The Vision for the Future of Greater State Street* had a number of permutations and phases. It was produced by a team under the oversight of the City of Chicago DPD. Throughout, there were progress reports for the phases. The main document used here as an overview was produced in 1997. It encapsulates most of the prior plans as played out or as expected to be. For the purposes of simplicity, all of these will be referred to as the Vision plan.

Additional resources, most notably interviews with key players in the plan's conceptualization and implementation, bring the plans and designs to life. Two of these key players are architect Peter van Vechten, who was head of the design team for Skidmore, Owings & Merrill (SOM), the architectural firm selected to implement construction of the new streetscape design for State Street, and Tyrone Tabing, who was assistant commissioner in charge of retail recruitment on

State Street, was later the DPD assistant commissioner, and is currently CLA executive director. Van Vechten and Tabing—along with other members of the city's DPD and the GSSC, representatives of architectural firms working on State Street, merchants, and residents—provided invaluable insights, the backstage view, if you will. My fieldwork, carried out between the year 2000 and early 2005, allowed for verification of the plans' and the interviewees' stated objectives while my own ethnographic observations provided a way to sustain an ongoing sense of the development of the street in real time. Interwoven throughout this analysis are echoes of the first, second, and third generations of the Chicago schools of architecture and sociology. The earlier generations are responsible for giving the city its physical and social frameworks. And while contemporary architects and sociologists do not always follow their predecessors, they nonetheless continue the legacy of forging new frontiers.

The first chapter provides an analysis of the renovation process of each layer of the street, from planning to completion, in order to show how each unfolded to reveal the new street, beginning at ground level with the resurfacing of the street, followed by the intermediary or tonal layer created by palette (materials and fixtures), and proceeding to the refurbishing, new construction, and ultimate use of the buildings. With the pieces in place (specifically a retail, theater, and educational district housed within landmarked buildings), the second chapter provides a view at street level. That is, it offers verbal and visual observations, in real time, as I walked along the street during my visits over the course of 2000–2005. The purpose is to revisit the street with new insight, but also to assess how well the street has succeeded in its goal to be a node of nodes in a new Central Area. Does it manage to connect with other parts of the city while simultaneously retaining its distinct character? Does it bridge past and present, and open a vista to the future? Has it achieved mixed use by bringing together a diversity of business enterprises and entertainment venues, as well as educational and residential facilities? Most significant, has State Street become a more open, more welcoming, more inclusive space for diverse users? What statement does State Street make today?

THE VISION PLAN

Despite its indisputably prominent place in Chicago's history, the status of State Street in recent times has been more tenuous. Why, then, would the city invest so much effort in saving it? Perhaps Ty Tabing of the city's Department of Planning and Development (DPD) best encapsulated the motivation behind the tremendous momentum to save State Street when he said: "I think [State Street] . . . is the retail spine of Chicago and always has been and people . . . root for it in the same way that you know Frank Sinatra's going to sing a song about it 'cause it really is . . . a microcosm of the city and its ups and downs and its bright future" (Tabing 2000). Chicagoans wanted to see State Street make a comeback because, in many ways, it is the story of the city in microcosm. State Street's story begins with the birth of the city itself. It is the first and oldest street, named for State Road, which ran along the eastern boundary of Chicago when the city was incorporated in 1831. And in 1908, when the decision was made to create a definite dividing line on which to base a consistent numbering system, State Street became that east–west base line (GSSC 2005).

Almost from its start, Chicago emerged as a premier entrepot city. It was the jumping off point for the western part of the country as well as the commercial and business center of the Midwest. The railways greatly contributed to the city's role as a transportation hub and to its growth in population and economic status. State Street was also defined by the role it played for the growing resident population and for those coming from and going to other destinations. The intersection of State Street and Wacker Drive was the last outpost for shopping for the thousands of immigrants from the east who were heading for government lands in Nebraska, Kansas, and the Dakotas.

Like much of Chicago, the shape and character of State Street grew out of the ashes of the Great Fire of 1871. Rebuilding infused the city with a new vitality and determination to transform an inhospitable environment into a desirable place to live and work. Remarkable engineering and architectural feats in stone and steel replaced the destroyed wooden buildings. Those who built the city at this time must have known they were not merely restoring a single city but they were, in effect, creating a new vocabulary for urban design—the commercial style. It was an indigenous vocabulary, yet it was able to produce the most ubiquitous symbol for all urban landscapes—the skyscraper.

Whole streets, including State Street, were developed around this new vernacular. The buildings that arose here were shaped by the need for sunlight for interior illumination, by the dimensions of city lots, by city regulations, and by the desire to use "new potentialities which had hitherto been exploited only in bridges and industrial structures of various kinds . . . in buildings which were permanent and essential parts of the structure of Chicago's daily life" (Giedion 1941, 292, 303). From the turn of the century through the 1910s, the dominant form for office buildings was the "big boxy building penetrated at the center or rear by a large light court," a design that came to be known as the Chicago style (Willis 1995, 65). More than "a style," its underlying ethos reflected the attitude indigenous to Chicago and to its original line. Reflecting on this attitude, Peter van Vechten, architect with Skidmore, Owings & Merrill (SOM) and head of the team that renovated State Street, observes: "Chicago's attitude clearly is that it's a Midwest city. It's a product of Midwestern sensibilities which are clearly different than New York and West Coast cities. There is a quiet/calmness of the city; in the attitude of the people of the city. Things are done with a certain parochialism and there's a comfort with that. There's a confidence issue potentially that exists that's inherent in the Midwest" (van Vechten 2001). This description helps explain the bolder aspects of the design; but even more, it describes the activity housed inside the quiet facades that formed the streetscape. On State Street, the art and craft of salesmanship found a new home and new meaning.

State Street was the unparalleled retail and entertainment hub of Chicago and the Midwest until the middle of the twentieth century. According to van Vechten: "If you needed something to buy you went to State Street. It was America's super block of department stores—Marshall Field's, Carson Pirie Scott, Goldblatt's, Rothschilds, Gimbel's, Sears—all of these." The street also became a vital part of people's collective and individual image of the city. Van Vecten continues: "And [for] civic celebrations and where did you go? State Street. . . . State Street, then, has this really powerful meaning to people in the city. . . . It was clear to us when we talked to anyone about State Street they . . . had a thousand stories. So there's a chord" (van Vechten 2001).

Early Chicago sociologists such as Ernest W. Burgess documented and formalized the upheavals and new patterns of urban living occurring in Chicago during the late nineteenth and early twentieth centuries. Of particular interest was the commercial hub, since, as Burgess noted, "In all cities there is the natural tendency for local and outside transportation to converge in the central business district. In the downtown section of every large city we expect to find the department stores, the skyscraper office buildings, the railroad stations, the great hotels, the theaters, the art museum, and the city hall. Quite naturally, almost inevitably, the economic, cultural and political life centers here" (Burgess, in Park 1967, 52). This center, termed the Central Business District (CBD) by Burgess and his colleague Robert E. Park, also became the focal point of the Chicago school's special brand of sociological inquiry. As part of this construct—real and ideal—State Street, as a key artery of the CBD and frequent focus of study, served as source and prototype for a typical hub and thoroughfare within the CBD.

One of the best-known activities of the Chicago sociologists in the 1920s was "producing maps of the distribution of social phenomena in the city" (Harvey 1983, 9). The mapping method was central to the assessment of indicators of social mobility and social order and disorder. From these concepts, Burgess and his colleague at the University of Chicago, sociologist Robert E. Park, developed their theory of urban growth and mobility. They derived their Concentric Zone Theory (CZT) most directly from observations of Chicago, although they recognized that similar changes were occurring in other American cities during early stages of industrialization and urbanization. The CZT portrayed the city as an entity that included a downtown core, surrounded by neighborhoods beginning with slums and becoming progressively better as one reached the "commuter zone." Much of the growth and transition was precipitated by the arrival of new immigrants and conditions for socioeconomic mobility, that is, as new immigrants arrived, the wealthiest inhabitants moved to the outskirts (Burgess, in Park 1967, 47–62). "This chart," Burgess wrote, referring to a graphic representation of the CZT, "represents an ideal construction of the tendencies of any town or city to expand radially from its central business district. If applied to Chicago, all four of these zones were in its early history included in the circumference of the present business district" (Park 1967, 50–51).

State Street exhibited many of these social and physical changes. Writing in 1925, Burgess noted: "The present boundaries of the area of deterioration were not many years ago those of the zone now inhabited by . . . residences of the 'best families'" (Park 1967, 51). The succession of changes, along with several depressions and natural disasters in the early part of the twentieth century, tested the CBD generally and State Street in particular. These changes left Chicago's CBD in a state of increasing deterioration and its social scientists searching for ways to ameliorate the problems of the city's inner core.

FROM CRISIS TO OPPORTUNITY— A NEW VISION FOR STATE STREET

Perhaps the most difficult challenge for State Street came from demographic shifts and planning mistakes that began in the 1960s and lasted through the 1980s. During this period, substantial residential and commercial outmigration to the suburbs and other regions in the U.S. severely hurt the entire CBD, but State Street was especially hard hit. State Street might have been able to fend off the challenge from suburban shopping malls alone; but within the city limits, it faced growing competition from North Michigan Avenue. Water Tower Place opened in 1976, followed by other mixed-use, high-rise complexes including Olympia Center–Nieman Marcus, One Magnificent Mile, City Place, and 900 North Michigan Avenue, as well as some highly visible stand-alone megastores, such as Niketown, Crate and Barrel, and Banana Republic in the late 1980s and early 1990s (N. Harris 1993; Smith and Enquist 1996).

In 1979 the city countered with a mall plan for State Street. Like many other cities at that time, Chicago took advantage of Federal Urban Mass Transportation funding and created a pedestrian/transit mall along a nine-block stretch of State Street. From Wacker Drive to Congress Parkway, State Street was closed to automobiles and taxis. The street was widened and slightly curved to allow for two-way bus traffic. State Street's sidewalks were also curved and widened, in some cases to up to fifty-two feet, nearly doubling their expanse. One-of-a-kind dark gray asphalt hexagonal pavers were used to give the street a distinct look and feel. Reshaping the street and sidewalk necessitated replacing the existing street-lights. The modest lights that had once lined the street were replaced with fifty-foot-tall, high-intensity cluster fixtures reminiscent of the original ones. New subway entrances, bus shelters, and information kiosks were also installed.

Architect Adrian Smith and planner Phil Enquist from SOM comment that "the mall created an oddly non-urban, non-Chicagoan ambience" (Smith and Enquist 1996, 16). Van Vechten goes further: "[A]lmost from the first day, everyone knew it was a mistake. By making it a singular kind of idea really in my mind hastened its problems and brought on more unanticipated ones" (van Vechten 2001). The design itself created many problems. Prohibiting automobiles and taxis isolated the street from the rest of the downtown area. Pick-up and drop-off for restaurants, hotels, and other venues was difficult. The line of the street was lost, and with it, its legibility. Newsstands, information kiosks, and bus shelters along the streetscape seemed jumbled, which impeded pedestrian flow and people's views of storefronts across the way. The street appeared dark and dingy, in part because of the gray asphalt used for the sidewalks and in part because of the diesel fumes that collected during morning and evening rush hours as a result of moving most of the Loop buses onto State Street. At night, the new light fixtures cast harsh shadows, leaving parts of the street in the dark; and pedestrians sought more inviting streets to walk along.

Inadequate maintenance of the street compounded the design flaws. The side-walks became dirty, the streets needed repair, and many of the street elements such as the information kiosks were often broken. State Street began to attract vendors selling poor quality items and "adult" oriented products, and newsstands, for example, began to display X-rated magazines in full view of passersby. The presence of panhandlers added to the decline in image of State Street (Smith and Endquist 1996, 16; Coffey 1997). The department stores and retail stores that had originally helped to create and foster State Street's success and recognition as the city's retail hub continued to leave. Once central to the city's Loop, State Street moved to the margins of the cityscape—although its physical location did not change. Perhaps the final blow came with the flooding of the street in 1992. Things were so grim that some Chicagoans wondered if this once proud and grand artery might cease to exist.

But once again, State Street turned crisis into opportunity. Aided by another federal transportation act, the city decided to undo the redevelopment and re-cover State Street's original line. Not only would the street itself be physically re-aligned, it would be reintegrated with the rest of the downtown area. This time, the "retail spine" of the CBD would respond to the new and growing number of people who were both working and living in the downtown area. This renova-tion plan would involve more than simply rebuilding State Street as a great retail hub. But the street had to be more. As stated in the Vision plan: "State Street, for many years, Chicago's premier shopping street, will be reborn as 'classic State Street'—a dynamic mixed-use district that will build on the Street's traditional strengths and complement them with exciting new uses" (Vision plan, 2). Func-tionally and visually, a new pedestrian-oriented main street would be created that would set the stage for future development in the Central Area in order to attract Chicagoans and out-of-towners seven days a week (Coffey 1997).

In 1987 the Greater State Street Council, with the consent of the city, formulated a plan, *Vision for the Future of Greater State Street*. Intended to offer recommendations rather than directives, the plan quickly precipitated a collaborative effort between private and public sectors to produce the formal guidelines and designs for State Street's renovation. *State Street Development Plan and Urban Design Guidelines* (1993) provided the framework for redevelopment, specifically of the one-mile stretch of State Street that extends south to north from Congress Street to Wacker Drive, and established specific standards for evaluating proposed planned developments and other improvements within the district. Design principles were incorporated into the State Street Renovation Project in 1995. Funding for planning and construction was provided through the federal Intermodal Surface Transportation Efficiency Act of 1991 (ISTEA) and matching grants from the City of Chicago, drawn from Tax Increment Financing (TIF; see below).

The overarching goal of the Vision plan was to make State Street a viable and vibrant component of the new CBD by making the street a viable and vibrant space of place. The two most catalytic provisions of the Vision plan involved strategies to reintegrate State Street with the rest of the Loop and to preserve the historic character of its remaining buildings, while introducing new uses for them. Once these provisions were set in motion, others fell into place, including the reintroduction of cars and taxis onto a four-lane straight-curbed street, narrowing the sidewalks, improving the mass transit infrastructure, and bringing street lighting to a pedestrian scale. The city sought landmark status for twenty-two buildings and for the nine-block district bounded by Lake and Congress streets. Street elements were introduced to complement and reinforce the street's classic image, which meant incorporating landscaping to green and shade the streets, lighting the historic buildings to emphasize their architecture, building new subway entrances and information kiosks, and providing guidelines for signage that would not visually clash with or obscure the architecture (Smith and Enquist 1996, 15; Coffey 1997; Gallagher and Enquist 1997).

In conjunction with the design plan, the city initiated an aggressive marketing campaign to attract the widest possible mix of users to State Street: office workers, city residents, suburbanites, business travelers, and tourists. The State Street Mall Commission, created by the city in 1979 to oversee mall upkeep, was restructured to fill a new management role that included marketing. This eleven-member committee consists of four city representatives and seven private-sector representatives, appointed by the city (Gallagher and Enquist 1997). Funding and marketing projects through the collaboration of public and private sectors facilitated diversification along State Street. By situating new retail/commercial, entertainment, and cultural/educational establishments in existing structures, through retenanting or adaptive reuse of the upper stories of existing structures for residential and other "people-intensive" uses, and by creating new development that was responsive to the current urban context, the image of "classic State Street"—i.e., "the Great Street" and "street of the people"—could continue to serve as a space of place, while now fitting into the context of the city's changing needs and options (Vision plan, 2). The result was the creation of three zones or districts (retail, entertainment, and educational/cultural), each one distinct, yet deliberately designed to spill over onto one another.

SOCIOLOGICAL FOUNDATIONS—
FOOTSTEPS ON THE STREET

The view from the street is never single or enclosed. It has to admit a variety of other perspectives and by its nature is shifting and contradictory. The evocative power of the word
'street' derives precisely from its vagueness . . . whether used by fashion magazines or political journals, it always implies a common touch, a feeling of how everyday life is lived by
most citizens appealing to some demonic, sometimes democratic urge. (Jukes 1990, xiv)

The ideas that inform the Vision plan for State Street draw from the tenets and
ideals of urban sociology and architecture that emerged here a century earlier, in
particular the notion that the street is as much a social entity as it is a physical
one. As Park asserted: "Much of what we ordinarily regard as the city—its char-
ters, formal organization, buildings, street railways, and so forth—is, or seems to
be, mere artifact. . . . The city is, finally, a state of mind, a body of customs and
traditions, organized attitudes and sentiments" (Park 1967, 2, 1). The relationship between physical and social is reciprocal and reflexive and must be viewed
as such in planning and designing the street. While this may seem obvious, such
a view of the city owes its origins to the Chicago School of Sociology, which
emerged and developed at the University of Chicago between 1915 and 1939.
The ideas of these urban sociologists, integrated into the Vision plan itself, provide the perspective necessary for examining and understanding State Street.

The members of the Sociology Department at the University of Chicago
were strongly motivated by the desire to view the city as an object of sociological analysis through firsthand empirical investigation. The creation of a program that successfully combined theory and empirical research marked a departure from departments that emphasized general theory, social philosophy,
or purely historical work. The use of personal documents, observations, and interviews conducted within an implicit general theoretical framework became
the hallmark of the department, as did the incorporation of ethnography, especially life histories as proposed by Park and pursued by other members of the
department. These methods and subsequent works created a new tradition, one
that put a face on otherwise anonymous, often ordinary or nondominant, marginal inhabitants. They made a significant contribution to the body of literature and to investigative work in the field. "Life histories, where it is possible to
secure them," wrote Park, "illuminate some aspect of social and moral life
which we may have known hitherto only indirectly, through the medium of
statistics or formal statements. In the one case we are like a man in the dark
looking at the outside of the house and trying to guess what is going on
within. In the other, we are like a man who opens the door and walks in and
has visible before him what previously he had merely guessed at" (Park 1974,
2:208). Park had twelve years of experience as a newspaper reporter prior to becoming a professor at the University of Chicago, which no doubt impacted his
focus and style, and subsequently those of the department. By the end of the
1920s, members of the Sociology Department had produced a series of intimate
studies depicting life in the everyday world of the city. W. I. Thomas and Flo-

rian Znaniecki in *The Polish Peasant* (1918), Nels Anderson in *The Hobo* (1923), Louis Wirth in *The Ghetto* (1928), and Harvey W. Zorbaugh in *The Gold Coast and the Slum* (1929) exemplify this research style and the Chicago School's ethos of inclusiveness.

The Chicago School is most often characterized by its emphasis on qualitative research methods in contrast to the quantitative approach exemplified by Columbia University or the theoretical approach exemplified by Harvard. Ethnography was the preferred research approach for many Chicago sociologists and often considered their defining characteristic, but it was not their only methodology. What really set them apart was their openness to all methodologies, a creative eclecticism that enhanced knowledge of the city. They went further, using the city as a "natural laboratory," because they believed that the only valid field of experience was the street. As sociologist Morris Janowitz notes, in the introduction to a 1967 reprint of *The City,* they were fascinated with "the complexities and contradictions of the urban community and the prospect of discovering patterns of regularity in its apparent confusion" (Park 1967, viii). The university, an island of architectural and intellectual grandeur, was itself surrounded by Chicago's slums, making it too an example of the city's contradictory ecology and of urban space's duality of physicality and sociability. "The growing city was the big story of the day," according to Park, so he sent his students out to find "the big sociological new" in the everyday world around them.

Sociologist Martin Bulmer summarizes: "This tradition of local social involvement was the soil that nurtured the urban studies of the Chicago school of sociology and made the relationship between the university and city different from that in New York and Boston" (Bulmer 1984, 25). The Chicago School, moreover, endeavored to discover the meanings assigned by ordinary people to places, behaviors, and institutions. By injecting observable, everyday reality into analyses, sociology became more than a distant abstraction or a static, depersonalized accounting of behaviors or attitudes.

The Chicago sociologists injected dynamism and humanism back into the science of the study of people and communities. Their concerns and methodologies gave sociology the opportunity to become a science in the deepest sense of the term. In the words of sociologists Philip J. Ethington and Martin Meeker, we come to know the street by the concepts of the two Spanish verbs "saber" (personal knowledge)—surveying the street—and "conocer" (acquaintance with)—walking the street (Ethington and Meeker 2002, 405–20). This bifocal analytic framework is especially useful in conceptualizing and analyzing the whole streetscape, as well as its components—buildings, parks, public spaces, street furniture, and human activity. Each element has a presence, but it also has to be seen from the wider context of the street or community. Further, the street is the place where buildings and people continuously intersect and interact. In this way it achieves a dynamic quality. The result is a sense of the street as a sort of harmonious but polyphonic composition where spontaneity and people's experiences are as significant as the formal rules and structures that ground their activities. Form and action merge to create a whole that is more than the sum of its parts.

Second-generation Chicago sociologist Erving Goffman formally developed this notion for understanding "the organization of experience" and termed it "frame analysis" (Goffman 1986, 11). Extrapolating from the works of psychologists and philosophers including William James, Alfred Schutz, W. I. Thomas, Charles H. Cooley, and George H. Mead, Goffman views reality (that which occurs inside the frame) as dynamic and subjective, defined by the intersection of socially created conventions or rules and by the individual's vantage point (his or her prescribed and perceived position in that frame). Framing, or defining the situation, is comparable to what the viewer sees inside a picture frame, but from the vantage point of standing on the frame. By stepping outside the frame, one can make the frame itself part of the picture (the content), thereby creating a new frame with new content. Reality, then, consists of boxes within boxes if we do not make certain social moves to focus it within a controllable frame. "Individuals are always concerned with keeping their frameworks in order; even when they step into and out of those same frames, there is no escaping the impact of our framing behavior" (Collins and Makowsky 1978, 236–37).

REFRAMING STATE STREET

Employing the concept of frame analysis to read the Vision plan for State Street, in fact, does something quite radical: it transforms the street into a frame, which is itself framed or bracketed by form (convention) and activity (the experiential). To use Park's term, it "thickens" the idea of the street. The Vision plan's working definition for State Street deliberately incorporated its social and physical dimensions, drawing from the street's two predominant images as "the people's street" and "the Great Street." This allowed a new image of the street to be built both upon vibrant and diverse activity and upon the presence and legibility that its structures project. Activity is as significant as form, and content as important as context. While this sense of the street was clearly absent from the 1979 mall plan, it was infused into all levels of the Vision plan and design programs, from the street's overall scheme down to the smallest of details.

Resurfacing the Street

The plan embodied other dualities. The most immediate change resulted from the Vision plan's reconceptualization of the street both as a pathway that facilitates movement and as a node that situates and orients. Juxtaposing these seemingly contradictory roles was necessary to achieve presence as well as fluidity for vehicles and pedestrians. Therefore, in addition to bringing cars back onto the street, the roadway was straightened and widened to accommodate four lanes of vehicular traffic, with a painted median for exclusive-left-turn lanes where applicable and new traffic signals at each intersection. People could be more easily dropped off or picked up from the hotels, stores, and theaters. The impact of this new accessibility was almost immediate. "It was," in van Vechten's words, "huge. Just the ability to be able to go by your destination. It was incredible . . . and it removed this stigma on the street" (van Vechten 2001).

2—A view of State Street looking South, with Marshall Field's, November 2000

State Street's sidewalks were also reconfigured (see Plate 8). The mall sidewalks were ripped out and completely rebuilt. The hexagonal sidewalk pavers were replaced with new light-rose-colored concrete to give the street a brighter and more cheerful look and to tie it visually back into the Loop. The gentle curb line that had been given to the sidewalks in the mall plan was straightened, in order visually to unify streetlights that lined the street in orderly rows (Smith and Enquist 1996, 16). The sidewalks were also narrowed to between sixteen and twenty feet, which placed people in closer contact with each other, thereby providing the sense of bustle that had been lacking on the excessively wide walkways of the transit mall. The fact that most foot traffic is directed into a corridor adjacent to the display windows of State Street shops increases the likelihood of impulse buying and enhances the street's economic viability (Vision plan, 3). In essence, the narrowing of the sidewalks pushes pedestrians closer to the storefronts and to one another. Together, these modifications created effective and aesthetically appealing pathways for pedestrians and vehicles.

The relative width of streets and sidewalks were only part of the problem. When State Street was viewed in the context of the surrounding streets, other design flaws became glaringly apparent. Van Vechten explains: "It was very curious because it was only State Street. The minute you turned off to go to a cross street, over at Wabash, it was a different feel. The stores on Wabash were doing fine. Go over one block, it's just a whole different ball game. So it was clear that something was going on right on the street" (van Vechten 2001). It was also clear something else had to be done to create a positive image.

Streets and their sidewalks, the main public places of a city, are its most vital organs. Think of a city and what comes to mind? Its streets. If a city's streets look interesting, the city looks interesting; if they look dull, the city looks dull. . . . Streets provide the principal visual scenes in cities. (Jacobs 1961, 29, 378)

The visual scenes of a street or more generally of a city are, in urban planner Kevin Lynch's view, the result of an overlap of publicly and privately held images. The shared images are necessary for people to operate successfully within their environment and to cooperate with their fellows. "Each individual picture is unique with some content that is rarely or never communicated, yet it approximates the public image, which in different environments is more or less compelling, more or less embracing" (Lynch 1960, 46). The renovation design plan for State Street therefore had to provide the street with cues that could elicit positive responses in overt and subtle ways, for collective as well as individual interpretations. The tonal layer—that is, the palette, materials, shapes, and especially the lighting for the street—was in great part responsible for accomplishing this image change.

Palette, Materials, Shapes—The Tonal Layer

One of the single, biggest problems identified with the 1979 mall plan was the choice of materials, palette, and street fixtures. Looking back, it became clear that this aspect of the street greatly contributed to its success and failure. While these may seem almost invisible features of the streetscape, they are essential to the image and identity of the street, acting in much the same way intonation and punctuation do in speech or writing. The tonal layer bridges the physical and psychosocial dimensions of the street. Therefore, new colors, materials, and street fixtures were selected to provide a more pleasant pedestrian environment and to create a more vibrant image for the street. The planners' choices for these elements illustrate what happens when the frame is shifted so that background becomes foreground, and then background again.

Of all the design elements of a city's infrastructure, exterior lighting most conspicuously captures people's attention. In many ways the image of modern cities was created by the interplay of natural light on built forms by day and by the way artificial lighting presents the city and makes it accessible at night. Artificial lighting obliterates darkness, or perhaps more accurately, it fractures it. Good lighting can put people at ease, foster interaction, and enhance a setting. But just what constitutes good lighting? For State Street, this proved a complex question, and the answer was as much a psychosocial as it was a technical one.

In fact, State Street had employed a number of lighting programs over the years. It was, according to van Vechten, "almost like a laboratory for lighting," beginning with the streetlights created specifically for State Street in 1926 by the Chicago architectural firm of Graham, Anderson, Probst & White. In 1958, the original lights were replaced by futuristic-looking florescent fixtures, which came up on prongs. The lights had a turquoise tint to them, further enhancing the futuristic or surreal look of the streetscape. The tint proved unflattering, however, if not a bit frightening, for people caught underneath the lights, so in 1979, these were replaced with the hovering, fifty-foot-high cluster fixtures described in the mall plan. Their scale and appearance seemed more appropriate for airports or parking lots than for an urban street. Van Vechten recalls their impact:

One reason no one wanted to go on State Street at night was that . . . there was a perception of it being dangerous which was directly linked with the lighting. I remember going late and you couldn't wait to get across State Street. . . . It was foreboding, there wasn't anybody around. It [had a] very different character than the rest of downtown. In fact, it had that project look to it. (van Vechten 2001)

Therefore, when the Vision plan was conceived, finding an appropriate lighting program became a priority. Lighting would have to fulfill a number of roles. It had to provide visibility and a sense of well-being for users; it also had to provide, in Kevin Lynch's terms, "legibility"—apparent clarity—and "imageability"—the probability of evoking a strong image for viewers (Lynch 1960, 2, 9); and it also had to work with lighting on other streets in the Loop. The city, in conjunction with the SOM designers, prepared a Downtown Lighting Master Plan with a five-year (1997–2002) implementation schedule. The plan, in fact, encompassed all streets in the Loop, with a future option including the illumination of the Loop's bridges, bridge houses, and the EL. The plan was based on a palette of ornamental light fixtures. Each of the main streets would have its own distinctive style, but all of the styles would be compatible with one another (Vision plan, 18). In this way, the plan incorporated the dual values of individualism and community. These form the core of what sociologists are concerned with in any setting, and which were of greatest concern with the rise of modern cities. These notions were also embodied in works such as Goldberg's as he sought to infuse aspects of modern urban living into his works.

For State Street, the design team opted to use recastings of the 1926 fixtures. While they have the look and appeal of the originals, they embrace new technology and respond fully to the street's current needs (see Plate 2). The placement of the lampposts—eight on each side of each block—orders the street visually and provides proper lighting for pedestrians and automobiles. The new "Washington Post" units (so-called because they are manufactured by Washington Series Fixtures) employ a two-tiered lighting system with glass acorn-shaped lighting at twenty-seven feet and pedestrian-scale globes at ten feet. Tiny blue globes support the larger acorn-like ones in order to add a touch of subtle color to the street. State-of-the-art color-corrected light fixtures, 250 watts at the twenty-seven-foot level and 50 watts at the ten-foot level, were supplied by the Holophane Corporation (Smith and Enquist 1996, 19; see Holophane 2002). An advantage of the fixtures is "the prismatic glass optical system, which places the light where it is needed—not as glare, but as usable illumination" (Bruce Worthington, City of Chicago DOT, Bureau of Highways, Holophane 2002).

One of the primary goals for the choice of lighting was to humanize it, or bring it down to a more human scale, so that people could see each other's faces. And according to van Vechten, that goal seems to have been met: "It had a direct cause and effect. When you walk down the street now, we can recognize each other and you don't look like an axe murderer, right. If somebody's all in shadow and they have a hat on with a brim, my gosh, [you think] what is this person going to do?" (van Vechten 2001). While most agreed that the choice was a good one in this regard, some criticized the style, claiming that the lights resorted to nostalgia and imposed a "period look" that would keep the street tied to its past. Van Vechten, however, makes it very clear that nostalgia was not the design team's chief goal:

It was more of a response to the physical surroundings and to what State Street mean[s] in a deeper sense. . . . We brought back what we felt was part of the essence of the street. We actually started designing custom lights but [the] concern was, how do you fuse it with what exists because it's brand new and how does it survive the inevitable budget crunch at the end? By going back to something, which was very much of that street. There're great stories about that light. Calvin Coolidge turned it on . . . and the celebration cost more than the lights. When you see the street in its golden era, that was the light that was associated with it. . . . It was less I think a stylistic choice than a meaning. (van Vechten 2001)

This interpretation is supported by other features of the streetlights. Each lamppost is adorned with natural features of the city and this site, including ornamental plant forms such as acanthus leaves and the distinctive "Y" that represents the confluence of the north and south branches of the Chicago River. The tavern-green palette recalls the State Street most people see when they look at historic photos or postcards. However, the streetlights also complement the newly placed rose-colored sidewalk pavers, which in turn enlivens and defines the current State Street. The intricacy of layer upon superimposed layer of meaning brings to mind what has become the symbol of the city itself—the onion.

The streetlights illustrate that the way in which people are engaged by lighting is more complex than is often assumed. While illumination offers people freedom and security, these fixtures demonstrate that more is not always better and less not always bad. The lampposts also engage people in a variety of ways. The appearance of the lampposts helps people orient and situate themselves. Distinctive lampposts for each street in the Loop serve to distinguish and identify one street from another. At the same time, they help connect disparate sections of the Central Area in nonobtrusive but visually appealing ways. The lampposts also engage people through touch. As Park observed: "Touch and sight, physical contact, are the basis for the first and most elementary human relationships" (Park 1967, 24). Many people, almost unconsciously, touch the adornments on the lampposts in the way one might interact with real leaves or natural elements. Van Vechten notes: "One of the most heartening things I remember was a little elderly lady standing there just running her hands on it. That happens in Chicago. People stop and say, well what do you think of it? They're very much tuned in" (van Vechten 2001).

Experiences such as these bring the meaning of the street very much into the present. The role of streetlights therefore expands and deepens beyond their most obvious function. In addition to providing light, they become affective symbols that can evoke memories or create new ones, and bring the street to the people and people to the street at the individual and the collective level. Evoking and sustaining the connection with history is important. As architectural historian Dolores Hayden astutely observes: "Urban landscapes are storehouses for these social memories, because natural features such as hills or harbors, as well as streets, buildings, and patterns of settlement, frame the lives of many people and often outlast many lifetimes" (Hayden 1995, 9). Finding ways to recover and utilize these memories in lively and relevant ways is a challenge, as exemplified by the choice of lighting fixtures and other street elements for State Street.

Subway Entrances, Bus Stops, and Information Kiosks

Integral to the city's vision for State Street is the revitalization of the mass transit infrastructure. The plan reverses the dark, dank feel previously associated with Chicago's urban transit by redesigning subway entrances. The below-grade spaces are opened up and the stops are made more transit-friendly (see Figure 3).

The functional concerns for State Street's new S-curved subway entrances, bus stops, and information kiosks revolved around several issues. For a shop-driven street, visibility is important. "[W]hen you look at the photographs and see the simple boxes of the subway entrances [created by the mall plan] and ask, well how's that bad? [The answer is], well you can't see the stores" (van Vechten 2001). So, functionally, the new subway entrances had to maximize pedestrians' views of store windows and other people on the sidewalks. "The soft 's' [of the newly designed entrances] comes from the family of kiosks that exist down Michigan Avenue and is playing very much into that. . . . It's also very much of a functional thing because by keeping the backside low you increase the visibility from the street into the stores across the street" (van

3—Detail of subway entrance
on State Street, July 2001

Vechten 2001). Subway entrances connect the street to mass transportation and to pedestrian paths that are above and below street level, thus inviting multilevel vantage points from which the street may be comprehended and used. The newly designed subway entrances and information kiosks also frame the storefronts. The contents of the information kiosks orient and inform pedestrians while their design and form reinforce the street's role as a place to (window) shop and as a multimodal pathway. In addition to designing for pedestrian, automotive, and train traffic, new features have been put in place for buslines. Bus stops have busline indicators for passengers that display the same tavern-green ornamental frame of the lampposts. New waiting spaces provide seating and standing space for passengers seeking shelter from harsh weather.

There were other considerations for the design team. "The subway entrances and kiosks are very much tied to the architecture of their surroundings, to the street itself, to other features on the street and to its history, even to the vegetation of the larger landscape" (van Vechten 2001). Layered onto the polished-brass subway entrances and tavern-green information kiosks are ideas of the onion and other natural indigenous plant forms. "And if you look closely, you will find a little bit of prairie school motifs, which is very much associated with Chicago. This brings to the entrances and information kiosks a sense of detail and craft. This brings to the foreground the unique creativity that comes by way of the human hand" (van Vechten 2001). The goal was to create a sense of belonging, entitlement, and pride through color, design, and detail of these street fixtures:

When you look back at what Burnham and Bennett did in terms of the construction, there was a sense of civic pride and we were very conscious of not necessarily the specific vocabulary but just the level of love that went into what they were doing. We wanted to also strive for that too because I used to always think it but now really believe it, that if you give people great things, they respect it. (van Vechten 2001)

Van Vechten's explanation reveals the design team's desire to connect their work with the city's history, especially its architectural legacy, and to offer citizens that opportunity to access the city's past. It was important that the connection occur at the collective or symbolic as well as at the personal and experiential level. The design features also captured and connected people with the city's culture and to some extent with its natural forms. A more direct provision for a connection with nature was made in the Vision plan's provisions for the landscaping and greening of State Street.

Landscaping and Greenspace

Landscaping serves as a frame in a way no other device can. "The greening softens what is a pretty tough street. . . . There's quite a difference in the feel from this very tight place and when it opens up it's much more gracious" (van Vechten 2001). People realign their view of the street by looking up, down, and to the side. They can and do slow down to admire the greenery, read the maps, and look at various buildings, displays, or features, thus switching to a more natural tempo as opposed to the pace inspired by urban living. The omission of greenery in city and street design denies a perspective that is part of the urban landscape, even if it is not easily seen or remembered. Such an omission also denies access to part of State Street's history and identity. It is interesting that there was always some amount of vegetation, including trees, on the street prior to 1979.

Soon after landscape architect Jens Jensen came to Chicago in 1886, he began working for the city's Park Commission. His greatest ongoing contribution was the commitment he made to reuniting urban residents with the Midwestern landscape that so enthralled him: "to give the people of Chicago a bit of native Illinois, something most of them have little chance to see or feel" (Jensen 1990, 113). Jensen's concerns were understandable. Chicago, at the turn of the twentieth century, not only epitomized the modern city, in many ways Chicago had created it. The idea that the urban landscape should be a vista of massive structures, symbolizing great feats of technological and human innovation, quickly and easily replaced Jensen's idea. This built-up image for cities persists, creating a conceptual barrier no less formidable than the physical ones landscapers encounter in their efforts to bring greenery into urban spaces. But greening efforts such as those found on State Street today reveal that Jensen's goal can and should be met. Not since the 1909 Plan of Chicago has such effort been put into greening the city. Plans and programs emanating from the Office of the Mayor downward testify to the real desire to inject into the built environment a softer and more natural side. The Vision plan offers ways to reconnect these seemingly disparate frames on State Street. There were, however, several physical barriers to overcome.

The lack of undeveloped space on State Street precluded the possibility of large spaces of greenery such as are found elsewhere in the nearby area, most notably in Grant Park, the newly built Millennium Park, the revamped Navy Pier, and spaces closer to the Lakefront. The notable exception of vacant space is Block 37, the largest and last undeveloped area along State Street. Over the past two decades, plan after plan for this site has fallen through. (Although, new plans were being "finalized" in August 2005, and ground was broken at the end of the year.) Given Block 37's past, its future remains unresolved. The Vision plan, however, did include provisions for greening "two of State Street's least appealing locations" (Smith and Enquist 1996, 19).

Benton Place and Quincy Court are alleys opening onto the northern and southern ends of State Street, respectively. They are evidence of Jensen's observation: "Culture and a good life do not grow where gorgeous boulevards border on filthy alleys" (Jensen 1990, 97). Now mostly used for deliveries to adjacent buildings, these alleys are shunned by most pedestrians because the sidewalks and curbs are neglected or nonexistent and the lighting is poor. Plans to enliven

Benton Place and Quincy Court include the addition of new sidewalks, lighting, curbs, trees and curbside plantings, and the curtailment of deliveries at midday. Through these measures, Benton Place and Quincy Court could become gathering places. With outdoor cafés, in good weather they could become more popular hubs, much like Maiden Lane at Union Square in downtown San Francisco. Given its proximity to the Chicago Theater, Benton Place could become a node for people to meet or gather, before performances and during intermissions (Smith and Enquist 1996, 19).

The Vision plan focuses on Pritzker Park, at the southern end of State Street. This is a "special project" in part because of its irregular shape and weak grade relationship to surrounding sidewalks and in part because of new activity around it, generated by the new EL station and the increasing student population (see Plate 4). One proposed solution is the creation of a development parcel, with provisions for residential or dormitory facilities, a park-oriented café or restaurant, and another visitor-oriented amenity, one that allows use of computers, for example, or where performances might be held (Vision plan, 14). While its physical and social idiosyncrasies may require greater attention to security and other concerns, stemming from its proximity to the elevated train, Pritzker Park has the potential to draw from a substantially large and diverse population from the early morning to the late evening hours. Currently it offers an island of greenspace; but it is in dire need of better landscaping, lighting, and seating. On warm days, nonetheless, people find their way to Pritzker Park, use it as a place to sit, read, socialize, lie down, or be alone in thought—activities that the street prohibits.

Greening was not to be limited to only certain sections of the street. Working with smaller gestures, the plan included ways to incorporate greenery all along the street. Trees were planted, which "in summer . . . provide a handsome green canopy above the street and offer welcome shade to pedestrians. And in winter, . . . branches festooned with sparkling lights, create a festive air" (Smith and Enquist 1996, 18). Planters were hung from the lampposts, strengthening the connection between natural and built forms, and granite curbside planters were installed just above the sidewalk. Encircled by low iron railings, they contain colorful flowers and shrubs that are changed with the seasons. Looking at the street today, it is hard to imagine that plants have not always been part of the street, or that they grew here naturally even before State Street existed. Their seamless fit into the texture of the street, however, obscures the physical barriers that had to be addressed, specifically the limitations imposed by the entrances to the subways and vault supports underneath the cement blocks of the buildings. "All the buildings have vaults that extended out to the curb. And so to put in any kind of generous landscaping was very problematic. So we basically put a bunch of bathtubs on top and suspended them. That's how we were able to achieve this" (van Vechten 2001).

Trees, hanging plants, and sidewalk planters may be viewed as inconsequential gestures; nonetheless, they have had a profound effect on people's reactions both to the street and to the other people they encounter there. They slow down, look up and down, change expression, and make contact with these features and other people, if only for a moment. They also recall the spirit and creativity that past Chicago engineers and architects called upon in order to give Chicago what nature had not. As writer Robert Herrick noted in *The Gospel of Freedom*: "Chicago had none of the natural advantages found in great cities elsewhere around the world. . . . its creation depended solely on the force of human will. Man must make all—buildings, streets, even the green plants" (Herrick 1898, 102). From reversing the flow of the river to make living in the city possible, to designing windows that offer substantial lighting and ventilation for the newly developed commercial structures along streets such as State Street, to "planting" trees in places never imagined, Chicago is continually fueled rather than deterred by its many challenges. Moreover, these innovations synthesize engineering and landscape architecture. The greening elements display and highlight nature rather than the built form or, rather, give stature to what might ordinarily be overlooked. Greening, too, is a reversal of sorts, something that resonates with Jensen's hope for Chicago: "Cities move countrywards in solid formation like an army on the march destroying all in its path. History or beauty mean nothing. Let the cities move in groups, leaving fields and native landscapes between these groups to penetrate the city and be an harmonious part of the whole" (Jensen 1990, 92). So, "the green street" may well be a name that can be added to the other nicknames for State Street.

ARCHITECTURAL FOOTPRINTS—BUILDINGS

Chicago is a city of architectural excellence; it is probably the best city in the country for building quality. (Huxtable 1988, 155)

Old ideas can sometimes use new buildings. New ideas must use old buildings. (Jacobs 1961, 188)

With State Street's new foundation in place, attention turned to the buildings and their uses. Years of neglect and misguided planning had obscured their value and potential. So too did the ambivalence exhibited by most American cities toward preserving urban vernacular buildings, even architecturally attuned cities such as Chicago. This was especially true for work sites such as factories, foundries, and offices (Lefebvre 1991; Hayden 1995; Huxtable 1988; Newman 1998; Muschamp 2000). Under these circumstances, it would have been easy to justify the demolition of many of the buildings on State Street. The Vision plan's emphasis on the historical importance of the street, bolstered by financial incentives for refurbishing these buildings, enabled planners to envision new life for them. State Street would not give way to—but would rather lead the way into— the next century, using its architectural bounty.

Marketing this idea to potential developers, owners, and tenants involved appealing to their civic pride and their sense of history as much as to their financial astuteness. At stake was not only the preservation of the physical structures that greatly contributed to the character and success of State Street but also access to the origins of the industrial American city as it had emerged at the end of the nineteenth and beginning of the twentieth centuries. State Street was in fact an epicenter of a new architectural vernacular: the Chicago commercial style.

More than just expedient containers for commerce, the buildings embody and emphasize the vigor, raw energy, aspirations, and ideals of the Chicago and the businesses of that time (Cohen 1976, 18). The cadre of architects who came together in Chicago—among them William Le Baron Jenney, Dankmar Adler, Louis H. Sullivan, Frank Lloyd Wright, Daniel H. Burnham, William Holabird, John Welborn Root, Ernest Graham, William P. Anderson, Edward Probst, and Howard J. White—possessed the remarkable ability to synthesize engineering, architecture, and art in order to address the exigencies of large-scale commercial building. Architectural historian Carl Condit contends that "the whole forward movement of contemporary architecture moved in the direction of that synthesis (Condit 1964, 12).

But rather than call for a singular vision, the Chicago School embraced a diversity of approaches and missions. Some, including second-generation Chicago architects Stanley Tigerman and Stuart E. Cohen, believe there were, in fact, two schools within the first Chicago School—an ego and an alter ego, in a manner of speaking. Tigerman explains:

The first Chicago School of Architecture grew out of a need to urbanize . . . it was revolutionary and narrow in its solution to the rebuilding of a great American city. . . . The "alternative" Chicago School reveled in an open America on the prairie through an open plan and a purportedly open mind that began with Sullivan and grew with Wright into a civilizing philosophy. The first . . . was direct, obvious and forward looking. . . . The "alternative" . . . was individual, constitutionally American and free, if self-conscious, non-directive and nostalgic for a simpler time. (Tigerman, in Cohen 1976, 8)

Cohen suggests that Chicago architecture can be "understood as 'both-and' rather than 'either-or' . . . not necessarily of words but of *ideas,* precisely because both defined and continue to define the city and its ways of building" (Cohen 1976, 26). John Entenza, publisher and editor of *Art and Architecture,* goes further in this assertion: "In order to understand Chicago Architecture [or Chicago the city], it is necessary to be aware of important particulars . . . rich in a diversity of attitudes and talents. [These] are an intrinsic part of what had to happen to a city on its way to developing and bringing into reality major contributions to the practice of architecture" (Entenza, in Cohen 1976, 7).

Nowhere are these ideas and "important particulars" more apparent than on State Street. Here, architects designed with the intention of letting the building do its jobs without drawing attention to itself; they went after broader and deeper statements. In their understatement there was a powerful creativity and sensitivity to the users and to a new urban landscape. The buildings are constructions in and of space, but they are also layers in and of time. They ask users to be patient, to get to know them from outside to inside, from one level to another. Even without knowing anything about architecture, one feels a difference when approaching or being inside these structures; it is indeed a feel more than a look.

Rather than conceive the forms in abstract terms, architects designed with the users' most basic and routine activities as the starting point. Then, advancing from this common starting point, the architects broke through the existing vernacular and style and produced buildings that were innovative and that, by attending to human scale and design elements, elevated the status of the ordinary individuals who inhabited them. One only has to enter Sullivan's, Carson Pirie Scott department store, Burnham's, Marshall Field's department store, Reliance Building, or Jenney's Second Leiter Building, for example, to understand the complexity of these buildings and experience what the architects were seeking. This focus on everyday people and everyday activities, especially work, in architectural design parallels the interests of the Chicago sociologists of the same era who not only charted the city's growth and change from stage to stage but also documented the lives of its inhabitants. Changes and life histories, these urban sociologists believed, could be traced architecturally, especially in and around the CBD.

Throughout the late nineteenth and early twentieth centuries, the buildings along State Street were frequently torn down and replaced by larger, taller ones. One reason for this was the growth in population, from 298,977 in 1870 to 2,185,283 in 1919 (Smith and Enquist 1996, 15). Another reason was the changing nature of the economy. As State Street continued to evolve and then devolve, there was an ever-present sense of its many past lives. Its buildings and their uses exemplified multiple stages of what Chicago sociologist Robert D. McKenzie described as "invasion and succession." He explained: "the introduction of an innovating element into . . . a community may be designated as the initial stage of an invasion which may make for a complete change in the structure and organization of a community" (McKenzie, in Park 1967, 72). The changing tones and meanings of the streetscape reflected attitudes toward the past that ranged from imitation and repetition to contestation and disregard. "The general effect of the continuous process of invasions and accommodations," according to McKenzie, "[was] to give the developed community well defined areas, each having its own peculiar selective and cultural characteristics. These units of communal life may be termed as 'natural areas'" (McKenzie, in Park 1967, 78). On State Street, the clarity of these units of communal life began to blur, as did the imageability of the buildings themselves.

So, when planners in the 1980s began to contemplate the renovation plan and look at the street's history, it became clear that State Street suffered more from a lack of vision than from a lack of order. The decision was made to keep many of the structures and, instead, to strip away some of the layers of meaning—imposed by prior plans and occurrences—that obscured the intrinsic character of the street. This was a critical decision. By holding to the richness of diversity of attitudes as exemplified by these historic buildings, the organic line and the important particulars of the street could come through. The buildings could reemerge once again to form an essential and elegant layer of the new streetscape.

Prescribing a more complex life for the street than it had experienced in the recent past, the Vision plan introduced a set of roles involving three subdistricts: a theater and entertainment district at the northern end, a retail center in the middle, and an educational and cultural district at the southern end. The plan's creators believed that these well-defined yet reinforcing uses, supplemented by residential units, would intensify the fabric of the street and knit it more tightly together (Vision plan, 2; Smith and Enquist 1996, 19). A combination of strategies, from renovation to new construction, were developed to meet this goal. Renovation projects fostered the continued use of Carson Pirie Scott, the Palmer House, and Marshall Field's, for example, while the De Paul University Center (1993), formerly the Goldblatt Brothers Department Store, and the Hotel Burnham (2000), formerly the Reliance Building, both underwent renovation and adaptation. Other projects such as the Harold Washington Library (1991), the Renaissance Hotel (1992), and the Goodman Theater extension (2000) required new construction.

When the city became serious about the renovation of State Street, both planning and implementation had to reflect the need to turn the street around (Tabing 2000). The plan's decision to restore the historic character of the street not only provided a vision for renovation and a selling point for winning the support of developers and city officials, it also suggested strategies for raising funds for the plan's implementation. Spurred by the urgency of revitalizing the street, the mayor, the DPD, the GSSC, developers, and architects launched an aggressive funding campaign employing Tax Increment Financing (TIF) and landmarking. These are the key vehicles that enabled the plan to move forward.

TIF and Landmarking

Tax Increment Financing (TIF) was created in 1984, by Mayor Harold Washington. The TIF program was developed in order to offer governmental incentives to private developers or companies to stimulate new investment, and job creation and retention. TIF is a public finance tool, which allows the city to finance long-term economic development in areas that are "blighted" or in danger of becoming blighted (conservation areas), according to the state law that governs TIF, by tapping into the future tax revenues it is expected to generate. The city issues bonds to pay for the projects, which include anything from renovating historic buildings to subsidizing private developers. The bonds are later paid off by using the new tax revenues captured in the district over the life span of the TIF—twenty-three years in the case of State Street (City of Chicago DPD 2000c; Schwartz 1999, 9–10; "Downtown Is Up," 22). TIF is available for three types of districts—commercial, industrial, and residential—and provides funding for theaters, the rehabilitation of landmarks, transit improvement, and rehabilitation and conversion of existing properties.

In the early 1980s, new office development in outlying areas presented a challenge to the Loop's aging but architecturally significant buildings in competition for business tenants. In response to this and other challenges facing the Loop, the city created the North Loop TIF district. In 1997, when federal funds were running out, Mayor Daley implemented an additional $300 million ten-year redevelopment plan that expanded the North Loop TIF district to include part of the East Loop, and renamed it the Central Loop TIF district. The Central Loop TIF was given an expiration date of 2007, with the expectation that the revitalization would be complete (City of Chicago DPD 2000c). Five times larger than the original North Loop district, the Central Loop TIF district is the largest TIF district in the city. It was hoped that the expanded district would help building owners remodel or convert space to residential use.

In the Central Loop, TIF was used to create new office buildings and parking structures, to renovate and restore landmark buildings, to create a new downtown theater district, and to provide crucial assistance in the resurgence of State Street. As part of the DPD arm involved in retail recruitment for State Street, Tabing explains, "A lot of these buildings were dogs that had no future so what are you going to do when you want to preserve the character of older buildings? The City and Department of Planning and Development became pretty instrumental in converting some older class C [that is, a real estate classification for low-rent, low-quality buildings] office buildings to residential, hotel and commercial use" (Tabing 2000).

Among the projects along Greater State Street that benefited from the Central Loop TIF are Carson Pirie Scott, Sears, the Page Building, The Goodman, Ford Oriental and Nobel Fool Theaters, the Mentor Building, the Hotel Burnham, the Hub (formerly the Lytton Building), and the Dearborn Center (on State, Adams, and Dearborn). Some of these were designated Chicago landmarks or were listed on the National Register of Historic Places. As such they were also eligible for a number of financial incentives. In fact, twenty-two landmark buildings lining State Street represent three distinct architectural periods: the late nineteenth century's Chicago School, the Mercantile Classicism of the early twentieth century, and the Beaux Arts and Art Deco styles of the 1920s and early 1930s. The number and concentration of examples of architectural styles were among the reasons behind the push to designate part of State Street a landmark district. When the State Street streetscape renovation phase was completed in 1996–1997, the City of Chicago and the GSSC began a drive to add the area bound by State and Wabash, and by Lake and Congress, to the National Register of Historic Places. In late December 1998, federal approval was granted to this eight-block stretch, which is now known as the Loop Retail Historic District.

Designated landmark buildings are eligible for a number of financial incentives. The listing of State Street on the National Register of Historic Buildings allows buildings that do not individually qualify as landmarks to benefit. The first is federal-income-tax credit equal to 20 percent of the rehabilitation cost for income properties. To qualify for this credit, projects must comply with federal historic rehabilitation standards for any proposed alterations, demolition, or new construction. The second incentive is a "façade easement donation," in which the property owner essentially relinquishes the right to make substantial changes to the structure's facade. The value of the easement then may be deducted from federal income tax as a onetime charitable donation (Vision plan, 31).

Landmarking provides other benefits for State Street. It guarantees State Street a permanent place in American history. It can be used as a marketing and promotion tool for the commercial and retail sectors as well as for residential, cultural, and educational ones. It ensures that the buildings—both individually and as they relate to one another—will continue to set the standard for new construction. Landmarking, as framed by the Vision plan, prevents buildings and public spaces from being viewed as static environments, distinct both from the time and space they occupy and from the things and people they house. Rather, they are seen as dynamic, living entities—made so over time by the diversity of activities they facilitate or accommodate. Thus landmarking provides the context for structures and people to align and interact and, together, to define the street.

Cognitively, landmarks help order space and time. Often structures are chosen as landmarks because of their unique physical features, but to see them merely in this way ignores the role people's experiences with them have in viewing them as significant. Structures can become landmarks because of the meaning they acquire through people's experiences with them (Lynch 1960). Park clearly understood this when he wrote:

Local institutions, like works of art and literature, are symbolic expressions of common life. . . . They have extension and form, but at the same time they have a fourth dimension, namely meaning . . . not immediately accessible to us. We get the meaning . . . by observing the ways in which they are used; by investigating the occasions and incidents of their origin and growth, and by taking account of whatever is unusual or unique in their history. (Park 1974, 2:201–2)

On State Street, buildings whose history and distinct features are once again apparent and which are brought into the present by their adaptive uses are more readily perceived as vital (organic) components of the streetscape and of the larger urban landscape because they are connected to personal frames of reference and memories as well as to collective ones. The juxtaposition of old and new forms and functions, of one style of building with others, is diverse and varied without being incompatible or competitive. Each building reinforces the other, enlivens the street, and allows Chicago's architectural legacy to continue. The impulse to annihilate difference disappears. Architect James Stewart Polshek believes that "if you view architecture as a bridge then there is a kind of interfacial potential for it to carry certain opportunities and responsibilities. The opportunities are there to create forms that will be understood by future generations not to recreate the old so that it is comfortable" (Polshek 2000). Sustaining the tension of old forms with new ones holds on to time and place or rather allows the old forms to show their connection to the present. The dynamic and texture afforded by preserving older forms may be considered another benefit of landmarking.

In a global context, preserving local identity can help reverse the growing trend of ahistorical flows and irreducible identities of local communities. Sociologist Manuel Castells contends: "The symbolic marking of [local] places, the preservation of symbols of recognition, the expression of collective memory in actual practices of communication, are fundamental means by which places may continue to exist as such, without having to justify their existence by the fulfillment of their functional performance" (Castells 1989, 350–51).

TIF and landmarking on State Street, in fact, relied on guidelines to "justify" the choice as to which buildings would stay or go, and how those that were saved would be used. These guidelines themselves rely on criteria for establishing how value, more essentially, is determined. Early in the city's development, Park and colleagues such as Burgess, McKenzie, and Hoyt determined that value could not be based solely on market terms. The intangible, unpredictable, and intrinsic components of value, stemming from people's tastes and use, had to be factored in. Park explained: "Under our system of individual ownership, it is not possible to determine in advance the extent of concentration of population which is likely to occur in any given area. The city cannot fix land values. . . . Personal tastes and convenience, vocational and economic interests, infallibly tend to segregate and thus to classify the populations of great cities. In this way the city acquires an organization and distribution of population which is neither designed nor controlled" (Park 1967, 5).

Yet plan after plan seemed to want to do just that: design and control. In the mid-1970s, architectural historian Ada Louise Huxtable echoed Park's observation and warned of the danger of utilizing this singular definition of value to determine the fate of buildings in Chicago. "Chicago is currently caught in the trap of backlash zoning and economic expediency and a City Council that is on the one hand loathe to designate landmarks or explore remedial zoning, and on the other unwilling to buck the developers' version of manifest destiny" (Huxtable 1988, 160).

The Vision plan, to some extent, bucked this view of value by including history and aesthetics into its value equation. The plan called upon a new vocabulary and grammar for evaluating structures that was based on a synthesis of utility and aesthetics. The surface structure is site-specific while the deep structure is grounded in a more comprehensive view of style and worth. In this way, State Street—to borrow from preservation architect James Stewart Polshek (2000)—offers an occasion to expand the thinking of architects, planners, and the populace, or at least to enter into a more profound dialogue among all the participants, in dealing with spatial and temporal parameters, local with global, and past with present. The outcome of this expansion of thinking synthesizes seemingly disparate components. It is a "both-and" rather than an "either-or" mechanism in matters of value. The first couplet makes justification for preservation plausible, if not necessary, whereas in other frames, preservation would not have been as readily apparent.

REIMAGING STATE STREET

Whereas the grid and the buildings of the street provide the order, the variety of colors, styles, materials, and activities can inject the volatility of the metropolis that gives it energy and dynamism. It becomes possible to open up the street functionally so that it can be "congested with difference" (Jencks 2002). As van Vechten notes: "That was the whole point [of the streetscape plan or design]—to try to lay a framework that doesn't preclude something and yet is an instant change" (van Vechten 2001). To accomplish this, the street had to be conceived of as space rather than just as a line. The Vision plan conceptualized the street as a series of interfaces, registering how people live in and move through the space. In a way, the plan is a playful conception of the street, something that perhaps distinguishes and humanizes it. The plan indeed goes to the original line of the street in order to provide a frame that allows for spontaneity as well as order. "What you had prior [was a singular kind of idea]; what you've got [today is] a subway, some transportation, and you still have the bus lines, but they're co-existing with people, allowing for more interaction and other kinds of urban activity, rather than it's their world" (van Vechten 2001). Thus, the street is framed by the larger cityscape, which itself defines and is defined by notions of frontières (as borders) and frontier (as the wilderness or unexplored).

But, to paraphrase Park, ultimately State Street is the marriage of its physicality and congeries of the mind; it is footsteps on footpaths, in front of architectural footprints. Footpaths and footprints are literally set in stone. Footsteps are as fleeting as the blink of an eye. But what is experienced can create a lasting image, an experience set in the mind's eye. The next chapter offers both fleeting and permanent views of State Street and, in the course of that experience, considers how successfully the Vision plan has achieved its goals.

TAKING IT TO THE STREET

Observations and Reflections

The first street I thoroughly walked was State Street. State Street is undergoing massive redevelopment. Signage all along the way indicates, "State Street—the Great Street" as well as what is coming into the area. Sears, new condos and apts., other stores are being incorporated into many landmark buildings. A nice interweaving of old and new. Lots of traffic in part because of the construction, but also because it is heavily used—the EL, buses, people use this street. The Chicago Theater, Marshall Field's, and Carson Pirie Scott, my first stop. . . . When I walked back towards the River, I was drawn to the Reliance Building (Hotel Burnham). These amazing structures hold their own, enhance and in some cases easily outdo many of the newer structures. Amazing how graceful Carson and the Reliance are. (Satler journal entry, September 7, 2000)

A description of selected buildings in each of the street's new districts is offered here in order to provide a virtual walk along State Street. I chose particular buildings and not others because they were repeatedly noted in personal interviews, in the DPD's summary report (January 2001), or in the GSSC's summary and minutes of meetings through August 2003, or because I was drawn to them especially during my own walks along the street. While not inclusive, the buildings are representative of first- and second-generation Chicago architecture, and of the new generation that is currently defining State Street.

State Street has always been defined by its buildings (its forms) and its commercial activity (its functions). But perhaps, more now than ever before, it is helping to provide the CBD with a new and revitalized identity, which is emerging from a melding of old and new forms and functions. While it is true that "form and function" are reflexive, State Street's prototypical buildings offer a window into the street's history, and the activities within those buildings provide the street with a present and a future. Together they make State Street timeless. The buildings selected here will be explored to reflect State Street's formally induced presence, that is, as form and function. The buildings also invite activity *on* the street. We find men and women operating street-cleaning machines, for example, clearly making an effort to keep the street clean, and in winter clear of snow. And we also encounter homeless people selling papers to support various programs and the panhandlers simply asking for change or food. They are also part of the texture of the street and the city. Therefore homelessness is an issue to be grappled with and interwoven into the new story of the street and of the city. State Street has cleaned itself up, but we need still to ask whether it has cleaned up the social messes that plague this and many cities' streets. So in viewing the clearly diverse aspects of this street, perhaps we can also take a look at how democratic and inclusive it has become?

Our walk begins in the retail district, which not coincidentally is found in the center portion of the street. The retail hub is at the heart of people's collective memory of State Street and forms the common ground from which new collective memories are emerging. We then head north to the theater/entertainment district and finally move to the southern, educational section of the street.

THE RETAIL DISTRICT

While Chicago did not invent the modern department store, the city's retail merchants took the idea to a different level than was done elsewhere in the country. Innovations such as window decorating, counter and floor displays, sales and promotions, and new customer services, all revolutionized retail merchandising, making department stores places for entertainment as well as for shopping. In some ways, entertainment helped take the shoppers' minds off the prices. Along with marketing innovations, the stores' architecture while assisting people in their shopping also created a diversion. Technological innovations made possible the construction of large buildings with immense floor plates, providing literally acres of open selling floors. These "retail palaces" offered volume and variety of merchandise, with individual departments devoted to particular types of goods. By the turn of the century, State Street was a nearly continuous row of specialty shops and enormous department stores. By World War I, it housed the largest, tallest, and most concentrated area of department stores in the world. Seven of these, known as the Seven Sisters, encompass a half-mile of the street, with a combined five-million-plus square feet (GSSC 2005; Gopnik 2003). These seven buildings are still standing. Marshall Field's, Carson Pirie Scott, and the recently reopened Sears continue to perform their role as retail emporiums. Ty Tabing speaks for most of those involved in changes on the street when he observes: "this street would never have made it were it not for Marshall Field's and Carson Pirie Scott, and everybody takes their hat off to them because they stuck with the street and downtown Chicago when it was really pretty grim down there" (Tabing 2000). State Street continued to build on the success of these famed merchants to create a stronger retail core, adding to its diversity as the stalwarts underwent significant renovations of their own. Merchants, unlike businessmen or salesmen, have what has been described as "a gift for the where and what. The specifics and particulars are the whole of [their] craft" (Gopnik 2003, 102). The merchant knows how to order a shop always with an eye to the details and to the shopper. Mercantilism is clearly apparent on State Street once again.

Marshall Field's and Company—111 North State Street

Architects, Daniel H. Burnham and Company (1902–1914)

Marshall Field has been a presence on State Street since 1852 (see Plate 3). In 1902 he commissioned Daniel H. Burnham and Company to build a modern steel-framed structure to replace the existing palatial French-style store. Occupying an entire city block (1.4 million square feet), the twelve-story neoclassical structure, with a grand State Street entrance, may well be considered a "retail palace" (GSSC 2005). The Field's store is the prototype of other large urban department stores designed by Daniel Burnham in London, New York, Cleveland, Philadelphia, Boston, and other cities worldwide (Schulze and Harrington 1993, 49–50). Field's 800,000 square feet of retail space make it the city's largest and the world's second-largest department store (second only to R. H. Macy's in New York). Its structure consists of a three-story base, a seven-story central section topped by an entablature, and a two-story columned top with a classical cornice. The neutral color of the granite blends with the street, offsetting the building's size and allowing the window displays and the most familiar exterior feature—the elaborate bronze Tiffany clocks at the corners of the State Street facade's first level—to be more visible. The clocks orient the pedestrian and help direct attention to the window displays, and then ultimately to the store entrances. By design they remind "the shopper that Field's is the grandest of the grand emporiums" but in an elegant and understated way. The human scaling of the store's display windows, entrance doors, and clocks maintains the integrity and value of those who pass by or who go inside by not overwhelming them in size and scale (Marshall Field's archival brochure, GSSC 2005). Once the shopper is inside, this impression—of the value of people as individuals (and customers)—is only enhanced.

Louis Comfort Tiffany designed a dome in the light court at the southwest section of the store. It is the largest unbroken example of Tiffany Favrile glass in the world. The green marble Daniel Burnham Fountain graces the atrium and serves to orient customers or offer a spot to people watch. Green marble accents can be found throughout the store, in water fountains, flooring, and other amenities. They surprise the shopper with their beauty and detail. Perhaps intentionally, they also distract.

Between 1988 and 1992, Marshall Field's undertook a $120 million restoration, signaling to other merchants that it intended to stay and grow with State Street. In 2003, the store initiated another transformation. This eight-month-long facelift had two goals: to open more of the space visually to patrons and to appeal to a more diverse customer base. Lighting was increased by 50 percent, and facades were removed to make merchandise and structural features more apparent to patrons. "Boutiques" were created within the store, each with its own look and feel. Many offered items found nowhere else in the city. In essence, Marshall Field's created a mall within the store.

Marshall Field's is in every sense of the term a landmark on State Street, forming a central node for the new Central Area's activities. More than just a physical prototype for urban retail stores, Field's prides itself on having been a prototype for service, retail, and innovation. It was the first store to offer personal shopping service, to initiate money-back guarantees, to grant exclusive product licenses, to create the "bargain basement," and to provide a multilingual information desk. It continues to serve as a prototype today. The latest renovation fractured the store into a cluster of distinctive diverse spaces, with unusual and diverse offerings. Bob Giampetro, vice president of the Target Corporation (parent company of Marshall Field's from 1990 through 2005), explains that "the gist of this move is introducing newness, introducing the unexpected. You won't find an Aprilia motorcycle dealership or a Levenger anywhere else." Other venues unique to the store are Merz Apothecary, Thomas Pink, and Whittard of Chelsea (Giampetro 2003). Marshall Field's hopes to attract the growing number of young people who go to school, reside in nearby dormitories, or work in the area, as well as older persons returning downtown to live who have money to spend (Jahn and Schwartz 2004). The ability to attract the next generation as well as to keep older patrons coming back is the key to the department store's revival. Field's is poised to attract this diverse clientele through its look, merchandise, and service.

Today, the store is a blend of old and new meanings. For example, the stately Walnut Room Restaurant on the seventh floor is a retreat into elegant dining of times past, whereas the Food Court on the lower level offers ethnically diverse, well-prepared food and drinks to eat in or take out at reasonable prices, referencing food courts in suburban malls and the hastened lifestyles of city residents and workers, all while maintaining the Marshall Field's style and service. Underground paths allow access to trains and to City Hall and other nearby buildings, which offers Chicagoans easy movement in unpleasant weather. And if plans go through as intended, Field's will connect not only to other hubs in the Loop but to hubs outside the Central Area as well, by way of a Chicago Transit Authority (CTA) station located in Block 37 (midway between Field's and City Hall) that will offer express trains to Midway and O'Hare airports (Tabing 2000–2005, e-mail dated June 4, 2004).

According to G. Brent Sr., vice president for retail financial services at the LaSalle Bank: "Looking back, Marshall Field's bold commitment in 1989 to the expansion of its State Street flagship store was the turning point in State Street's fortunes" (Smith and Enquist 1996, 17). Mr. Field is credited with coining the motto "Give the lady what she wants" (Wendt and Kogan 1952). It may be fair to say that the store continues to follow this mandate. It may also be fair to say that Marshall Field's and Company is indeed State Street and epitomizes the spirit that is Chicago. Another change lies ahead for Marshall Field's, State Street, and the city. In September 2005, Terry Lundgren, the CEO and president of Federated Department Stores, Field's new parent company, announced that Marshall Field's would become Macy's as of September 2006. The Tiffany clocks and name plaques will remain. Reaction is mixed, but Mayor Daley noted, "If you're not willing to accept change, then you stay in the past. We're never going to stay in the past as a city" (Spielman 2005).

Carson Pirie Scott and Company—1 South State Street

Architect, Louis Sullivan
(1899, 1903–1904)

Carson Pirie Scott and Company was Louis Sullivan's last large commission, and today it is regarded by many as "the architect's greatest masterpiece and the ultimate achievement of the Chicago School of Architecture" (greater statestreetchicago.com/Directory/Architecture/HistoricPlaces.asp) (Figure 4). Carson Pirie Scott was, in fact, built in several stages by several architectural firms. Sullivan built the first portion in 1899. This consisted of three bays and nine stories on Madison Avenue. The main section, built in 1904, replaced the old Schlesinger and Mayer store. This section was twelve stories high and extended seven bays, so that it wrapped around State Street.

The upper floors, sheathed in cream-colored terra-cotta and filled with Chicago windows to flood the interior with light, articulate the building's underlying steel frame. Elaborate iron scroll work in the form of intricate flowers and leafy vines surrounds window displays like ornate picture frames and also demonstrates Sullivan's commitment to organic form. The curves, colors, and ornamentation help the building to appear as if it has simply grown out of the street. Later, in 1906, D. H. Burnham and Company extended Carson Pirie Scott five bays south on State Street, and much later, Holabird and Root extended this another three bays south in 1960–1961 (greaterstatestreetchicago.com/Directory/Architecture/HistoricPlaces.asp; Schulze and Harrington 1993, 52–54).

4—Carson Pirie Scott,

August 2004

Carson Pirie Scott, like Marshall Field's, was a thriving retail venue during State Street's early twentieth-century heyday. It stands at the corner of State and Madison, one of the Loop's busiest intersections in the early 1920s. In 1922, in fact, sociologist Ernest W. Burgess reported that during rush hour, 31,000 people passed the southwest corner of State and Madison, and over a 16.5-hour period, a total of 210,000 people passed through (Burgess, in Park 1967, 61). Like Marshall Field's, Carson Pirie Scott is also a symbol of persistence in the face of hardship and despair. By the 1990s, for example, the level of traffic in the once busy intersection had plummeted. In 1996, the DPD reported a daily average of 23,100 automobiles and 70,000 pedestrians on State, between Madison and Monroe (City of Chicago DPD 1996). While Carson Pirie Scott continues as an important retail presence on State Street, its new role as a mixed-use space distinguishes it from Field's in the street's renovation. In 1985, Carson Pirie Scott invested $57 million in renovations. In 1999 additional interior and exterior renovations began. The organic and natural dynamic of the store has been enhanced by the recent landscaping and detailing. Current exterior renovation plans include the addition of a cornice (Tabing 2000; GSS Status Summary Report January 2001; City of Chicago DPD 2001).

The interior upgrade program involves over 50 percent of the retail selling space. Upper floors are being converted to office space (City of Chicago DPD 2000, 4; DPD 2001). The store's conversion to a mixed-used space along with its landmark status reflect the benefit to Carson Pirie Scott of bridging old and new in order to encourage viability of its existence and that of the street. Having an office in the Carson Pirie Scott Building, for example, has potential marketing advantages in terms of cache, easy recognition, and desirable location in the Loop. In addition, the interior improvements and upgrades along with financial incentives offered to commercial tenants on the upper floors should further empower the building's presence on State Street in new and significant ways. Carson Pirie Scott has strengthened its position on State Street by accommodating the new commercial enterprises that the city hopes to attract.

Sears, Re-deux—2 North State (2001)

The new Sears occupies 250,000 square feet of retail space on the lower level and first four floors of the seventeen-story historic building on the northwest corner of State and Madison streets (see Plate 5). The old Sears resided at 401 South State Street. Its new location, 2 North State Street, was originally the Boston Department Store. At 325 feet, the Boston was the second-tallest of the seven sisters. The upper floors now house offices, including Novopoint; SBC Communications; Divine, Inc.; and Bank One (Guy 2001a, Newbart 2001). Sears now resides diagonally across from Carson Pirie Scott, recalling Sears's historic connection to another of the original retail giants on this street. Outside, the gold-toned awnings with lights over the entrance ways on Madison and State resemble theater marquees, complementing and referencing the nearby theater district. The awnings also reference the newly renovated subway entrances, which were designed to improve the visibility of store windows such as the ones found here, creating multiple interlocking frames from which to view the street. Inside the new store, murals depict city landmarks, and boutiques such as Unity Square, which has an African theme, are intended to appeal to and reference the African American customers Sears hopes to attract.

Sears views itself in its traditional role as a full-service department store offering a variety of moderately priced products. The difference is that it is providing this convenience downtown (Newbart 2001). Sears is keeping a close eye on the new city population. Of the 800,000 people who live within five miles of the new store, whites, African Americans, and Hispanics appear in equal numbers. Sears products and displays reflect an awareness of this diversity. By store estimates, 112,000 people now live downtown, and this number is expected to reach 150,000 in the next ten years. About 46 percent of State Street shoppers are men—a statistic merchants would like to see rise (Guy 2001a). Like Marshall Field's and Carson Pirie Scott, Sears was a presence on the street from 1932 until 1986. Its return, to quote Tabing, "is one of the big hits the street needs to succeed. For many, Sears is also an old friend that has returned. One customer said, 'I hated it when they moved. I'm glad they're back'" (Newbart 2001, citing Tabing 2001).

Sears is a new old store in an old new space. It is a new hybrid and prototype—very much in character for Chicago. While many of the retail, entertainment, and even educational facilities have revamped in either or both form and function, as time and need dictate, some such as Sears evoke an additional meaning or message for the street. The presence of Sears on State Street today symbolizes optimism, if not a leap of faith in the return of the street's viability. The store's physical image reflects the street's current image as a marriage of old and new materials and shapes; its contents likewise mirror the city's changing population. Sears's local roots are important, serving as a source of pride and inspiring the power to draw customers. As with Carson Pirie Scott, the building can potentially become a good marketing tool for rentals in the upper stories. And the Sears name recognition in other parts of the world can help better position Chicago in the global economy. Sears itself has become a globally recognized corporation. It represents an entity whose vernacular draws simultaneously and reflexively from the local and the global. Another example of this duality is Mc-Café, which opened on North Wabash in May 2001.

McCafé—115 North Wabash Avenue (2001–2002; closed)

"The idea of a gourmet café at McDonald's is unnatural, even laughable for some. . . . But judging from McCafé's opening day, McDonald's may be on to something" (Smoron 2001, 14). My own experience there echoes this:

I came upon McCafé at 115 N. Wabash. It shared an awning with a traditional McDonald's. In contrast to the bright and sleek design of McDonald's, McCafé had French curtains, ceiling fans, bistro tables, wood counters, and leather couches. The menu included a large variety of coffees, à la Starbucks but without its nomenclature. It also offered tea, fruit drinks, and pastries. At the counter where you got sugar, milk, and so forth, I noticed the preserves were the little Kraft packets. . . . The two Hispanic female workers were obviously new to this and the computer cash register, but very friendly and willing to please. I got a French vanilla/hazelnut iced coffee—regular—and sat down on the leather couch near the window. . . . The atmosphere was anything but McDonald's, yet the two stores opened up to one another at the back so people could move back and forth from one statement to the other. It was an-other contradiction or paradox that somehow made sense here. Many people came in and did a double take. One man laughed and said "it would never fly in Iowa." Another woman, who was on the McDonald's side, came over to see what the deal was, turned to her party and said, "it's just desserts" and went back to her table. (Satler journal entry, July 7, 2001)

It took the "attitude" mentioned by van Vechten to open McCafé on Wabash, a no-nonsense Chicago street dimmed and rattled but somehow also buttressed by the EL running above it. And yet, there it was in 2001, fitting in, somehow (see Plate 6). In some ways this vignette captured, in microcosm, the differences between Chicago and cities such as New York City or San Francisco, where sensibilities might cause people to turn up their noses. They might call it a "Starbucks rip off or wannabe." It also took daring to meet Starbucks on their own terms. By this Mc-gesture, we un-derstand how profound an impact McDonald's continues to have on our collective identity, that is, on how we work and live (see Ritzer 1992; Schlosser 2001). The fact that McDonald's has its origins in Chicago made this experiment all the more ap-propriate. Like the juxtaposing of old and new structures in Chicago's Union Sta-tion, the two McDonald's venues coexisted in absolute contention or counterpoint formally but in support of one another functionally. And like Sears or McDonald's proper, McCafé reified local innovation that has now become a part of the American and global standard. McCafé was closed in early 2002 when the building in which it was housed was razed to make way for the new Heritage at Millennium Park. Plans call for relocating and reopening McCafé once construction of the Heritage is com-pleted, but no further specifics have been given to date.

The Hub (Lytton Building)—247 South State

Architects, Marshall and Fox (1913)

In 1999 the City of Chicago began working closely with the real estate industry to create an affordable, technology-friendly work space to support its growing technology sector. As a result, downtown Chicago is quickly becoming adept at renovating structures in order to offer a full complement of high-tech tools in-cluding fiber-optic connectivity, redundant power grids, backup generators, and sophisticated around-the-clock security. The Hub-Chicago "was the first poster child building in helping to transform Chicago into a player in the new econ-omy. The Hub combines technology and a unique environment to meet chal-lenges of the New Economy" (Chicago Tech Today 2001, 1).

The Hub, as it is now called, was the Lytton Building. Occupying what once housed a three-story retail space, which acted as the base for H. C. Lytton and Sons' "Hub Store," and professional offices on the upper nine stories, "The Hub" went about redefining its new (old) name so that it could meet the needs of the street and assist in the city's entry into twenty-first-century economic viability (see Figure 5). The Hub literally sought a new profile by changing its old address of 14 East Jackson to 247 South State, reflecting a desire to be a presence on the main, rather than on a side street. This was partially necessitated by new guidelines for State Street. The Vision plan calls for new buildings to incorporate store entrances facing State Street but not the building itself (Vision plan, 23; GSSC 2000). In seeking to fit in with its neighbors, The Hub complied with building codes, which required that the restoration of facades reflect their original character or that facades, if replaced, be made of terra-cotta, stone, or cast stone material. Metal panel and glass curtain walls are discouraged (Vision plan, 23; GSSC annual Summary Report 2000). While The Hub's exterior adheres to the Chicago commercial style, its interior is far from traditional. The Hub has 280,000 square feet of office space for technology companies. The old skeleton affords the possibility of ceilings as high as fifteen feet, large windows to allow for maximum natural light, and a pre-built floor for small-space-using tenants ready to move in immediately. Within the skeleton, renovation has provided spaces with access to a fully redundant SONET (synchronous optical network) in telephone closets at each floor, turn-key telecommunications infrastructure, building intranet to connect tenants to building management, and customized Category V fiber-optic cabling. Other newly added features include tenant lounge areas complete with pool tables and vending machines, fitness and locker rooms with showers, shared conference and training rooms, and a first-floor retail space that currently houses a coffee house and restaurant. The Hub has easy access to DePaul University and Robert Morris College, as well as city buses and Metra and South Shore trains. There are also nearby parking facilities for commuters (Chicago Tech Today 2001a, 2).

5—The Hub on State Street, September 2000

Retail tenants include Zoom Kitchen, Radio Shack, America's Best, and Chipotle Mexican Grill, while the list of corporate tenants includes Telenisus Corporation, Qwest Interactive, United Charities of Chicago, Planned Parenthood, Arthur Andersen Works, Addus Healthcare, Eolas Technologies, and Pangaea Technologies. This roster reflects the shift into the information and service sectors yet shows the building's and the city's continuing commitment to socially and community centered enterprises.

■   Getting behind the facade, or going beneath the surface, is useful for uncovering the many layers that comprise the life and evolution of State Street. Two other retail establishments will be mentioned here because of their significance in the rebuilding of this street. One is a new addition, now gone; the other is an old staple that shows no signs of leaving. Their contrapuntal origins and outcomes reflect the character of the street.

Toys R Us—20 South State (1999–2002; closed)

Toys R Us was the first company to commit to building when State Street began to recruit new retail under the auspices of the Vision plan. The space was designed specifically for this retailer. Tabing recalls: "Toys R Us coming here was a real pioneer in the renovation. They were one of the first national retailers to go onto State Street because there had been such disinvestment that had occurred for so long that everybody was like wow—thank god they have a retailer. What that did was signal an upturn for the health of the street" (Tabing 2000, 2001).

Early in 2001, however, the store announced its plans to leave, citing poor sales in the area. The 54,000-square-foot space remained vacant until late 2005. The vacancy was not just the result of potential tenants' not showing an interest. People involved in retail recruitment for State Street did not want to repeat what, in some ways, may have been a mistake. They took time to reassess what would best suit the goals and needs of the street. In late 2005 it was announced that Urban Outfitters would open a branch in this space. The store, which opened in February 2006, features elements of a Victorian mansion inside the retailer's traditional warehouse setting. The customer base is geared toward college students, whose presence is growing thanks to the street's new educational district (Guy 2006, 61). The presence of Toys R Us on the street, though short-lived, was important and appreciated by those who understand the courage needed to take a risk when no one else will. Toys R Us was a pioneer on this street in the way other retailers were a century ago, moving into uncharted territory—the terrain of an unknown future. While the store did not succeed monetarily, it paved the way for others who have seen that monetary return. Old Navy, for example, came onto State Street shortly after Toys R Us, and it has been extraordinarily successful. In 2001 this branch recorded the highest sales of all Old Navy stores in the city, and it continues to generate robust sales.

Central Camera—230 South Wabash Avenue (1907)

Central Camera, on the other hand, is a store that came early and stayed (see Figure 6). Established in 1899, Central Camera is still owned and operated by the originals, the Flesch family. The business first opened at 31 East Adams, where it remained until 1907, when it moved to the old Palmer House. When the Palmer was demolished to make way for the new building in the late 1920s, Central Camera's owner, Albert Flesch, moved it to Wabash (Ferkhenoff 1995, 2). Don Flesch, grandson of the original owner, currently operates the store. Its location on South Wabash draws from the Art Institute School and Columbia College, as well as from the other colleges on State Street, from Michigan Avenue and State Street, and from the Metra and bus stops nearby. The store helps reify the idea of a "Greater State Street" and benefits from this reframing as well.

In some ways, Central Camera is a place that has barely changed in form or function. "For those who are uninitiated in the downtown places where trade and culture collide, Central Camera remains a must-see in the one-of-a-kind

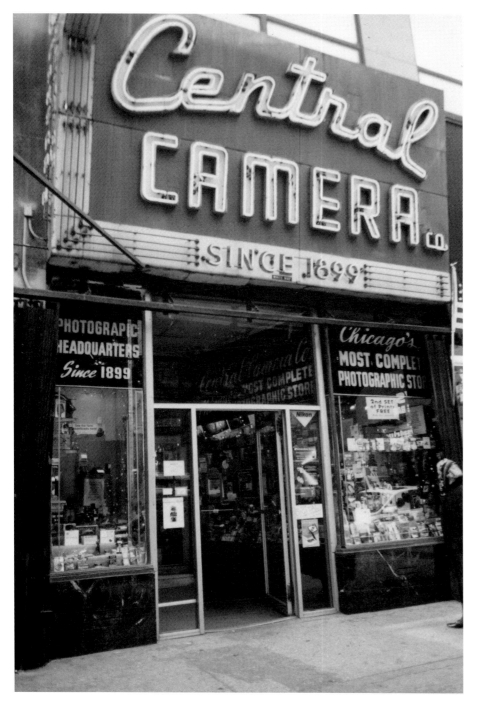

6—Central Camera on South Wabash, January 2002

fixture league, with the likes of The Berghoff [which closed 2/28/2006], Billy Goat Tavern, tobacconist Iwan Ries & Company, and the Jazz Record Mart. Each business invites with neon and serves customers with a nod to history, nostalgia and tradition" (Pierce 1999, 1). A White Way steel and neon streetside sign has been there since the store's opening; and a portrait of the owner's grandfather, hanging lovingly and prominently above the crammed glass display counters, greets you as you walk in from the street.

This matchbox of a store bustles with staff members who know everything about selling and caring for cameras and for customers. Many have been employed there for decades, in some cases starting out while they were still in school. Given the size of the store, a visitor is surprised by the vast selection of merchandise, some items displayed in vintage glass-and-wood cases and others in boxes and bins that cover the area of the store's twenty-two-foot-high walls. A second floor houses the repair area and office space, where desks are lodged among piles of papers, brochures, and additional equipment. The store's appearance does reference another time, but its contents—both in products and in service—reflect the continuation of the character of the Chicago School's sense that style must be concerned with meeting the needs of the street and its users today. Accommodation to the present is reflected in what has been an invasion of newer technologies and venues for still photography. Longtime customers and those venturing in for the first time, including students from the nearby colleges, return repeatedly both to investigate the latest products and to explore cameras and equipment from decades past. Flesch is as philosophical as he is practical, noting:

> The ethos of the store demands that accessories and parts for the camera one buys today will still be available back at the store for years to come. We like to be diversified and carry things that some people don't care about anymore. We're a landmark as far as what a camera store looks like. Just because you've been here [this long] doesn't mean you have all the business. You have to stay up with it, find customers and win them over. We have a wonderful, soft feeling for people who walk in. I think it's comfortable. (Pierce 1999, 4)

Customers confirm this assessment of the store's atmosphere by their continued patronage and their looks of satisfaction as they engage in transactions. There is a pride in longevity, but Central Camera does not rest on past accomplishments. The staff, many of whom have also worked at Central Camera for decades, are well informed and adept at communicating their wealth of knowledge. The store has a Web site, which draws customers from around the corner as well as from around the world. Equally useful is the word of mouth advertising. Flesch has no plans for expanding or moving the store. So those who have been coming to 230 South Wabash for decades can be as confident that, in form and function, Central Camera is there for them as they are confident that there will be a supply of cookies on the counter for them while they wait to be served (Flesch 2001). In retail, past and future can find a good fit if, to paraphrase Marshall Field, "you give the customers what they want." Central Camera seems to have found that fit with merchant Don Flesch at the helm.

Palmer House Hilton Hotel—101–129 South State Street

Architects, Holabird and Roche (1927)

Built in 1927 for Potter Palmer Jr., son of the real estate magnate responsible for State Street's emergence as the retailing center of the Midwest, this modern-looking hotel was actually the fourth Palmer House. The Holabird and Roche design replaced a massive granite-faced hotel that had been built in 1875 by Chicago architect John M. Van Osdel when the city's growing number of tourists rendered the seven-story building far too small. When the 2,268-room current building was completed in 1927, it was the largest hotel in the world. Interior features include an opulent two-story interior lobby, an indoor swimming pool, elegant ballrooms, and a T-shaped shopping arcade.

Even at the time it was built, the Palmer House in many ways presaged how other buildings would be used, that is, as mixed-use structures. It also presaged the importance of tourism for the city's economy. Aside from its role as a place of lodging, the hotel continues to serve as a premier, well-recognized gathering place in the city's downtown area. Presidents and world leaders as well as heads of business have come to the Palmer House and used its grand ballrooms and meeting centers. As tourists and businesspeople from the city and from all over the world become more important to the city's economic viability, a hotel that offers space for meetings and conventions as well as dining and sleeping in a central location has greater relevance. In a way, the Palmer House bridges work and residence, for travelers at least. This type of mixed-use space is becoming increasingly common in developments for more permanent residents and businesses. It is fitting that the CLA, another force in the history of State Street, resides in the adjoining Palmer House Hilton Office Building at 37 East Monroe, overseeing the changes along the street and ensuring continuity with its past.

20 North State Street

Interior remodeling by Booth Hansen, architects (2003/4)

The building at 20 North State Street is one of the many buildings on State Street adding "new life" in its role as a residential space. It is not a remarkably designed building in comparison to many of the other commercial structures built during the first generation of the Chicago School on this block. In its former life, it served as a distribution center for Woolworth. Supportive and efficient, the building got the job done quietly. Nonetheless it played a vital part in commercial enterprises of the city and of this street by facilitating the movement of goods. Today, the building is significant because of its function and location. Condominiums at 20 North State are the first true lofts within the Loop district; 106 totally restored units occupy the third through tenth floors. The building retains much of the detail common in the early commercial structures, including clay brick tiles. All the units have eleven-foot ceilings. The tripartite Chicago-style windows—with a wide central sash flanked by narrower sashes that open, topped by transoms—were specifically designed to offer maximum light and ventilation. These windows can be found in many of the buildings along State Street. They are part of the legacy of the Chicago School and are testament to the synthesis of function, aesthetics, and human scale. The location on State and Washington streets offers proximity to the nexus of State Street's retail and entertainment hubs. Nordstrom's Rack and other prominent fashion stores occupy the street level. In addition, the building literally envelops one of State Street's and the city's premier architectural achievements, the Reliance Building, now the Hotel Burnham.

The Reliance Building—32 North State Street

"The Reliance Building was a remarkably advanced structure for its time. Once the skeletal frame relieved the exterior walls of the bulk of a building's weight, buildings could be sheathed almost entirely in glass. No building of its day came closer to this than the Reliance" (greaterstatestreetchicago.com/Directory/History/Archives.asp). Taking advantage of the unrestricted height that was allowed in the heart of the Loop at this time, the Reliance was one of the few tall thin buildings that occupied lots small enough to take advantage of a compact core (see Figure 7). Rising fourteen stories on a corner lot of fifty-six by eighty-five feet (Willis 1995, 54), the Reliance is sometimes described as the world's first glass skyscraper. The first part of the Reliance was designed and built by John Welborn Root of Burnham and Root in 1890–1891. It was completed by Charles Atwood upon Root's death (greaterstatestreetchicago.com/Directory/History/Archives.asp).

In October 1999, after a massive four-year rehabilitation effort, the Reliance reopened as the Hotel Burnham. The Atwood Café was added in 2000 (City of Chicago DPD 2001). Architectural critic Herbert Muschamp describes the current building: "The building's white terra-cotta façade, set to rhythm by bay windows, stares out from the pages of many books on architectural history. The windows are immense" and contribute to the openness of the facade (Muschamp 2000). The building is sited on the corner of the busy intersection of State and Washington, where its elegance becomes even more evident. The hotel gracefully meets the street, an intersection made even less intrusive by the addition of landscaping and, in warm weather, an outdoor eating area that wraps the corner. These features facilitate the possibility of chance encounters—the happenstance and bustle so desired for this urban street.

"On the ground floor, the reflections from the glass panels two stories high put you in the picture. You'll lose the blues at the Burnham [Reliance]" (Muschamp 2000). Although this advertisement may sound like a salesman's hyperbole, it actually offers an appropriate description of the building's deeper function. The interior and exterior boundaries between hotel and restaurant are fluid (see Figure 8). The hotel lobby entrance to the restaurant is on Washington Street, diffusing congestion and offering a bit of private space to those who will come to eat or sleep. The lobby has a cozy sitting area with a fireplace, which allows a view of the café. Few real walls exist here; open space easily flows into open space. For example, across from the original and still operating elevators, on a "wall" forming part of the alcove that once was the State Street entrance, there are displays

(now Hotel Burnham, main entrance at 1 West Washington Street); architects, Burnham and Root (1890–1891), D. H. Burnham and Company (1895); renovated by Graham, Anderson, Probst & White (1999)

7—Hotel Burnham (Reliance Building) and 20 North State Condos, July 2002

of historic photos of the Reliance Building. On the other side of the wall is the Atwood Café. The colorful tile floors that line the alcove are also original to the building and form the palette for both old and new spaces. They also serve to denote the transition from outside to inside, and from hotel to restaurant.

The Atwood Café draws patrons from among downtown workers, shoppers, and visitors. The café's expansive windows offer an unobstructed view of State and Washington streets, a growing entertainment hub, and of Marshall Field's and Company as well as activity on the street. Outdoor seating further blurs boundaries between inside and outside while it enables the sidewalk, as a path, to become a place where people can gather and interact, and shift their attention and pace. Interior and exterior meld past with present and invite those who are willing to shift the temporal rhythm from that of work to that of leisure and easily drift from public to private space—a necessary transition on urban streets. Beyond its overt function as a hotel and a restaurant, the Reliance Building can be considered an educational or cultural facility (and an elegant one at that), thus encapsulating the goals of retail, entertainment, and education in one space. For example, an exhibition hotel room is open for viewing.

The building has been transformed into a structure of multiple uses, for diverse users, much as the rest of State Street has. Its roles as hotel and restaurant are not new to the street, but now these have greater relevance to the city's transforming economy, which relies on tourists and businesspeople. In serving these new users, as well as locals who can enjoy the café while shopping or visiting the street, the building joins the Palmer House as another historic hotel on State Street that hopes to expand its own role and, with that, the role of State Street and the city.

THE ENTERTAINMENT DISTRICT

The renovation of North State Street's Chicago Theater Center is generally acknowledged as the pioneering effort toward the goal of making State Street an entertainment hub. The project, completed in 1986 with private funding and the city's endorsement, converted a 1921 movie theater and adjacent 1870s building into a mixed-use entertainment, retail, and commercial complex. The record-breaking success of the show *Joseph and the Amazing Technicolor Dreamcoat* sparked interest in other theater and entertainment properties on the north end of State Street and the bordering blocks. As a result, the expanded area has become known as the North Loop Performing Arts District. Randolph Street is, in Tabing's view, "really shaping up as the city's downtown entertainment district," thanks to TIF and other public funds. According to Tabing:

There are several theaters that were barely existing but have been brought on line. . . . [T]he reality is that with such ornate architecture, the private sector is not going to restore things in this manner. It's not economically doable and there's no economic sense behind it. So the public subsidy has really come in and bumped the caliber of these building up to a level that's really amazing. We have the streetscape with kiosks, just like on State Street—so Randolph and State streets are really the two focal points of what we're trying to do to all of downtown Chicago. (Tabing 2000)

Randolph Street now spills over to State Street, in the sense that the entertainment facilities and retail enterprises are mutually supportive. Together, their diverse offerings draw a variety of users downtown. This deliberate blurring of place and usage extends to other parts of Greater State Street and beyond to create a new Central Area. Plans work from the premise that buildings and public spaces must attract a diversity of people and that businesses must collaborate to achieve this goal. The intertwining of State and Randolph forms the command center of Chicago's theater and entertainment district. This area is rich in history, housing several cultural landmarks—some old and some new, each of which respects the others' temporal and spatial frames of reference, while very much working toward the Vision plan's present goals. Block 36, in many ways, encapsulates these goals for Greater State Street, in microcosm. Randolph Street also serves as a vital artery for the burgeoning West Loop and east to Millennium Park and the Lakefront.

Block 36 Complex—from State to Dearborn/Randolph and Lake Streets

Conceptualizing this area as a complex is appropriate, because it was conceived as a "social" group rather than merely an aggregate of buildings in proximity to one another. Framing it as a "block" fosters its form and function goals of offering a mix of entertainment, education, and retail facilities that intertwine and intercommunicate one with another. At the same time, this frame allows the area to be viewed in the larger context of State Street and other parts of the downtown area.

The State Lake Building (1917), located at 190 North State, was built by C. W. Rapp and G. L Rapp, architects. Rapp and Rapp were famous for designing over four hundred movie palaces across the country, including the Chicago Theater (1921) across the street at 175 North State. An elegant twelve-story white-terra-cotta office building, the State Lake Building originally housed the State-Lake Theater. The broad archway on the first floor, surrounded on either side by broad fluted columns, framed a grand marquee. Inside, the former twenty-seven-hundred-seat auditorium—converted by Skidmore, Owings & Merrill in 1984—still serves as a venue for entertainment, but now as broadcasting studios for ABC-WLS (television and radio).

Potbelly Sandwich Works (2000) occupies retail space at 190 North State. This eatery was designed by Aria Architects (see Figure 9). Potbelly's is a Chicago-based enterprise, one of the small but significant success stories along this street. The original Potbelly's opened as an antique store in 1977. When the owners started serving sandwiches in order to draw more business, the patrons' enthusiastic response convinced the owners to abandon antiques and focus on food. Bryant Keil bought the business in 1991. Although Potbelly's now operates over fifty branches, each one remains friendly and has its own style, one responsive to its siting. The business is still privately owned, and Mr. Keil has no intention of changing this aspect, or the feel of each place, personalized by kitschy antiques he and others often find in flea markets.

Tabing spoke enthusiastically about the impact of Potbelly's on the street: "One nice thing that happened in September/October [2000] was the result in part of students' moving into the dormitories. I talked to the owner last week and he said that their business had gone up 25 percent since the kids moved in, so they're really excited about that. And the increase is in dinner as well as lunch, which spreads their business—which is about 80 percent lunch—out a

9—Potbelly Sandwich Works
on State and Lake streets,
August 2004

little more evenly during the course of the day" (Tabing 2000). Small ventures can flesh out the city street and make State Street an active scene around the clock, seven days a week. Potbelly's offers a space for students and workers to gather and escape their concerns for a while. Like the Atwood Café, it offers outdoor dining and a view of the Loop including what, in fact, helped frame it, the elevated railway (the EL).

Designed by engineer John Alexander Waddell in 1897, the Chicago Union Loop Elevated Railway (the EL) is the only surviving elevated rail structure of its kind in the world. It was constructed as a "rapid transit" alternative to congested, at-grade electric streetcar lines (GSSC 2005). The EL wraps around this vital area of the city like a ribbon around special packages such as the State Lake Building. The synthesis of art and engineering on the level of street life, both staid and fluid and functioning on multiple levels, the Elevated offers itself as a singular gift of form and function to the downtown area, and as a reminder that transportation is vital to the vibrancy of not only the center but also the areas connecting to it and that movement networks can exist above or below street level.

Architects, Booth Hansen &
Associates (2000)

160–62 North State Street

160–62 North State Street, on the corner of State and Randolph, was designed by the Chicago firm of Booth Hansen & Associates and opened in 2000. The new seventeen-story, three-hundred-thousand-square-feet construction was horizontally connected to the renovated sixteen-story terra-cotta-clad Butler Building. In form and color, its design intentionally mirrors the Reliance Building, its neighbor to the south on State. A respectful and symmetrical counterpoint to this landmark building, 160–62 North State helps to bracket Block 37 (the space that separates the two), which remains undeveloped at present.

In 160-62 North State many of the Chicago traditions are referenced, from the Chicago-style structural bays and the Chicago-style windows, to the design and proportions of the building base and the cornice on top. While its form references a time past, 160 North State and the adjacent Butler Building are more than imitative. Glass-reinforced concrete (GRFC) panels introduce twenty-first-century technology to the beauty of nineteenth-century terra-cotta detailing. Maximum visibility reinforces the retail aspect of State Street. The streetwall is maintained and the existing height is extended (www.boothhansen.com). The thirty-four-thousand square feet designated as retail space currently houses Borders Books (three floors), Jamba Juice, and AT&T Wireless at street level, all of which opened in 2000 and early 2001. The complex provides student housing for the Art Institute in 165 loft-style apartments in the Butler Building and 325 residences in 162 North State; the Gene Siskel Film Theater; and the Art Institute's Film Center. Upper spaces are residential and commercial.

The real heart of the theater district actually begins around the corner on Randolph, from the Old Heidelberg/Nobel Fool Theater (see Figure 10) to the Ford Center for Performing Arts/Oriental Theater to the Goodman Theater (see Figure 11), all of which have been revamped to reflect their distinct form. Perhaps *disjuncture* and *fluidity* best describe the narrative they create. The Old Heidelberg, at 16 West Randolph (1934), was built by Graham, Anderson, Probst & White, Architects, in the rare style of German Revival. It was inspired by a popular restaurant concession at the 1933–1934 World's Fair. Renovation was undertaken in three stages at a cost of $2.5 million. The building offers a fitting context for the quirky Nobel Fool Theater Company, which opened in 2001 in the former Old Heidelberg Restaurant. The Nobel Fool adds a different dimension to the entertainment district, attracting late-night crowds with its special brand of comedy, improv, and cabaret performances. The Oriental Theater, at 24 West Randolph (1925), was built by Rapp and Rapp architects. It is at the street level of a twenty-two-story office building. It has a fanciful, Far Eastern–inspired auditorium, which seems appropriate for fanciful theater productions.

A counterpoint to these more modern theaters can be seen in the city's oldest and largest nonprofit theater, the Goodman Theater. The new Goodman Complex at 170 North Dearborn and Randolph consists of the older Harris and Selwyn theaters (built in 1922) and the new Albert Ivar and Bruner theaters (completed in 2000). The Harris and Selwyn theaters (1922) were designed by Crane and Franzheim and were home to some of the most famous plays and performers of the Broadway stage. Closed in the 1960s through the 1980s and then revamped and designated official landmarks in 1983, they both inspire and inform the complex. Sheathed in Mankato limestone, the original Goodman incorporates the classic terra-cotta facades of the landmark Harris and Selwyn. The new Albert Ivar and Bruner Goodman Theater Complex was added to the Harris and Selwyn in 2000. The $46 million, 170,000-square-foot building was designed by

10—*left*—View of Randolph at State Street (Theater District), July 2002

11—*right*—New Goodman Theater—Randolph and Dearborn, January 2001

the Toronto-based firm of Kuwabara Payne McKenna Blumberg Architects. The Albert Ivar Theater seats 850, and the Bruner, built within the Selwyn, seats 400. At the far end of the new complex lobby is a restaurant and retail corner. The vocabulary used by the new portion of the Goodman Complex makes it a thoughtful neighbor to the older building it conjoins (the Harris and Selwyn). Its interior and exterior synthesize technology, engineering, and aesthetics for a particular set of functions in the tradition of the early Chicago School of architecture. Patrons are offered a magnificent view of the area from the second-floor lobby while pedestrians walking along Dearborn or Randolph streets are engaged by its distinct curved-glass wall. The Goodman Complex is a vibrant and contemporary addition to the existing theater- and streetscape. Like Marshall Field's, it is understated and elegant.

The Block 36 complex straddles the line dividing the planned and the unplanned. While multiple intentions and activities fill State and Randolph streets, the block's main thrust follows the tradition of the former theaters and movie houses along this street. Many of these were demolished in the 1960s, including the Schiller (1892), later renamed the Garrick, and the Central Music Hall

(1897), both designed by Adler & Sullivan (Lowe 1985, 180–82). Van Vechten laments this physical and cultural loss: "When I first came here [twenty-five years ago], I think there were still some theaters up towards the north. The Woods Theater was still around on Madison and within the State Street vicinity. All those were right there with assorted other small scale things, like restaurants, some in basements, offering sort of an energy amid the messiness" (van Vechten 2001). In discussions concerning State and Randolph streets, comments such as this one arose frequently, reflecting the cognitive mapping that people use to sort out place and meaning. The landmarks are sometimes large, but often they are small, and they are based on experiences that increase the desire to return to something familiar, comfortable, and yet, as van Vechten notes, energizing and memorable. The disappearance of the old theaters was strongly felt.

Consequently, their recent reintroduction has encouraged the twenty-four-hour use of the street or at least has provided reasons for workers to stay on in the area beyond the regular office day, in a way that builds upon Chicago's tradition of varied and world-renowned cultural venues. Randolph quickly became recognized as the theater/cultural hub, and it soon inspired marketing strategies such as Hot Tix, at 78 West Randolph, which offers a variety of same-day half-price theater tickets. Hot Tix attracts customers with a Web site updated twice a day. It also hosts, on site, a video monitor playing clips from Chicago's top shows and an exhibit of theatrical posters. The SFX Theatrical Group and the Nederlander Organization teamed up to create BROADWAY IN CHICAGO, a promotional organization that joined the staffs, programming, marketing, and subscription series of three major theaters. And all along the street, there are kiosks and embossed "theater district" logos in the sidewalk itself that give this area imageablity and legibility.

The new Block 36 Complex is the product of a concerted effort by both private and public entities. It is probably fair to say that without the assistance from the city and the state, this successful revitalization could not have taken place. The entertainment forms in this hub span the spectrum from light and fanciful to masterful and cutting edge and, in doing so, provide a functional bridge between pure commodity and culture. This is being continued on the eastern portion of Randolph Street with smaller theaters such as the Storefront Theater at Gallery 37; the Loop Theater, also a storefront venue; and the Joan and Irving Harris Theater on Randolph just east of Michigan Avenue in Millennium Park, which crosses the vast divide that has existed between the Loop and the Michigan Avenue/Lakefront area.

So, too, in a physical and formal sense, the entertainment hub links State Street's retail and education districts. While the education hub is more squarely centered at the southern end of State Street, several educational institutions exist at the street's northern end. Among these are the dormitories for the Art Institute and Harold Washington College (HWC). HWC, at 30 East Lake Street, designed by architects Lowenstein and Lowenstein (1982), is part of the City Colleges of Chicago. Founded in 1962 as Loop College, it was originally sited at 60 East Lake Street, in the heart of the downtown business district, to serve Chicago's business community. The college moved when the current building was completed in January 1982 and, in 1987, changed its name to commemorate Chicago's late Mayor Harold Washington (Wozniak 2002).

Bounded by Lake, Randolph, State, and Wabash, HWC has the advantage of being in the heart of the Loop. It is a low-key and unremarkable beige concrete building, almost invisible in terms of design and signage, reflecting a no-nonsense approach to education or perhaps attuned to the sensibilities of the surrounding business district. HWC is a product of its time and place both literally and philosophically. In some ways it presents a postmodern statement, which views the workplace as a small urban village. In the words of Charles Jencks, an office becomes "a small city turned inside out. Part of the reason is pragmatic: these externally disguised informal types turn their back on the real, hostile street for security reasons, or they retrofit an old structure because it is cheap" (Jencks 1993, 66).

Today, the college is showing signs of structural wear and tear. A master plan proposed by the firm of Holibard and Root would repair elevators and escalators and liven up and expand spaces for socializing and add child-care facilities. However, because the facility is land-locked in terms of gross footage, it cannot grow physically to accommodate any new needs. Growth, therefore, must take place in virtual space, by means of distance learning and off-site instruction as well as through more creativity and flexibility in scheduling classes. HWC is dealing with the scarcity of physical space in all these ways.

Adding evening and weekend courses further enlarges the college and contributes to expanding temporal and social use of the Greater State Street area. Both approaches to defining form and function are especially important not only for this college but also for the Central Area if it is to reclaim its presence and vitality. As a public two-year college, HWC is not in competition with Northwestern University, Loyola, or the University of Chicago, all of which have a presence in the city's Central Area, but it does draw from the same student pool as Robert Morris College, DePaul University, Roosevelt University, and other institutions located just blocks away. In order to compete, HWC has taken cues for framing its curriculum from its location, Chicago's demographics, and the city's economic needs.

Job growth in the future will concentrate almost entirely in nonmanufacturing sectors. Booms in the hospitality and financial services sectors serve as the college's beacons. HWC offers both regular and continuing education programs in Culinary Arts, Business Information and Management, Information Technology (in partnership with Microsoft), Travel and Tourism, Video Production, and Healthcare. These programs reflect the changing economy of the city, the nation, and the students who attend. Profiles of HWC students indicate that a vast majority (75 percent in 1997) attend school part-time and that they are older than the traditional college age. A surprising 54 percent of the students work downtown, yet only 7 percent live there, although 54 percent report that they live on the South and Southwest sides of the city (Office of the President, HWC, 2002). Because not all those coming to HWC are interested in degrees, recreational course such as dance, yoga, and photography are also offered.

HWC's strategic and accessible location help the college to draw from the existing and emerging population. It is situated near trains and buses, in an area where people shop, work, and reside. It is at the nexus of the burgeoning Millennium Park area, as well as the Theater/Entertainment District and a developing riverfront occupied by information-based businesses and new residences, so the college also becomes an important resource for all these entities. But as the building is physically limited in space, the college's distance learning and virtual space becomes more critical, allowing HWC to expand its campus in ways not allowed by brick and mortar. HWC's look, like its mission, is no-frills. The college is less about place and more about activity.

THE EDUCATIONAL/CULTURAL DISTRICT

The third district finds its more literal center along the 400–500 blocks of State, west to Michigan Avenue, an area that includes Columbia College, De Paul University's Loop extension, Roosevelt University, Robert Morris College, and the School of the Art Institute. In 1993, as part of the university's expansion, the DePaul Center opened in a former department store building on State Street. This reuse project interwove educational, office, and retail functions and spurred a growth movement. Along with the city's new Harold Washington Library Center, DePaul firmly established what would be the city's cultural/educational district, a hybrid space anchored at State Street's south end. All but the Harold Washington Library occupy old structures, and several are housed in landmark buildings. Roosevelt University, for example, occupies the Auditorium Building at 430 South Michigan, which was designed by Adler & Sullivan and completed in 1899. The Robert Morris College is housed in the Second Leiter Building at 401 South State, which was designed by William Le Baron Jenney and completed in 1889. As with Block 36, this area should be thought of as a district or a hub, with paths that easily flow in and out of other parts of the street and the central area.

Robert Morris College—401 South State

Architect, William Le Baron Jenney (1891)

The Second Leiter Building, now housing Robert Morris College, is internationally known as an early Chicago School skyscraper. It introduced a new age of architectural design with a simple grid-line exterior reflecting the building's interior metal-frame construction. Occupying a full city block, the eight-story building was developed by Levi Leiter and constructed for the Siegel, Cooper and Company Store. Later it became the flagship store for Sears, Roebuck and Company (1932–1986) (GSSC 2005). The narrow exterior piers suggest the metal frame within them as do the slender piers and high ceilings inside. Ornament often is sparse, and the general effect is simple and direct. Renovation for the college includes a bookstore at street level with an entrance on State Street, as a concession to the Vision plan's desire for uniformity/order in appearance and as a way of situating its face on that street. The building is a prime example of the commercial style for which Chicago was famous at the end of the nineteenth and beginning of the twentieth centuries.

Jenney trained many of the eminent architects of the Chicago School's commercial buildings, including Louis Sullivan, William Holabird, Martin Roche, and Daniel Burnham, who in turn trained others and whose works also graciously line the Loop area. It is perhaps fitting that a structure designed by Jenney, one of the most significant of the first-generation Chicago School architects, now houses a place of higher learning where the tradition of passing knowledge and skills along to others thrives. One block north, in fact, the former A. M. Rothschild's (later Goldblatt Brothers) Building at 333 South State was converted by Daniel P. Coffey and Associates into the Loop campus for Depaul University, as well as spaces for retail and commerce. The university resides in a terra-cotta structure with wide projecting cornices and prominent brackets. It was designed and built by two of Jenney's students, architects Holabird and Roche, in 1912.

Several positive consequences brought about by the presence of students in the downtown area warrant mention. Students have changed the demographics of the downtown area by extending hours of use and by creating needs that require fulfillment. Tabing comments:

There are fifty thousand [part-time and full-time] students who attend classes in the Loop sometime during the week, . . . mostly at the South end of GSS . . . and as a result there's been a couple of retailers that have come in that really cater to that sort of crowd, like Rag Stock, which opened a couple of months ago, on South Wabash up on a second floor space. They're advertising in school papers down there and people love them. They're doing great. Another one is Reckless Records which just opened, and there is already a buzz. (Tabing 2000)

Newer stores such as Forever 21 and Urban Outfitters are clearly responding to the growing presence of this cohort group. Without this demographic, it is doubtful these stores would have come to State Street. Another observation on the increase of entertainment venues that cater to an educated but not necessarily wealthy population comes from architect and longtime city resident John Lahey (of the architectural firm Solomon Cordwell Buenz and Associates), who recalls: "I remember in 1976 on a weekend looking at how many places you could go to see live music and there were like four [places to go] and now there's four hundred" (Lahey 2001).

Architects, Hammond,
Beeby and Babka (1991)

Harold Washington Library Center—400 South State

Directly across from Robert Morris College is Chicago's main library. It takes its cues from the city's rich architectural heritage, including State Street's historic department stores. The ten-story classic structure has a rich terra-cotta-colored rough-face granite-and-brick exterior, five-story-high arched windows, which recall Sullivan's Auditorium Building, and metal ornamentation inspired by his own Carson Pirie Scott (see Plate 7). Like the Second Leiter Building and many of the first-generation commercial structures, it occupies a full city block and extends right up to the lot line. Inside as well, "the theme is much like that of department stores on State Street" (GSSC 2005). Escalators are located in the building's center; elevators, restrooms, water fountains, and phones line one wall. The light-colored wood floors and seating create an airy feeling as does the glass-roofed winter garden on the top story. Banners outside remind citizens of the importance of reading and of various library programs. Space has been allotted for a coffee shop on the first floor of the library.

Aside from its obvious role, this repository of information and culture is committed to being a democratic space, highlighting the diversity and contributions of the city's and country's racial and ethnic populations. The library houses large collections of artwork celebrating the links between African music and jazz, blues, and gospel. These not only reference the contributions made by African Americans to the city's and nation's shape and character; they also honor the library's namesake—the first black mayor of Chicago.

The library's and the city's commitment to the future is apparent in the growing number of free courses and programs offered to both children and adults. Computer workshops are particularly popular. On most days, the computer rooms are full, and there are long lines of people waiting for computer and internet access. Reference and reading areas are also heavily used. Patrons represent a good mix of the city's populace, including some of the city's homeless.

The Harold Washington Library—like Carson Pirie Scott, Marshall Field's, and other venues along State Street—has also become a place for the homeless to sit and read or use the bathrooms and lounges. In warmer weather, they also use nearby Pritzker Park to sleep. Seeing this, it becomes clear how the Chicago School of Sociology was compelled to consider marginality as well as centrality in cities as a topic worthy of careful investigation. Evidence of people living on the fringes within the center is all around—there to be seen, documented, and resolved, or to be avoided, ignored, and made invisible.

REFLECTIONS

It is perhaps fitting that the Harold Washington Library Center—a newer structure—references State Street's formal and functional heritage, while also extending it, at what marks the most southern edge of the street covered by the renovation plan, much like 160 North State does to the north. State Street is drawing in new populations and uses from its peripheral areas, just as the center is spilling outward. Now, however, a more reflexive relationship exists between periphery and center. In McKenzie's terms: "The process of population sifting produces not only increasing mobility with approach from the periphery to the center of the formation, but also different cultural areas" (McKenzie, in Park 1967, 78). And appropriately, new construction has begun, extending the street's southern end still further.

The Street as Marketplace—Economic Issues

State Street today seems to be making a successful transformation. By some standards the Vision plan has been successful in accomplishing what it set out to do. But State Street still faces problems. While the renovation has ignited some interest on the part of businesses, there is still concern about recruiting new industry and more retail onto the street. John Lahey observes: "In terms of corporate headquarters, no one wants to pay the high rents to have headquarters downtown, so they are out and still looking elsewhere. It will take a strong support system and other incentives to entice them back to the downtown area" (Lahey 2001). Attracted by such financial incentives, in 2000, Boeing moved its headquarters to Chicago's Loop. The company has had an important impact on development along the riverfront as well. The city hopes to send a signal to other companies that Chicago is a strategic and viable location for establishing their headquarters or branches.

For some areas of the Central Loop District, including State Street, TIF is due to expire in 2007, and there are concerns about securing the necessary funds for renovation and new construction. While some of these redevelopment projects are being fueled solely by private funding, developers and city officials believe some of the redevelopment will be impossible without TIF, which makes projects profitable for developers. Other affected programs would include the State Street Special Service Area (SSA), which was created to fund supplemental city services for State Street such as sanitation, signage upgrading, and maintenance by generating a special property tax levy on SSA property owners, with additional moneys provided by the city (Steele 2000; Tabing 2001; City of Chicago DPD 2000c, 2001; GSSC 2005).

Ty Tabing, among those who support TIF, noted: "Without this vision plan, and TIF, the probability is so many of these projects would not have gone forward. One effect is, it probably has pushed down the cost of office space downtown just in the way of supply and demand" (Tabing 2001). Figures for the Central Loop TIF district in 2000 bear this out. For the first time in a decade, the retail space in all of State Street's larger buildings was fully leased. Between 1999 and 2000, nearly forty thousand square feet of retail space was absorbed—the second-highest total in the last ten years. (Net absorption is the change in the amount of space leased and occupied and is a key indicator of supply and demand.) The Central Loop TIF has created and retained more than twenty thousand jobs, which otherwise would have been lost to surrounding communities or places outside city and state limits (City of Chicago DPD 2000c; GSSC 2000). Former planning commissioner Christopher Hill perhaps correctly observes: "The numbers show State Street is in the best shape it's ever been in a long time . . . but there's room for improvement" (Corfman 2000, 2).

Others are not so enthusiastic about TIF. Critics argue that it puts money in developers' pockets for doing things they would have done anyway. They also contend that there is not enough accountability in how moneys are spent; hence there is the possibility of waste. They add that success stories like State Street draw tenants away from other parts of the city. Thus these gains have not spread to other parts of the city that are also in need of economic boosting. Even in places like State Street, where successes are conceded, there are claims of inequity. For example, critics disclaim some of the gains in jobs, noting that, for the most part, they have been low-paying jobs in the service and information sectors, offering little mobility. They also contend that TIF mostly benefits larger businesses, thus driving out small business. Finally, critics see TIF as an instrument that promotes gentrification, making it difficult for the middle and working classes to move into or stay in the area (Schwartz 1999; "Downtown Is Up" 1998, 22–24).

Clearly, no one program, not even TIF, can resolve all the problems ailing State Street. In the first comprehensive report on the state of TIF in Chicago, released in August 1999, the National Budget Group (NBG) found that "Each TIF district is unique, just as each neighborhood is unique. Every TIF needs a revitalization plan that fits in with specific goals, assets and aspirations of the community" (Schwartz 1999, 8). For State Street these goals include increasing the presence of minority-owned businesses on the street, meeting the challenge of continued competition from suburban malls and shopping areas with higher profiles in the city, and generating a critical mass that can support business and retail. Success depends upon building a residential base that can make "downtown a twenty-four-hour neighborhood" (Tabing 2001).

Why have proposed solutions failed? While substantively different, all of these issues exist in a frame that has predetermined centrality and marginality and how the two must intersect. In all cases, the groups are positioned to oppose one another. So what must be done? Planners must, it seems, begin by shifting the existing frame, or more correctly sit on the frame, so perspectives and policies can emerge from State Street's goals, assets, and aspirations. From this vantage point, issues might be viewed and understood differently. That is, "center" and "periphery" refer not only to physical locations but to social configurations. If State Street is going to remake itself as a vital part of Chicago's new center, it must foster mixed uses, serve mixed functions, and also draw diverse users.

The city acknowledges the absence of minority-owned businesses on State Street and the DPD has launched marketing campaigns that reach out to African American and Latino communities and businesspeople. But this has not yet yielded any significant results. Historically programs have centered around a separation of spaces and political jurisdictions, that is, programs usually treat one section and then another, independently. For State Street—and, more generally, the CBD and its surrounding areas—to succeed in recruiting minorities, plans must interweave the needs and concerns of the dominant and nondominant groups. Programs and policies that integrate marginal areas into a larger vista in strategic ways must replace more traditional approaches. The expediency of zoning as well as traditional social and political jurisdictions must yield to mixed use in all regards (Terkel 1967, 1985; Hayden 1995; Sassen 2001b). Small inroads are being made on State Street, but there is room for improvement.

The continued challenge posed by other retail venues in and around State Street requires an internal as well as an external shift in how the street relates to difference and similarity. State Street finds itself needing to create a niche market in an economic environment that is growing increasingly uniform. Tabing sees the site-specific goal for State Street as one that focuses on assets rather than on competing with these venues. He notes:

We really want State Street to be a destination point for retailers and we have no illusions that State Street is going to be competing with Michigan Avenue because they're different markets. . . . six hundred thousand people a day work downtown and there's plenty of a market for retail shopping and destination shopping hopefully. I don't mean one of a kind upscale shops or products [as you might see on Michigan Avenue], but just something you couldn't get anywhere else, where you also get the service and you get a different kind of experience. That's the sort of thing we'd love to see on State Street. (Tabing 2000)

The deals currently being made may be smaller and the tenants not as glitzy as Michigan Avenue's, but they reflect a more fundamental change for State Street (Corfman 2000, 2). Part of that fundamental change reflects the street finding its place in an increasingly global market. As Park observed nearly eighty years ago: "[Modern cities] are, by their position . . . integral parts of a system of international commerce. They are way-stations and shopping centers, so to speak, on the main street of the world. Politically and administratively, these cities are of course independent of one another, but commercially they are all bound up together and as interdependent as the spokes of a wheel" (Park 1974, 2:134).

Today, this relationship is more intensified and complex. One important difference between today's global cities and markets and world cities and markets in earlier periods is that global cities are a function of a cross network of strategic sites. The grid is vastly larger and more intricate. Global cities are still the central site for production. But now instead of things, they produce information and innovation. The dispersion of some activities, such as manufacturing or assembling, has occurred, often to cities in other parts of the world. This leaves cities once defined by manufacturing struggling to find new identities. It also means they must realign with first-tier cities and cities in what is a vastly more complex, competitive, yet more interdependent grid (Sassen 2001b, 1998b).

This new arrangement exacerbates the already tenuous balance between localism and globalism that must be sustained by cities and their components. Manuel Castells (1989) asserts that localities such as cities and regions can find their role in the new informational economy by becoming indispensable elements in the new economic geography. While the main source of productivity here is to generate and process new information, this is itself dependent on symbolic interpretation, which is locally generated. "Production in the informational economy becomes organized in the space of flows, but social reproduction continues to be locally specific" (Castells 1989, 351–52). So, localism can actually save the city's identity and viability when confronted with spaces of flows, rather than becoming "meaningfully meaningless" (Castells 1993, 254). State Street is a prime example of this. The term *space of place* refers to areas defined by specific concrete or material sites and local parameters, or place-boundedness. The term *space of flows* references areas defined by trans-border connections, especially through virtual networks of connectivity, i.e. telematics. "Space" here is unbounded and defined by parameters external to it. The distinction is made to reflect shifts in economic orders—"place" referring to industrial/manufacturing and "flows" to information-based industries/economics.

The postmodern city Castells describes is a site where people live as well as work. This means that the CBD must expand beyond its traditional role as marketplace and become a residential area as well. To do this, it needs to find unique features it can offer residents as well as businesses, spaces that can house both activities such as mixed-use venues, so that, in itself, State Street must be "both-

and" rather than "either-or." Residential spaces will give the street added form, complexity, and diversity in use, and potentially more profitability. Residents will then provide the needed source of density and association to support business and infrastructure; without these, the lifeblood of the city, the street, falters.

Van Vechten's reflections on the current condition and feel of the street give voice to these concerns: "There's an air of, it's not artificiality—of thinness. I think if there're enough people downtown you'll start to see the need for a shoe repairer, Blockbuster video, and mom and pop delis. There used to be—The Dill Pickle Deli and Bev and Bob's—and that whole level that kind of thing that you currently have to search to find. There's still a few of them around but most of them are dropping like flies. Maybe if more people lived here, maybe that will come" (van Vechten 2001). But Tabing notes:

The reality is that the folks in the retail business are not really known for their risk taking. Our goal has been trying to get better bars, better restaurants, better everything downtown and everybody says well you know you've got to . . . show me the money here first. So they need to see numbers. In order for businesses to be willing to come to this area, they need to see a residential community that provides potential customers besides just the ones who are here nine to five everyday—with a lunch hour. (Tabing 2000)

What we have is a catch-22 situation. That is, how do you generate the necessary critical mass if there is nothing to lure people in, if businesses will not come unless they are guaranteed a critical mass prior to making a commitment? The answer is multifold, and it requires a new and deeper reading of urbanism and of urban forms and functions.

Today, perceptions about urban and nonurban areas, and consequently their uses, are in a state of flux. This ambiguity could be used to State Street's advantage. State Street's re-creation coincides with a larger realignment of urban with suburban and exurban spaces, which in part is the result of demographic shifts that have been occurring for the last twenty years. Empty-nesters, people tired of long commutes, young people eager to take advantage of the new economy and city amenities, all are helping to resuscitate the city as a place to live. Architect John Lahey reflects on these trends as they have impacted Chicago:

In the '60s and '70s when I was growing up . . . everything was suburban, still the nostalgic version of American living. Now everything is situated in the city. It's hot and the place to be—to live. And in Chicago, it's right in the downtown area. . . . In the '60s and '70s there was Old Town. . . . Now River North, West of the Loop are areas that are really thriving . . . and areas that would not have been considered by many . . . but are situated close to the downtown area are also surging. (Lahey 2001)

So while State Street does not want to be perceived as a competitor with North Michigan Avenue or suburban malls, it must still establish a corelational position and role with the surrounding residential spaces. For State Street, this means focusing on what is distinct in its form, how it can provide for a new pool of residents, and how it can better coexist with surrounding areas. The relationship between the spaces may very well be contested at times, but now this contestation can be viewed as precisely that which will sustain the identity and vitality of the new whole and its parts.

Rather than risk a recurrence of the oozing or seeping tendencies that characterized movement out of the cities, new plans need to be clear, focused, and pliable. This includes positioning the city in the global terrain. One outcome of globalization is a sharpening inequality of strategic resources and activities. Central to the development of this new core of cities as well is high-income commercial and residential gentrification (Sassen 1998b). In order for State Street and the larger CBD to thrive, the flip side of gentrification, extreme poverty and, with it, homelessness also need to be considered and addressed.

The Street as Meeting Place—Social Issues

According to Hayden: "place is one of the trickiest words in the English language," and "as a place becomes more economically and socially complex, change is rapid, layers proliferate, and often abrupt spatial discontinuities result that are difficult to identify, much less reconcile" (Hayden 1995, 17, 3). Thus space of places is a good characterization of State Street in 2005. But place, regardless of where or when we assess it, must incorporate identity: the identity of the area and the identity of those who inhabit it. For the inhabitants, that identity must be forged out of a sense of belonging. Therefore a space of place needs, according to Hayden, "to acknowledge and respect diversity, while reaching beyond multiple and sometime conflicting [social factors] to encompass larger common themes" so that more people feel a deeper sense of membership, without having to reject their identity (Hayden 1995, 9). "Place" needs to become "places." From these criteria, State Street has become an increasingly inclusive place. Plans deliberately include a diversity of users: students, residents, older people, and visitors. Retail is making efforts to reflect the city's ethnic composition (for example, Sears's efforts to attract Hispanic and African American customers). But as Hayden's commentary suggests, for State Street to be considered the people's street, it must also make space for those in search of a new sense of identity in an urban setting, including the most peripheral population of all—the homeless.

Homelessness is a noticeable and growing problem for State Street, as it is throughout the entire downtown area. But it is not a new problem. From the very start, Chicago School sociologists explored the city with an eye to its more marginal citizens and to the issues of stratification, distance, order, and mobility from a physical as well as a social context. They understood that people on the fringes of life were as much a part of the city as those who were firmly entrenched in what was understood as normal life. Marginal people, including the homeless, therefore had to be included in any description and analysis of urban community and of the life of the street. Sociologist Martin Bulmer believes: "The tradition of local social involvement was the soil that nurtured the urban studies of the Chicago School of Sociology and made the relationship between the university and city different from that in New York or Boston" (Bulmer 1984, 25).

More recent analyses of urbanism tend to reject the early Chicago School's portrayal of marginal individuals (as, for example, Park's "hobo") on the grounds that this portrayal romanticized and misrepresented what was actually a structural problem as a problem that was more idiosyncratic in derivation and ultimately solution (Park 1967, 156–60; Stoner, in Dear 2002b). Nonetheless, studies of the homeless, especially those done in the past twenty or so years, point to critical differences in who the homeless persons are and in the causes of homelessness. Today, along with single males there are women, children, and families. The homeless are predominantly people of color and are often severely and persistently mentally ill. They are "the faces of extreme poverty and cycles of systematic disadvantage in postmodern society" (Stoner, in Dear 2002b, 221). Sociologists point to the crucial connection between an increase in poverty (in part caused by inflation and by unemployment in low-skill sectors) and a corresponding decline in the availability of affordable housing (Stoner, in Dear 2002b, 220–31; Hoch and Slayton 1989; Shinn and Gillespie 1994).

While differences clearly exist between those comprising the floating population of Park's time and those occupying that position today, there are characteristics they do share. Both types of studies focus on people who belong to severely marginalized groups and who are little understood by mainstream society. Both depict such people whose connection to productive labor is tenuous at best, who are disaffiliated from their early associations and locations, and yet who are interested in and in need of re-creating new associations and personal spaces. Indeed, today, the homeless are comprised of a greater diversity of people as well. Both old and new versions of homeless studies note that social distance is intensified by their presence at the physical center of the city. Both versions suggest that the floating population is part of the rhythm of the city. In essence the homeless people are the silence between beats; the presence of an absence. It is this silence that Greater State Street must give voice to.

State Street must therefore consider how to include the transient population as well as other marginal populations in its plans for greater economic and social viability. If cities and their components have become the nexus for the homeless as a result of the convergence of urbanization and extreme poverty, attention must focus on cities and their relationships with these citizens. Policies must be responsive to both local and global issues, and they must offer economic incentives to rebuild areas that are—or are on their way to becoming—blighted in ways that include rather than exclude portions of the urban population. In particular, the policies need to resist the geographic containment and isolation of poor people because isolation creates border vacuums and hinders flow and interaction (Jacobs 1961). Architects and developers must resist designs that devalue and further marginalize groups of people by race or socioeconomic standing, as was historically borne out in the building of hyperghettos. This means not only resisting the urge to segregate groups of people by activity, function, or socioeconomic standing, but also, as Huxtable warns, avoiding the developer's version of manifest destiny known as gentrification.

Social historian Studs Terkel's view of the encroachment of one group upon another in his neighborhood pointedly encapsulates the dilemma: "Our rooming house is not there for these other-worlders. Our rooming house is not there for any guest. Our rooming house is not there at all. It is a vacant lot. . . . Not for long. The upwardly mobile young have discovered the neighborhood; so have the developers. . . . They simply sniff the air of a neighborhood—close to the Loop, close to where the action is, close to what is *de rigueur* for the young on the make. And so, it's bye-bye, McLaren School" (Terkel 1985, 48). Cities and their basic units—their streets—must make spaces that can accommodate all inhabitants in a respectful way. In urban environments, this means including a healthy presence and use of public as well as private space. Jane Jacobs reminds us: "Formal public organizations in cities require an informal public life underlying them, mediating between them and the privacy of the people of the city. . . . The difference between public and extended private life [or space] is subtle but city design needs public space" (Jacobs 1961, 57, 64).

Therefore, designs must balance public and private spaces so that they foster flow and interaction. This is not always easy, as shown when the homeless or other groups colonize space or create home-territories, often by necessity as businesses, keepers of public spaces, and other residents intersect with these inhabitants. This tilts but does not shift the frame. Policies and designs must be created to foster the delicate and ambiguous line that does not alienate patrons or residents and respects the rights and needs of the homeless in spaces inhabited by both. This is often frustrating and painful. After one visit to the city, I was particularly overwhelmed by the issue of homelessness and made the following journal entry from the stance of ethnographer:

As I waited for coffee at a Starbucks in the Loop, a homeless woman came in to use the bathroom. A patron waited to use the bathroom. It was a long wait. In the meantime the manager went outside and told the panhandler he couldn't stand in front of the door. When the woman came out of the bathroom, she was told they didn't allow people with satchels or bags to use the bathrooms. This was a more polite way of getting her message across I suppose. I understood and empathized with both sides. The presence of the homeless doesn't help business. This scene is repeated over and over, in department stores, in the library, in public parks. It is all around—visible in an invisible sort of way. I see how Chicago school sociologists were drawn to zones of transition and marginality in cities, choosing people living there as topics for study, and depending on your perspective, there to solve or at least document. (Satler journal entry, July 11, 2002)

The homeless use the street and its buildings; they use the parks and greenspace to sleep and rest. They are part of the rhythm of the street. But they too are framed by the street, although more loosely. Perhaps they are the real shadows, the in-between of beats on State Street; the presence of an absence that needs a voice.

Tackling homelessness and the greater inclusion of minorities in commercial, cultural, and educational enterprises on Greater State Street are tasks that still await resolution. Looking at the street, even in its unfinished state, through these problems provides a vantage point from which to observe part of the terrain that is essential to understanding the real essence of the street and the larger urban landscape, one not always readily visible. The frames formed by the unnoticed or unfinished also enhance the meaning of the street we see and inhabit. They help clarify the diversity of aspects that must be addressed by architects, developers, landlords, and inhabitants, if State Street, the CBD, and the city, more generally, are to continue along the road laid out by efforts such as the Vision plan.

So what do we see when we look at State Street today? In its most basic sense, State Street is a line and pathway. It is also a place of paradoxes, both solution and resolution, and unfinished business, much like the rest of the city. There is a new infrastructure in place. There are new residences and businesses, all of which are more attractive than before. A walk up and down State Street today reveals a well-choreographed composition of old and new. One can easily find the distinct retail, entertainment, and educational/cultural districts, while also experiencing the fluidity of the street. Here, spatial and temporal layers of the buildings overlap, and residential units interweave with commercial units to create a feeling of increased texture and depth. Van Vechten assesses State Street with appropriate understated pride and humility: State Street "has come a long way in ten years. While it's not quite at a level where it was, it's coming along" (van Vechten 2001). It is doing so, I would add, Chicago-style.

"Urban neighborhoods," Park wrote, "manage to retain their identity over time only occasionally and, even then, with the greatest difficulty. The increasing proliferation of transportation and communication facilities in the city stimulates population mobility and this tends to break up the tensions, interests and sentiments, which give neighborhoods their individual character" (Park 1967, 8). These processes have not only reshaped State Street, they are helping reshape the entire CBD. The Vision plan has taken State Street back to its roots. It has built upon these roots and given the street dynamism, fluidity, and the potential to expand and branch out in diverse ways, upward and outward. The reverse task awaits development on the riverfront—that is, creating structure and permanence on a terrain that is by definition unlimited and unbounded.

12—Overhead view of main branch of the river and river-bend from Sears Tower Observatory, January 2002

PART II

The Riverfront

If the renovated State Street can be considered a site where boundaries defined by meaningful existing structures were opened up through their use, then development along and on the Chicago River represents Chicago's new frontier, a terrain as yet unbounded and undefined, that offers potential—the energy of flow and (liquid) continuity in search of forms that can house or guide them. To put it another way, State Street represents the making of what sociologist Manuel Castells refers to as a "space of place," whereas the river represents the making of a "space of flows":

[S]pace of flows, refers to the system of exchanges of information, capital, and power that structures the basic processes of societies, economies and states between different localities, regardless of localization. . . . The new spatial logic, characteristic of the [Global] Informational City, is determined by the preeminence of the space of flows over the space of place. I call it "space" because it does have a spatial materiality. (Castells 1993, 254)

Just as an analysis of State Street provided insights into the city's efforts to redefine itself through formal and functional moves, an analysis of the developments on the Central Area's riverfront offers insights into the city's efforts to redefine itself through formal and functional means. Efforts on the street and along the river can provide a new understanding and interpretation of the new urban community, especially the relationship between center and periphery within local and global parameters.

In the late 1980s and early 1990s, Chicago, like many other older cities, began to experience the social and economic impacts brought about by globalization; in particular, there was growing emphasis on information-based industries as opposed to manufacturing, and increased levels of internationalization in the economic and social structure. For Chicago, these shifts were especially difficult. Not only did it lose its position as the nation's "Second City" (to Los Angeles), it was also displaced by Los Angeles as the archetype of the postmodern city. At this time, some observers even went so far as to question the very future of "cities" in a terrain where place-boundedness seemed to no longer matter. But Chicago's Central Area seemed to disprove this prediction.

During this period, Chicago's Central Area witnessed growth in the downtown office sector. New residential neighborhoods emerged, and the number of business visitors and tourists soared. Census data for the year 2000 indicate that population decline in most large central cities of the Northeast and Midwest slowed and in some cases reversed. This marked a significant change from the trend in the 1970s and 1980s (Krontoft, McMillen, and Testa 2001). According to one report: "Between 1990 and 2000, the population grew from 63,000 to 90,500, a growth rate of about 45% over the last decade" (City of Chicago DPD 2001, 63). Along with this growth came new questions and new issues tied to local and global factors: among them, the need to decide on the location, scale, and design of new buildings; how future land uses and population densities should be organized; and how to balance growth with quality of life.

In order to build upon its growth and successes and also address the new challenges it faced, Chicago adopted a bifocal approach. The city developed plans and programs for specific sites such as State Street to address local issues. In the process the city rediscovered some of its neglected assets. To respond to global exigencies, a different and more encompassing strategy was required. At the core of this strategy was the need to provide an infrastructure that could expand and reach beyond the existing central area and the city limits while still reinforcing the role of the city and center as vital hubs for the growing conglomerate of transportation, social, economic, and informational networks. To accomplish this dual goal, city and center had to realign with what surrounded them. And they had to do so in ways that responded to real as well as virtual time and space. Rather than focusing on a particular image or form, the challenge posed here was to locate or capture movement, without stopping it. This dynamic connectivity would create a new canvas for the city. As noted in the Central Area Plan (City of Chicago DPD 2000a; henceforth cited as CAP): "Successful cities are dynamic cities. They are linked to the world and are able to adapt to and conquer global challenges" (CAP, 1). In devising plans to address these issues, the city relied on one of its previously neglected resources. The city (re)turned to the river.

Precedents for this had been set by mixed-use projects such as Marina City and River City and by the Merc, whose repositioning through the selling of futures embodies the newer financial and informational sectors of the economy. For all these three projects, the river served as site and inspiration for design and function. Yet these were exceptions rather than the rule. This time, however, it was the city and not the river that changed direction. Using the river as both site and catalyst for new commercial and residential efforts, the city embarked on a transformation that has resulted in a Central Area that is new in scope and purpose, and ready to take on local, regional, and global challenges as well as those critics who are skeptical of the future of cities and city centers. This new Central Area would be "a vibrant place—a civic, high-density, mixed use and walkable area and the connection between city neighborhoods and the lakefront. The vision for the future of the Central Area is one that encompasses districts extending from Division Street to the Stevenson Expressway, from Lake Michigan to Halstead, with the Chicago River as a central focus" (CAP, 33). But it also became quite clear that the city intended to "preserve and enhance the local, regional and international position of the Central Area" (CAP, 1). To accomplish these goals, the Central Area had to be conceived as central to a much larger whole.

Traditional models of cities and urban growth, such as those posited by sociologists at the Chicago School, begin at the city center (the CBD) and extend outward. More recent models, such as those emanating from the Los Angeles School, contend that the notion of city center organizing the city no longer holds. Rather, it is the urban peripheries that organize what remains of the center (Dear 2002a, 432). These views about centrality and marginality are not quite as oppositional as they may appear. The challenge for twenty-first-century Chicago is to build upon an infrastructure shaped by a sense of great architecture and planning, including its public spaces, while incorporating new parameters created by globalization. As plans for Chicago's transformation began to take form in the late 1990s and the early 2000s, it was clear that the city was poised for change, movement, and redefinition.

(RE)TURNING TO THE RIVER

"Every advance in culture," wrote historian Carl Bücher, in his *Industrial Evolution* (1901), "commences, so to speak, with a new period of wandering" (347). Social historian Frederick Teggart concurred, noting that wandering is "considered as the liberation from every given point in space. It is the conceptual opposite of fixation at any point" (Teggart, in Park 1974, 1:351). "Wandering" and "liberation" provide an appropriate context from which to understand the impetus behind the re-creation of Chicago's Central Area and, particularly, for the rediscovery of the Chicago River.

The river offers the perfect literal and analytic tool for expressing the duality, complexity, and dynamism of Chicago's new phase of development. The river meanders through all parts of the city and serves as a kind of "disinterested" connecting force, which realigns and restructures everyone and everything along its path (including what exists in the river), both indigenous and constructed. It serves as a liquid spine, rather than a fixed core or boundary, creating what Saskia Sassen refers to as "analytic borderlands" (Sassen 1996).

Using the river as frame and viewing the terrain on either side as borderlands does several important things. It allows the focus to shift to the regions and their relationships, rather than the line that divides them. It also allows the relationships between regions to be understood as reflexive—that is, "both-and" rather than "either-or." Further, if centrality and marginality are used as analytic devices that denote social relationships (such as power or distance) rather than solely as physical constructs, it becomes possible to understand the status and concerns of the dominant culture while still respecting the vernacular and concerns of the nondominant or local cultures, or of a specific site, even if the relationship between them is asymmetrical.

So instead of reducing a terrain to a single parameter, the impulse now is to sustain and work with a multiplicity of perspectives and issues. This overlay expands the notion of place (a city, for example) and provides the possibility of more alternatives and outcomes, with greater inclusion than would have been the case using frames where many of these elements would be viewed as peripheral or out of the frame altogether. More specifically, it becomes possible to understand the impact of global and local processes on the city's morphology simultaneously. Rather than look at the Central Area as the source from which all else is derived and defined, its morphology and growth as well as those of the city can now be viewed as part of a larger network, where each aspect fuels and organizes the whole. Central and marginal regions become areas of discontinuity, rather than points of difference. In the global sphere, discontinuities are an integral part, indeed a necessary component, of economic and social systems.

REFRAMING CENTRALITY—THE PLANS

Current plans for the Central Area's development are firmly committed to this view. Three plans, in particular, *Chicago's Central Area Plan: Phase 1* (2000–2002), the *Chicago River Corridor Development Plan* (1999), and *A New Economy Growth Strategy for Chicagoland* (2001) provide for Chicago's new identity and direction. Together they lay a blueprint for building a center that confirms and is confirmed by the entire city composition. The Central Area Plan (CAP) provides a framework for economic and residential growth and establishes an agenda for the development of transit, open space, infrastructure, and environmental systems through 2020. Initiated by Mayor Daley with the assistance of Skidmore, Owings & Merrill (SOM) as lead consultants and a twenty-four-member steering committee of elected officials and government, business, and civic leaders, the CAP is the product of over two years of discussion and reflection. It is the first plan for downtown produced by the city since 1958. According to Alicia Berg, commissioner of the city's DPD: "This plan is driven by a vision of Chicago as a global city, the 'downtown of the Midwest,' the heart of Chicagoland, and the greenest city in the country" (Internal Publications).

The CAP recognizes that "Chicago's Central Area is actually many centers in one, operating within many geographic spheres, ranging from global to local. . . . The vision for the Central Area must address these multilayered relationships" (CAP, 1). In addition, the plan presents the new Central Area as "a vibrant place—a civic, high-density, mixed use and walkable area and the connection between city neighborhoods and the lakefront. Geographically, it encompasses districts extending from Division Street to the Stevenson Expressway, from Lake Michigan to Halstead, with the Chicago River as a central focus" (CAP, 33). Analytically, the CAP is framed around distinct mixed-use districts, waterfronts and open spaces, and good accessibility and connectivity (CAP, 33). For this reason, "[the plan] must be guided by a larger vision, one that looks beyond the current horizon to the challenges and opportunities presented by changes in the global marketplace" (CAP, 4).

Answering this call, *A New Economy Growth Strategy for Chicagoland* (NEGSC 2001) presents "a *dual-focused* growth strategy." The plan was created by the mayor and the city, in conjunction with a Council of Technology Advisors, various public-private partnerships such as World Business Chicago and CivicNet, and consulting and research firms, including McKinsey and Company. By fostering start-up businesses and technology transfer and by concentrating on key high-priority, high-tech areas and balancing the new enterprises with the city's existing viable economic sectors, the plan aims to transform Chicago into a leading center of the global new economy (NEGSC, 2–3). The key is to make technology a lasting and important part of the city's economy and, in doing so, to introduce diversity.

While the CAP and NEGSC inform the socioeconomic changes envisioned for the Central Area, the *Chicago River Corridor Development* (CRCD 1999) plan considers the physical site upon which these plans will be enacted—the riverfront. The plan was implemented in response to renewed interest in replacing or combining manufacturing with residential and commercial uses and in cleaning up the river for recreational use. To achieve this, the plan is organized around three linked spheres—combining authority, expertise, and more inclusive participation, and specifically, a steering committee to provide overall policy direction, key public sector partners, and public participation (CRCD, 6).

The steering committee was comprised of representatives from government agencies, nonprofit organizations, and developers with interest in river development and preservation (CRCD, 6). The key public-sector partners included the Chicago Department of Transportation (CDOT), the Chicago Department of the Environment (CDOE), Cook County Forest Preserve (CCFP), and the Metropolitan Water Reclamation District of Greater Chicago (MWRD). They offered financial and management guidance on specific implementation strategies. Public participation was achieved through a series of open houses held over a six-week period in March and April 1998. The overall plan for the river was presented at each open house, along with detailed descriptions of proposed improvements on adjacent areas in order to obtain public comment (CRCD, 7).

Along with the CRCD, the City of Chicago created a set of design guidelines and standards. Covering both renovations and new construction in all areas adjacent to the Chicago River, the guidelines are meant to ensure compatibility both with surrounding structures and with the environment (CRCD, 2, 76). Five key components frame the plan and design guidelines: building paths and green ways along the river, increasing public access through the creation of overlooks and public parks, restoring and protecting natural habitat and landscaping, developing the river as a recreational amenity, and encouraging economic development compatible with the river as an environmental and recreational resource (CRCDGS, 1).

The new economic and living patterns envisioned in the plans also call for different imagery in scale and function. The global terrain is characterized by hyperconnectivity, hypermobility, and flexibility. Much of its imagery is derived from the growing importance of telematics (telecommunications) in the economy. This requires a realignment of relationships and spaces organized by virtual or hyper-parameters in addition to local contexts, that is, plans for the center and the city must include parameters for framing and connecting the Central Area and the city beyond their actual spatial and temporal boundaries. The plans reflect awareness that the city must provide a terrain where people are connected in real space and time. Buildings, paths, and activities must therefore respond to the globally generated requisites while keeping in mind the more basic needs of quality of life on a local, human scale. This is especially significant because many conceptualizations of dual cities (and their marketplaces) often emphasize the virtual sites at the expense of real ones. As Sassen correctly reminds us: "large cities around the world are the terrain where a multiplicity of globalization processes assume concrete, localized forms. These localized forms are, in good part, what globalization is about" (Sassen, 1998a). So while Chicago and its center are being realigned and connected of necessity to areas that immediately surround them as well as to more distant areas, they remain essential and real components in this new terrain. In essence, the plans call for a perspective that focuses on the site, but that also reaches beyond it.

Chicago, like many cities, finds itself in the position of asking not only whether it can balance spaces for the new informational economy with older manufacturing sectors, but whether it can bring people back to the city to live, thus bridging the urban/suburban divide. And if so, how is such balancing and spatial formation best conceived? Mayor Daley holds a "strong belief that the cities that pay attention—really pay attention—to quality of life will be the cities that thrive in the 21st century" (Office of the Mayor 2002c). As the CAP acknowledges: "The City needs to strike a balance between preserving a healthy office environment and meeting the housing, retail and open space needs of new residents" (CAP, 27). Architectural critic Blair Kamin notes, "Ideally, a new building strikes up some relationship with the structures and the sidewalks around it" (Kamin 2001a). But Chicago architect James DeStefano points out: "there seem to be fewer directives from City Hall about fitting in with old-fashioned, stone-clad buildings. On the other hand, city planners will be right to insist that the new towers fulfill the social obligation of the skyscraper. That means ensuring that the buildings contribute to the liveliness of their surroundings with ground-floor shops, restaurants, and well-used public spaces" (DeStefano, in Kamin 2001a). As part of this frame, the CRCD raises other considerations and options for building on the riverfront. Freed of its industrial connotation, development along the river now encompasses other concerns, namely, the integration of public space.

COMPOSING DUALITY—ARCHITECTURAL DESIGNS

We can begin to see how the intersection of globalization and spaces of flows and local and site-specific spaces (spaces of place) frame socioeconomic and environmental planning. But how do they affect architectural designs? As with its economic and social mandates, architecture has to make space for the more globally informed views of aesthetics and functions while also maintaining a connection with its past. Architect James Goettsch believes: "The new aesthetic approach goes hand in hand with internal shifts, like raised office floors, that allow the workplace to better accommodate computers and adjust to future changes. After all, what good is a sense of permanence in a business culture that prizes flexibility and adaptability? Now the ideal is to make buildings that seem weightless rather than weighty. Technology has to do with reducing things. We're trying to use as much glass as we can" (Goettsch, in Kamin 2001a). But Benet Haller of the city's DPD reminds those building in Chicago that "Chicago likes buildings made of limestone, brick, concrete—not glass boxes" (Haller 2002). Chicago-based architect Larry Booth concurs: "We have a certain continuity over 150 years. If you begin to just ignore that and say, 'Oh, we want to keep up with the time and we want to do whatever happens to be in fashion,' we could end up losing that kind of quality or spirit of Chicago as a place, as a distinct town in the world" (Booth, in Hepp 1999).

This concern also echoes several economic realities of Chicago. One is that manufacturing is still an important economic sector for the city. While the city's business base has diversified in the last three decades and financial and service sectors are growing, more than 90 percent of the economy remains in slower-growing sectors—manufacturing, retail, financial services, and real estate—where overall employment growth is expected to hover at just over 1 percent annually through 2008. These sectors remain critical to the economic well-being of the city, but on their own they lack the potential to maintain the region's economic leadership (NEGSC, 3). The city aims to extend its reach, but recapturing the geography of places involved in globalization requires local places where the work of globalization gets done. For Chicago, this locality is the Loop. Chicago's downtown maintains a larger share of the overall metro-area inventory of office space compared to other major downtown office markets. With 56 percent of the total metro inventory in 2000, Chicago is second only to New York City, which captures 62 percent of the metro-area inventory, midtown and downtown (Manhattan) combined (CAP, 10). One issue for Chicago is that current building code restrictions limit the use of manufactured wiring systems ("modular" wiring systems), which reduce first costs and life-cycle costs (Krontoft, McMillen, and Testa, 2001). This transformation will involve institutional and structural changes. Sassen explains: "the new growth sectors, the new organizational capacities of firms, and the new technologies are contributing to produce not only a new geography of centrality but also a new geography of marginality. . . . This reorganization ranges from the spatial virtualization of a growing number of economic activities to the reconfiguration of the geography of the built environment for economic activity" (Sassen 2001a).

The integration of new spatial forms with older ones can take place in a number of ways. Some, like political economist Manuel Castells, believe that spaces of flows erode—or have the potential to erode—local vernaculars and ways of interacting. He notes, for example, that while "space of flows does have a spatial materiality, . . . the locales of the space of flows are meaningfully meaningless, both in their internal arrangement and in their architectural forms . . . due to their increasing differentiation between power and experience, [and] the separation of meaning from function" (Castells 1993, 254). Others, such as architects Rem Koolhaas and Maya Lin, see the shift in how one views the relationship between center and peripheries as one that can extend existing terrains. Koolhaas believes that, instead of using the old model that moves from center to periphery, one can begin with the experiences of the margins and create an entirely different work. The resulting frame or space is not based on knowledge from the dominant center; instead, "it starts with an absolute ignorance, and tries to create a knowledge about those kinds of particulars—for the project in question" (Koolhaas 2002, 8). In other words, building begins at the periphery or margins and then surrounds and solidifies to create its form. And architect Maya Lin suggests: "In choosing to break the symmetry of the existing building I am conveying a simple conceptual message—things don't have to be or look identical in order to be balanced or equal. . . . The base is not at the center point or circle" (Lin 2000, 4:28).

Regardless of perspective, there is consensus that coherence (or legibility) is primary, even if it now includes asymmetrical as well as symmetrical frames. These new perspectives have an impact upon the architecture and landscaping of Chicago's Central Area that is equal to the economic and social impact of globalization upon the city. These perspectives are necessary; more important, they make sense for development on the river. It is possible—and perhaps necessary —to include both frames of analysis when dealing with city-forms in the current global terrain. So it is therefore appropriate that the inspiration for what is emerging as the new Central Area begins along the riverfront, along the city's space of flows.

BUILDING ON THE RIVER

While Chicago has long understood the appeal and value of the waterfront, until now attention has centered on the lakefront, thanks to the 1909 Plan of Chicago, which made the lake the focal point for much of the city's planning and building. The lake has benefited from its role as both backdrop and boundary for the city, because of a rather placid, contemplative image and use of water. Journalist Paul Elie observes: "The Chicago skyline [is] set off by Lake Michigan: culture and nature, height and breadth, big buildings and big sky. Chicago is a place where the lakefront is a complement of the city, not an escape from it, where the city and lake seem suited for each other. Chicago's unassuming sense of its lakefront is apparent; [it] is for everyday pleasures" (Elie 2001, 25).

The lake and Chicago's development along it, however, do not reflect the potential and the power of water, especially not in ways that resonate readily with the global parameters of mobility and fluid connectivity, features that provide for dynamism, a trait the CAP recognizes as key to successful cities. But dynamic and successful cities are also the result of diversities that "arise from the richness of their cultures . . . making them places where people want to live, work and visit" (CAP, 1). It may appear paradoxical to ask that a site offer stability and also mobility, but in fact both of these are necessary to ensure viability. Urbanist Jane Jacobs believes: "To maintain in a neighborhood sufficient people who stay put, a city must have the very fluidity and mobility of use" (Jacobs 1961, 139). Architect Akio Kuroyanagi feels it is the very juxtaposition of land and water, when viewed in new and visionary ways, that can substantially add to the viability and aesthetics of a site and offer unique environmental opportunities. He notes: "The feeling of openness and other ephemeral qualities of the water such as buoyancy, waves, currents, tides, and light on the water's surface add a completely new dimension to architectural spaces for residential, leisure, and commercial facilities, offering the possibility of new lifestyle" (Kuroyanagi 1991, 16). Bertrand Goldberg underscores this, observing: "To build on the water is to affect our living in three ways: aesthetically, sociologically, and economically" (Goldberg 1991, foreword).

This changing vision of waterfront space contrasts with earlier developments that were primarily utilitarian in nature, devoted to shipyards and often cut off from the city by railroads or highways, precisely what the Central Area Plan seeks to overcome. The river affords the opportunity to infuse an undercurrent of constant raw energy by virtue of the very flow of water. It is a dynamic path, comparable to a liquid local area network (LAN) in the way it facilitates the movement of people and things. The river is, in a way, a double-coded site, one that marries place and flows, if only temporarily. Through frame analysis we are reminded that perspective can change at any moment—center can become periphery, or periphery can become center. For example, the development along the lake and on North Michigan Avenue, according to architectural historian John Stamper, helped "inspire" buildings whose scale required the city as frame rather than the immediate site or street upon which it was built, or the human scale of people standing in front of it. He notes of the Hancock Building that

it was not the building's image from the street that was important but rather how it was seen from several blocks away, or even a mile away. . . . It was impossible to comprehend the building's true architectural form from close up. It demanded to be seen from a distance, a point tower rising above a mass of generic low-rise buildings, with no specific reference to North Michigan Avenue. Its spatial realm was that of the city, not of the avenue. (Stamper 1991, 211–12)

In contrast, the river evokes—and perhaps demands, in design and use—the local and the human as its frames of reference, or at least it keeps them in the equation. In these ways, the river seems a more suitable vehicle with which to sustain the tensions of stability and mobility, of aesthetics and viability, paying attention to the natural and built environments described by Jacobs, Kuroyanagi, and Goldberg and to realize the goals of the three development plans.

While there is agreement that Chicago's riverfront is underused, there has been considerable debate concerning how it should be used. Traditionally, the riverfront, according to Peter van Vechten, "has been treated almost like an overly wide street or open space. The river, which is a strong interruption of the grid (almost like a tear) has not been very adequately responded to with the architecture. . . . There remain opportunities if there is vision" (van Vechten 2000–2002, e-mail August 3, 2001). But opposing, even controversial, visions for Chicago's vista have engendered the best and often most innovative of outcomes.

Divergence and diversity may well be appropriate in strategies designed for the site and current needs of the city. Together, the three plans provide the innovative vision needed to integrate the actual shape and character of the river into structures and activities for the Central Area. No longer merely a center for production, the Central Area is emerging as a central force. New economic spaces are rising along the river's southern and main branches, and residential and recreational facilities are being built along its northern, main, and even southern branches. The river has become an integral component of the Central Area's new image and purpose.

A closer look at the riverfront reveals visionary precedents for what is currently evolving both at this site and in the larger Central Area. Three outstanding projects are the Chicago Mercantile Exchange, or the Merc (1983, 1988), Marina City (1962), and River City (1987). They presage current development along the riverfront. They reference the diverse directions in which the riverfront, the Central Area, and the city are moving, especially the increase of residential and mixed-use spaces, as well as spaces that can house newer economic sectors. They also exemplify the breadth of experience that building on the water can evoke. Taking a closer look at them formally and functionally helps place newer developments into a context of continuity despite obvious discontinuity and change.

Chicago Mercantile Exchange

The Merc played a significant role in rerouting the city's economy after Chicago went into a tailspin in the mid-1980s as a result of the loss of manufacturing and nonmanufacturing jobs (Abu-Lughod 1999). In this context, the river serves as a metaphor more for the Merc's function than for its design, that is, the river reflects the emerging importance of space of flows, where the success of power-holding organizations in asymmetrical networks of exchanges do not depend upon the characteristics of any specific locale. The overall process of exchange, instead, becomes reintegrated through communication systems, telematics in particular (Castells 1989; Sassen 1998b). An example of the Merc's innovativeness in this regard was the development of GLOBEX—a twenty-four-hour computerized order-matching trading system launched in June 1992, which linked different exchanges in different time zones, thus freeing transactions from spatial and temporal borders (Tamarkin 1993; Abu-Lughod 1999). But the production process of even the most advanced information industries is partly place-bound. Global processes assume concrete localized forms in dual cities. From these auspices, the Merc's physical presence on the river assumes a deeper impact.

Anchored at the river's southern branch, the granite-and-glass structure offers strong legibility and symbolism. The colors and materials exude a cool, calm appearance that belies the powerful energy of the activity within, much like the steady surface of the river along which the building is sited. The forty-story twin office towers reference the institution's dual identity—past and present. They are joined by a ten-story granite-clad bridging component that houses the forty-thousand-square-foot trading floor with thirty thousand square feet of free space on the floor above. The bridge component is an admirable structural feat, achieved by cantilevering the top thirty-four floors of the towers over the low-rise building space. Symbolically, it emphasizes the relationship between the two towers and the strength of purpose that has sustained it over time.

The bridge is the most sociable area of the structure. The trading floor is visible from a gallery on the fourth floor, reached through a separate elevator that bypasses the many escalators carrying runners and traders back and forth (Sirefman 1996, 194). The environment is, essentially, controlled chaos. The bridge also houses Rivers, an appropriately named restaurant on the ground level, overlooking the water (see Figure 13). Outside, workers use the bridge to find brief respite from the activity inside. The gallery and restaurant inject a vital component of any marketplace—its public (social) persona. Almost any city or town can have fiber optic cables, but the combination of state-of-the-art office buildings, top talent, and the socializing networking infrastructure maximizes condi-

tions for success (Sassen 2003). The Merc makes reference to and provides impetus for Chicago's effort to attract and retain other institutions necessary for the city's long-term economic success. The Merc is a strong reminder that success is based, in part, on the ability to "go with the flow" while staying grounded. More correctly, perhaps, it exemplifies how doing so can make it a significant part of the city's space of flows.

Chicago intends to be on the upside of the growth curve. The Merc is driving Chicago's move forward and framing this part of the river as a place where the financial and informational industries can inhabit space alongside the more traditional sectors. Moving from literally selling "bread and butter" items (real commodities) to selling futures through telematics reflects the city's ability to keep one foot in the real and one foot in the virtual. In doing so, Chicago becomes a dual or global city, or at least a viable contender in the global economy. Ultimately, this transformation depends upon a variety of other assets: a technological infrastructure, a mass transportation system, an available labor force, a diversified economic base, amenities for office workers, and a residential base. The Central Area offers all of these. Yet liabilities are equally numerous, and they include high taxes, inadequate transportation, potentially unreliable electric power, possible corporate consolidations and mergers, and the uncertain future of the financial exchanges (CAP, 11).

The Merc offers other lessons for anyone trying to place Chicago or other cities in the global terrain. Sassen (2001b) notes that, for a century and more, Chicago was at the heart of an enormous agroindustrial complex and had a manufacturing-based economy. Even its financial markets have their origins in this complex.

added the landscaping. "Alfred," Goldberg recalled, "wanted to make the edges less distinct—to marry earth and water. He wanted to make it less of a designed pattern. He wanted an absence of pattern of development; I loved the idea" (Goldberg 1992, 195). The water gave identity to a community of people living on the edge of a densely built inner city. The walkway connected the complex to the rest of the city's CBD, fostering inward and outward movement and interdependence, presaging current visions for design and development.

Marina City represents several firsts. It was the first mixed-use building to be constructed in America. More specifically, it was the first building on Chicago's once heavily commercialized riverfront to offer residential housing. When it was completed, Marina City was the world's tallest apartment complex and the tallest concrete building. With a housing capacity of 637 persons per acre, Marina City was also the world's most dense residential complex. This density offered many opportunities for community formation (Goldberg 1991, 20–21).

Forty years after its completion, Marina City sustains its distinction as the building that brought water back onto the land and residents back into the city's center. Recent renovations include a hotel, recreational facilities, and restaurants. Smith and Wolensky's Steakhouse, in particular, reflects the ethos underlying Marina City's design. The entrance of Smith and Wolensky's spills out onto the street offering a fluid pathway for patrons. Outdoor seating, in season, affords a connection to the liquid pathway. Diners can see and be seen by passersby and boats that float along the river; all face the river. While the marina underneath Marina City prohibits the fluid continuity of the proposed riverwalk, it offers a reminder that one can build in as well as along the water, so that structures can literally interact with the water. And the marina offers the possibility for viewing water, in this case the river, as frame or framed.

Other renovations have not been as positive. Additions to the plaza at the tower's base, a feature that brought pedestrian traffic into the complex and allowed the river to be experienced from all parts of the plaza, have been seriously compromised. Recent alterations have enclosed most of the public space, creating the opposite effect of what the restaurant and riverwalk offer for the pedestrian. Efforts are currently underway to obtain landmark status for Marina City, in part to stop further alterations of Goldberg's innovative and organic intentions.

River City

Goldberg with his River City project continued his mission to revive the city using the river and an organic design. Phase one of the planned five-phase mixed-use complex was completed in 1986, fifteen years after it was proposed, on the site of an idle riverfront railroad yard at the southern end of the Loop. Many political obstructions prevented completion of the rest of the project. Even the phase that was completed suffered in its eventual design and construction. In 1998, American Invesco purchased River City and began converting the rental apartment complex into condominiums to be called the River City Private Residences. In 2001, prices ranged from $160,000 to the mid-$600,000s (Buck 2001). The overall complex consists of two ten-story S-shaped residential blocks housing 448 apartments and 52 townhouses that wind along the Chicago River. They are connected by an atrium that rests on a rectangular four-story commercial base. Amenities for the residential area include party rooms, leased parking, and twenty-four-hour doorman service. The retail/commercial section has a grocery store, a dry cleaners, a drugstore, Bally Sports Club, and a preschool. Beneath River City's mile-long structure is a harbor for seventy boats, all of which are moored in the water. Whereas Marina City was a high-rise high-density project (housing approximately 650 people per acre), River City was a mid-rise building of medium density (housing approximately 100 people per acre). Excavation of the riverbank after the building's construction formed a harbor, which brought the river's water into the building's interior. Like Marina City, River City contributes a great deal above and below the surface, reaching deeply into the city-ideal, while managing to stand firmly in the city-real (see Figures 14 and 15).

14—River City, September 2000

15—River City, July 2003

The project also testifies to what new technology can contribute toward planning and design. Architect Susanna Sirefman notes: "computer research allowed for the economic planning of cost-effective multiple use of internally fiber-glass lined standard steel formworks to cast the complex forms. The curvy cast-in place concrete is simultaneously structural and sculptural" (Sirefman 1996, 221–22). The building creates several small housing communities within its curves, and the entire design provides the sense of a new marine park in the midst of an urban streetscape at a city core. Each of its floors creates opportunities for people to form larger groups along the open sky-lit entrance walk and at the elevator lobbies. According to Goldberg, "River City's communities grow out of its horizontal spread; at Marina City, communities grow from vertical density. Though the buildings themselves are static, the water flowing beneath them contributes kinetic energy to the communities that rise above it" (Goldberg 1991, 22).

River City's pathways are designed to provide maximum exposure to the Chicago River. The entrance lobby, the corridors to commercial space, and a continuous walkway along the river, all work to marry the interior environment to its (natural) marine surroundings. Like Marina City, River City is designed to foster and symbolize connectivity, both internally and with the larger urban terrain. Goldberg achieves this connectivity with River Road, a walkway fashioned after a European streetscape enclosed by the atrium, and with Riverwalk, its outdoor counterpart. Thus "the street" in concept and design is, in essence, the life force of River City. These pathways seamlessly integrate part to part and complex to the site. Riverwalk's shape curves in ways that complement the river. Curves afford a more natural and interesting path for people to follow. On these paths, people are encouraged to meander and experience the spaces in planned and unplanned ways, alone or through interactions with others. Park benches, landscaping, and streetlight fixtures encourage interaction and a sense of community. Features such as flower planters in front of each residence and in common spaces on each floor encourage the individuality of each residential unit and subcommunity within the complex itself. For Goldberg, as for Park, community is as much a state of mind as a physical place. For this reason, Goldberg envisioned the architect as one who builds community by offering spaces that delight, stimulate, and provoke the senses and the mind.

It was Goldberg's belief that elements of surprise and excitement were not to be found walking (or living) in a straight line. Straight lines are not to be found in nature, and attending to the natural curve is one more gesture toward the natural landscape and to those who inhabit the complex. Goldberg understood the impact that curves, water, and other natural elements have on the quality of living. He was committed to proving that these experiences could be found in cities by moving beyond the grid. Fortunately, this idea did not go unnoticed when plans for new buildings and pathways along other parts of the riverfront were developed.

Goldberg's belief that the city offered the perfect place for setting in motion vital and dynamic communities inspired his designs for both Marina City and River City. Apartments in River City were designed to expand or contract as the needs of residents dictate, for example. As the vertical concrete tubes follow the

S-curve, the form between them varies, creating 22 possible layouts for the 448 residential units (Sirefman 1996, 222). Goldberg had observed that when families grow or shrink, they are often forced to move. He further observed that the very notion of family had been too narrowly defined by various housing agencies, including the Federal Housing Authority (FHA) and the Chicago Housing Authority (CHA). Acknowledging the diversity of family types, including singles, couples without children, and single-parent families, he then built to accommodate these and offered the flexibility of apartment size to accommodate expected and unexpected demographic or economic changes that might allow people the opportunity to stay put. This in turn would foster the stability of a neighborhood and increase the chances that a community could develop, not as self-contained but rather in a more inclusive way.

To this end, both River City and Marina City feature recreational, educational, and commercial facilities that are used by residents and nonresidents alike. They also offer communication and transportation lines, such as shuttles to the Loop and computer links to universities and hospitals, that connect residents to the larger downtown area. In both design and use, then, these projects foster the notion of (urban) community as an integral part of the larger urban landscape rather than as a closed off or isolated entity. While the relationship between inside(r) and outside(r) is more fluid, insiders are afforded an identity through the distinct design of the complex. It becomes their vernacular and also part of the texture of the city.

NEW CITY USERS

Not everyone viewed Goldberg's gestures as appropriate responses to Chicago's problems. Marina City and River City may look like attempts to create self-sufficiency, or to create "cities within cities" in the more exclusive sense of the term *cities*, but as noted, Goldberg actually intended to strengthen community in cities.

What planners today do agree with is Goldberg's conviction that the middle class has to be brought back into the city in order to create the tax base and population needed for the city to grow and function properly. As Goldberg stated: "As our cities shrink and atrophy, so does the life within them. If our cities are to remain a center of civilization they cannot serve a 35 hour a week city inhabited by our poor. The original American vision of the city is one of synergy, growth and community" (Goldberg quoted in Sirefman 1996, 220). Tabing concurs: "The real goal is to make downtown a twenty-four-hour neighborhood. Downtown Chicago in the past has been a lot like Wall Street. People get off work and they're out of there. There's no sense in staying. . . . We, being the City, have to give them reasons to want to stay" (Tabing 2000). Attracting today's middle class, however, has required new considerations. By synergy, Goldberg references the link between work, residence, and recreation. In his design of mixed-use complexes, he reinforces the idea that traditional views of placement require synthesis, or blurring. This blurring of boundaries parallels what must take place if dual cities are to realize their goals. What remains of the "old" notion of community in Goldberg's projects is helping to satisfy the basic human need of being social, being able to meet and interact with others. As architect Jack Hartray observes: "It's this kind of planning approach that can unify [and dignify] the region" (Hartray, in Bey 2001f, 15). This new understanding finds great importance in understanding the new middle class, or what has been referred to as the new gentrification in cities.

Gentrification was initially understood as the rehabilitation of inner-city decaying or low-income housing by middle-class outsiders. New gentrification is linked to processes of spatial, economic, and social restructuring, most notably the transformation in advanced capitalism, that is, the shift to services and the associated transformation of the class structure and the shift toward privatization of consumption and service provisions. These shifts have significantly affected the economic and social morphology of residential and business patterns we see today (Chall 1983–1984; Sassen 2000, 2001b; Friedmann 1986). In the 1970s and 1980s, the baby boom generation came of age, and the preference for urban living among the new high-income professionals was a key element in the gentrification of large sectors of the city.

The available evidence indicates that this trend toward urban living among professionals, managers, and service workers became even stronger in the 1980s and 1990s. Studies tracing such trends in New York City since the late 1970s, for example, find that Manhattan has an overrepresentation of professionals, managers, and service workers; the sharpest increase has been for professionals, followed by managers (R. Harris 1991; Sassen 2000, 2001b). Workers holding good jobs translate their incomes into lifestyles that clash with traditional middle-class values of saving and delaying gratification. A vast supply of low-wage service-sector jobs is required by high-income gentrification in both residential and commercial settings. There is also a large increase in expensive restaurants, luxury housing, high-end hotels, gourmet shops, boutiques, and the like, catering to this population (Sassen 2001b, 9).

There is also strong evidence that this new gentrification impacts planning and development in Chicago's new Central Area. Diversity is evident in occupation, age, and lifestyle. Professionals, managers, and service workers are all migrating back to the city. At the same time, the CAP notes, "Growth in households age 55 to 64 are driving demand for high-end primary and secondary housing. Younger households age 25–34 represent the other growing segment likely to be attracted to the Central Area. They are drawn by rental housing and moderately priced lofts" (CAP, 14). These new residents are not typically families with children. As Tabing points out: "The rise of empty nesters more recently and young singles wanting something more helped resuscitate the city" (Tabing 2000). Members of the new middle class share a large amount of personal and corporate income, yet they are a decidedly more diverse group than this one factor might imply. Plans and designs must reflect this diversity.

When Goldberg built Marina City and River City, he was building for people who were seeking "the convenience as well as the extraordinary experience of living in a building [whose design and features] attracted them" (Goldberg 1992, 191). Today, people are still choosing to live in the city not merely for convenience but because they want to. As Mayor Daley noted: "many suburbanites have found the city does a better job of creating human spaces than the suburbs" (Office of the Mayor 2002c). Tabing concurs: "I also think people . . . want a little more out of the quality of their lives than going out to Schaumburg and shopping at the Woodfield Shopping Center, where there are these huge stores and miles of parking, lots of the same thing over and over. . . . So the city of Chicago has tried to create something people want. The city has tried to create something that's not *that,* downtown" (Tabing 2000).

Chicago has become fully engaged in a transformation process that was only hinted at when Marina City, River City, and the Merc were built. Downtown is really down and around rather than just in Chicago's traditional center or at its fringes. The notion of what mixed-use can mean and look like has expanded and deepened, and the middle-class base that Goldberg hoped to lure back to the city is indeed returning. But it too has undergone dramatic changes. Goldberg's designs and theories of urbanism anticipated or required the strong presence of the middle class as well as the incorporation of ethnic enclaves. He anticipated people working from home through new technological advances. But it is uncertain just how much he could have anticipated the transnational businessperson or tourist as an equally strong presence. These shifts in lifestyle and economics provide new and difficult challenges for anyone involved in reshaping the city's Central Area. A walk along the riverfront today provides examples of efforts to respond to these shifts. And if we look closely at what has been and is now emerging along the river, we may discover that Marina City, River City, and the Merc were indeed merely ahead of the curve that they, in many ways, helped to create.

GOING WITH THE FLOW

A Walk along the Riverfront

Today I was very attuned to the water—especially the river. I noticed the bends of the river and buildings that incorporated them in their design and materials. What stops the lake is the land, so the line is clear and distinct. Nothing stops the river; it is about movement—on, over, under. And because it flows throughout the city, it affords as many perspectives as there are people and points of view(ing) along the way. At a certain point along the riverwalk, I looked up and noticed how the buildings fold into one another. The square into the curve into the round shaped; the varied textures, materials and styles fit together and stand apart . . . like a well-crafted collage. It is remarkable.

(Satler journal entry, July 12, 2002)

Once marginalized and overlooked, the river has become a driving force for Chicago's new Central Area. Unfolding along the riverfront is an expanding conversation of old and new forms and functions in distinct but fluid districts. The southern branch displays a more industrial, working image; the main branch in the CBD constitutes the most developed and diverse area; the northern branch displays its more natural character, which is being interwoven into the residential and recreational facilities that predominate here (Bey 2001f, 15). No effort has been made to meld these or to impose one vernacular upon the rest. And yet there is order, in many ways a more authentic albeit asymmetrical one, which responds to the curves and bends of the river and to the city's changing and multifaceted needs. Within these districts, built and unbuilt spaces are generating as much as responding to a broader vocabulary for conceptualizing and building community.

On the surface, one of the most significant contributions the river makes is to break the rule of the grid. Classical perspective generally is articulated at right angles off a central axis. This affords predictability, and perhaps too much predictability. It allows the viewer to look straight down a vista, to a focal point at the end, and stop. The effect is shallow. The river, with its curves and turns twists the axis upon which structures rest and interactions occur, creating a zigzag that forces the eye to move from side to side. This allows the viewer to look at the whole and its parts much more thoroughly than if the eye were drawn to the singular vanishing point of the classical perspective (Oudolf 1999, 84). And, as I discovered, if the structures found along the path of the river are also slightly twisted and staggered, more of the composition they create is noticeable and felt.

Yet perhaps it is what lies beneath the surface of the river that is more consequential. The ability to notice and engage in different kinds of relationships is reflected in the flow of the river. The calm of the surface structure belies the force and movement that occurs beneath. In the deeper structure, the essence and contradiction of space of flows are captured. As Castells notes: "The flows of power generate the power of flows, whose material reality imposes itself as a natural phenomenon that cannot be controlled or predicted, only accepted and managed" (Castells 1989, 349). It is this duplicity of movement, the tension created by the oppositional surface and deeper structures of the river, that invigorates— but only when it is thoroughly experienced, that is, through feel as much as through appearance. This duality can be found in some of the buildings along the riverbanks as they endeavor to interpret conditions of the new social and economic terrain.

The view from this liquid pathway is never singular or enclosed. It has to admit a variety of other perspectives; it is by its very nature shifting and contradictory. Further, each section of the river provides its own context, so that, although it is a fluid whole, temporality and spatiality are deliberately more ephemeral than in spaces of place. Not all the structures are going in the same direction on the surface; they do create a coherent and lively composition. The river, therefore, needs to be viewed for what is not visible as well as for what is visible, that is, it needs to be experienced in its movement as well as in what appears, formally, on the surface. To accomplish this, there must be a shift in perspective, a multisensory reading, one that is open to potential rather than just to finality. To view the river is to use it and its duality. The stance used to view the riverfront and to analyze its activity must be a stance that is congruent with the nature of the river and with how one conceptualizes a dual city. To this end, Park's "sociological stranger" provides an appropriate vantage point. Park explains: "If wandering is the conceptual opposite of fixation at any point, then surely the sociological form of the stranger presents the union of both of these specifications. The stranger stays, but he is not settled. He is a potential wanderer. That means that he is not bound as others are by the local proprieties and conventions. He is the freer man, practically and theoretically. He views his relation to others with less prejudice; he submits them to more general, more objective standards, and he is not confined in his action by custom, piety or precedents" (Park 1974, 1:351). It is from this perspective that the life and liveliness of the riverfront can be sustained for observers, and hopefully for the reader.

What follows is an excursion along this vital feature of the city's Central Area. The journey roughly follows the path of the river, beginning at its southern branch, heading north to the main branch and then east to the lake. The guiding thematic principle is to express the texture and diversity to be found in the forms and their uses. Each structure is introduced with an excerpt from one of the plans discussed, or from other relevant materials. Integrating theory and practice in this way reveals how the three plans and the three sections of the river work together through their divergences and discontinuities to create the new whole. Each site begins with its own theoretical auspices—a verbal sketch of intention if you will—derived from the various plans for this area. Then the actual form and use is described. In this way, the reader has simultaneous access to the architectural space created through the involvement of literal flow (the river) and the flow derived from new economic and social intentions for the riverfront and Central Area. Together, these create a composition which emphasizes that, although not all the structures are going in the same direction on the surface, they do create a coherent and lively new order.

<table>
<tr><td>Architects, Skidmore,
Owings & Merrill (1981)</td><td>

Gateway Center IV—300 South Riverside Plaza

The city seeks actions to build a nurturing environment to stimulate and retain new economy entrepreneurs. Needed is the development of geographic concentrations of new economy activity—for example, high-tech corridors, such as Route 128 in Boston, and incubators in New York and elsewhere. (NEGSC, 10)

</td></tr>
</table>

In the early 1960s when the rediscovery of the riverfront began, a plan emerged to redevelop the south branch of the river, where there was room to create a long, unbroken esplanade. Air rights for the area over the Union Station rail yard were purchased by Tishman Realty, who then hired Skidmore, Owings & Merrill to redevelop "an area that had chiefly served as a gateway to skid row" (Pridmore 2000, 21). While the plans to create a major transportation center there did not materialize, SOM did build four structures: Gateway Centers I–IV. Gateway Centers I–III typify the vernacular of the 1960s; they are glass-and-steel boxes that are efficient, but disconnected from their site. Gateway Center IV, completed nearly two decades later, makes a different response (see Figure 16). Its curving green glass follows the river, so that, as one moves along the river and the perspective shifts step by step, so does the profile of this twenty-two-story office building. The same profile is repeated on the west side of the building, which faces the street. A small greenhouse with staggered corners projects from the center of the east side, which faces the river, leaving space for a restaurant and outdoor seating.

Gateway Center IV does not entirely break the grid or the formalism created by Gateway I–III, but it begins to offer a design and a perspective that are more suited to the new economy and vision for the Central Area and to the river. A majority of the tenants in Gateway IV are firms and government agencies involved in the informational and service sectors. This clientele makes sense, given the facility's proximity to the Mercantile Exchange and numerous banks across the river, and to the city's financial district several blocks east on LaSalle Street. Its design, location, and function help Gateway IV strike a good balance between local and global parameters.

Recently, Gateway IV's name and address were changed to 300 South Riverside Plaza as part of the city's efforts to use the river as a frame for all buildings along the corridor extending to the northern branch of the river. Such a tagging device, applied on the other branches of the river as well, brings unity rather than conformity. It valorizes the river as an intrinsic part of each community

16—Gateway Center IV,

July 2001

that it seeks to frame while also serving as the common thread for all entities that line the riverfront, that is, it connects the buildings and activities along the riverfront. People will eventually orient themselves through this frame. Not all residents have reached this point. In my own search for 200 North Riverside Plaza, for example, many people were unable to direct me, in some cases even city officials from the planning department and people who worked in the area did not recognize the address. As Park noted, the city is as much a state of mind as a place. It will take time and some marketing for both notions of this building to become the reality for residents.

Boeing Headquarters—100 North Riverside Plaza

Architects, Perkins and Will (1990)

Chicago is home to 32 Fortune 500 companies, many of which manage their own IT. Chicago employs 31,660 computer programmers, more than any other metropolitan area (New York and Silicon Valley employ 24,280 and 22,400, respectively). (NEGSC, 12)

35,500 gsf in the upper floors, while the lower levels provide up to 44,000 gsf of office space. The landscaped plaza, pocket parks, and riverwalk link the tower with residences at RiverBend (DeStefano + Partners 2001a).

Architects, DeStefano + Partners (2001–)

Residences at RiverBend

Residences at RiverBend, a thirty-seven-floor condominium complex, consist of 144 condos, 4 townhouses, and 2 penthouses, with seven levels of parking (see Figure 18). By incorporating a landscaped plaza and riverwalk, this project will become a major contributor to the City of Chicago's riverfront redevelopment plan. All of the units offer balconies, with views of the river and the Loop through floor-to-ceiling glass walls. The predominantly glass tower with a concrete frame features an outward curving facade, mirroring the office building at 333 West Wacker diagonally across the river (DeStefano + Partners 2001a). Residents are typically "young professionals who find it appealing to walk to work. Some are people who are in love with the River North neighborhood. Some are upgrading to new construction. They previously owned a one-bedroom and now they are going into a two" (Nicole Kyros in Finley 2002).

18—RiverBend planned development, January 2002

The intention was to create "a signature building" (Handley 2001c; von Klan 1999). Yet the building is significant primarily for its understatement and for the attention it pays to the site. The design does not draw direct attention to itself. Rather, it is "virtual," acting more as a node for the multiple and varied activities taking place inside and around it. There is a transparency in its choice of materials and colors so that the building changes color or appearance as sun and clouds reflect off the water. There is also a sense of belonging to—as opposed to defining—the area in which it resides. It is a space of flows, of hypermobility, for the three sections of the river that conjoin here. It makes the eye move, to paraphrase Oudolf, in the zig or zag to different or multiple vistas.

RiverBend not only opens vistas, it opens potential uses for the space. Its design reinforces the difference between the symmetrical order of the street and the asymmetrical order of the river. RiverBend Planned Development does not make the statement Marina City or River City (or for that matter 333 West Wacker or the Merchandise Mart) makes. But then, it is a creature of the twenty-first century; it exists on another action plane both literally and figuratively. Yet, like River City and Marina City, which serve as nodal points or brackets for other corridors of the river, RiverBend could well serve the same function for this part of the river in the Central Area.

Fulton House—345 North Canal Street   Architect, Harry Weese

River Cottages—357–65 North Canal Street   (1981, 1990)

Adjacent to RiverBend is Fulton House, one of the city's first major condominium conversions. Architect and developer Harry Weese remodeled this former cold-storage building and in 1990 added townhouses (River Cottages) on a plot of leftover land. The two complexes (RiverBend and Fulton) now share part of the new riverwalk with benches, landscaping, and decorative lighting—a feature that circumscribes the riverwalk without isolating it from the rest of the Central Area. These structures comply with new building requirements and goals for construction on the river.

The city has been very strict about building requirements for all new construction along the river. All developments within one hundred feet of the river are treated as planned developments, which are reviewed by the DPD and the Plan Commission in accordance with River Plan and River Design Guidelines implemented in 1999 (Friends of the Chicago River 2001b). As of 1998, the city began to require that all new riverfront developments be set back thirty feet from the river and have a landscaped public path (Office of the Mayor 2002c). New riverwalks must be made accessible not only to the public in general but also to the handicapped. DeStefano + Partners negotiated both with the city and with environmental groups concerned about the impact of the riverwalk design. In the end, it was decided that the style of the Fulton House walkway would conform with the rest of the walkway along this stretch of the river, rather than attend to only the design of the complex. Bob Bistry of DeStefano + Partners agreed that in the end this decision made the most sense and afforded a more coherent line for the larger whole (Bistry 2002). "The greatest challenge to redeveloping the river is to blend or integrate the different uses and property owners along the river—both public and private" (Friends of the Chicago River 2001b). RiverBend Planned Development, along with other DeStefano + Partners riverfront projects, are working toward this end.

The completed portion of the walkway offers a spectacular view of the river and life along it. Scaled to encourage interaction while always keeping the river as its guide and meter, the walkway serves as a good buffer between the RiverBend/Fulton complex and the railroad running behind it. There is quiet and the feel of a real residential community, reinforced by entrances to townhouse units that open the building to the walkway and the walkway to both residents and nonresidents. On a warm summer day, employees from the nearby Merchandise Mart and other offices came to sit on the benches during their breaks and take in the river view, complete with new greenery and the birds and boats that travel by. The benches welcome such relaxation, and the building itself acts as a buffer between them and the noise and activity behind it. There is a sense that the building is open to all movement corridors and those traveling on them. Another consequence of the riverwalks and greenspace around RiverBend and Fulton House is that this portion of the riverfront is now connected to the Merchandise Mart and Kinzie Street for foot, bicycle, and boat traffic. Once again, the water is the guiding force of an area that was visually and physically cut off and therefore underused.

What 100 and 200 North Riverside Plaza share physically is an absence of color in their construction materials. This absence reinforces the role they play as spaces of flows rather than spaces of place and allows the natural elements— sky, water, and greenery—to give them an ever-changing complexion and image. Their organic, dynamic forms offer a new sense of what place might look like, thanks to the creative use of glass, granite, and concrete and the way their curves meld with the bends of the river. The riverwalk merges built and unbuilt forms in a fluid manner to create a welcoming public space. People can sit or meander with equal freedom. This public space gets heavy use, which is a good indication that the asymmetrical and less deliberate approach has succeeded.

Northwest of RiverBend, there is growing interest in developing the West Loop and Near West Side as an area of hi-tech enterprises, balanced by residences and retail. Canal Street, which forms one of the boundaries of RiverBend, is already showing signs of new development. Rather than hold to a traditional circumscribed CBD, new sectors of the global economy, especially telecommunications, foster a new type of hub, one that is central to multiple circuits and bridges other important types of places such as high-tech districts and export-processing zones (Sassen 1998b).

Architects, Richard E.
Schmidt (1908) and Gensler
(renovation, 2001–2002)

e-port (formerly the Montgomery Ward warehouse)— 600 West Chicago Avenue

Four new economy sectors offer Chicagoland the most attractive future growth potential: biomedical, wireless software, software development, emerging technologies—nanotechnologies. (NESCG, 10)

The irony of today's electronic era is that the older notion of the region and older forms of infrastructure re-emerge as critical for key economic sectors. But for this digital grid to work, conventional infrastructure—ideally of the most advanced kind—is also a necessity. (Sassen 1998b)

The city has an abundance of old warehouses and distribution centers with high ceilings and heavy-floor-load capacities perfectly suited for rapid conversion to telecom and data "carrier hotels," which house large computer banks of multiple companies. One of Chicago's most prominent new technology facilities, the 2.2-million-square-foot e-port, is giving newfound prominence to the old Montgomery Ward warehouse. The former warehouse is returning the favor, too, by affording the emerging businesses it houses the status that comes with occupying a landmarked building (I-street 2000).

Mail-order retailer Aaron Montgomery Ward kept the lakefront open and unobstructed, but his company constructed a sprawling complex on a great spot on the river north of Chicago Avenue. Built in 1908 by Richard E. Schmidt, with the firm of Garden & Martin, the 2.2-million-square-foot building was Chicago's largest and most beautifully designed retail-distribution center. The original design was noted for its large, well-proportioned windows along a curving facade facing the river. Renamed e-port, it is now the city's largest mixed-use high-tech facility, centrally located in one of the city's growing neighborhoods, Kingsbury Park.

Half of the nine-story, seven-hundred-foot-long building has been transformed into a hub for telecommunications and new media companies. The other half houses retail establishments and residences ranging from one-bedroom apartments to penthouses (One River Place 2001). A public riverwalk connects the parts and then connects the whole to the larger urban terrain. The owner of e-port envisioned the common areas and office space as places that would stimulate creative thinking. The Chicago office of Gensler was asked to create a "chic aesthetic" that would appeal to the high-tech mind-set. The decision was made to keep the industrial feel, with exposed ceilings and ducts creating a bright, open, and airy atmosphere, and at the same time to infuse a forward-looking feel by adding large atriums and elements such as a multistory video wall in the lobby. This curved five-story multimedia wall provides monitors for displaying web sites, flashing company graphics, or playing the tenants' newest commercials. Around the building's exterior, fifteen-foot-tall steel kiosk sculptures, lit from within, feature translucent interchangeable panels for tenants to display announcements. There is also a system of interior wall coverings for public lobbies and hallways that features steel-bar stock and metal mesh where tenants may hang brand identifiers. Gensler project executive Mary Festenstein notes that new-economy facilities typically require an aesthetic that can help with recruitment and retention. "The rough appearance of loft spaces highlighted by striking features is in alignment with the aesthetic of many new media companies. Branding," according to Festenstein, "is a very important issue for the potential tenants of e-port. So we created numerous opportunities for them to creatively display their company information" (I-street 2000).

Tenants including Qwest Communications, Level (3) Communications, Vertis Advertising, and Telocity, Inc., represent the new sectors that the city hopes to attract. Their siting in one complex exemplifies the process of agglomeration that occurs in dual cities, allowing like-and-kind industries to engage in social networking (Sassen 2000, 2001a, 2001b). Charles Bendit, partner in Taconic Investment Group, the firm handling technology development, notes that bringing any type of high-tech users to one area creates the possibility of "a community of common interests. . . . There are many other smaller technology facilities being developed throughout Chicago, but we wanted to create a critical mass to act as high-tech catalyst for the area" (I-street 2000).

A *New Economy Growth Strategy for Chicagoland* (NEGSC) profiles the Central Area's "superb transportation access and facilities" and notes that Chicago, the second-most-wired city in the United States, has available real estate at competitive prices. Yet entrepreneurs face a lack of both support mechanisms and community to help them launch start-ups. As businesses become geographically dispersed, many long for a network of mentors, information sources, and business contacts (NEGSC, 9). E-port is making efforts to create a community to support industries that, despite their being dispersed, require locally concentrated services such as residences and transportation for workers. Other sites along the river are doing similar things, some in newly built structures such as RiverBend Planned Development, and others in spaces with historical presence, such as this former warehouse of Montgomery Ward, the "granddaddy" and symbol of Chicago's rich past, both architecturally and economically.

East of 100 and 200 North Riverside Plaza is the heart of Chicago's Loop and the main branch of the river. The river is a constant amid all the changes happening here. The history of American and Chicago architecture is literally found in the reflections of this waterway and, in many cases, on the buildings themselves.

333 West Wacker

Architects, Kohn, Pederson, Fox (1983)

An architect who fails to recognize [the difference between building on riverside and building on land] and who fails to design for that is losing an enormous amount of message and significance and enhancement of spaces that he is creating for the use of people. (Goldberg 1992, 193)

19—View of 333 West Wacker and main branch of the river from RiverBend walkway, July 2002

Almost from the start, 333 West Wacker was one of Chicago's favorite buildings (see Figure 19). As van Vechten observed, this is perhaps in part because, like Marina City, it made real and original use of the river and of an irregular site.

"Emphasis has been on the continuity of the streetwall, having some buildings turn their backs to the river. A notable exception is the 333 West Wacker project" (van Vechten 2000–2002, e-mail August 3, 2001).

In effect, 333 West Wacker is two buildings. The side that faces the river bends with it, while the side that faces the Loop forms right angles that follow the urban grid. Its green-colored glass facade mirrors not only the river's hue but also the role the river plays in offering continuity through changing perspectives. Oudolf's notion of twisting the traditional perspective in order to allow the eye to look beyond the immediate or singular vantage point is exemplified by 333 West Wacker. The structure frames and is framed by its spatial and temporal contexts. Spatially, it is sited on a part of the river undergoing a great deal of development and change. Like the Merc, it serves to link expressions that typify spaces of place and those that typify spaces of flows. Temporally, 333 West Wacker distinguishes buildings that precede it from those that have come and will come after its construction. It is an architectural landmark and standard.

This structure also bridges and exemplifies the changing economic role of this part of Chicago's Central Area. According to Sassen: "Telecommunications and globalization have emerged as fundamental forces reshaping the organization of economic space. Whether in electronic space or in the geography of the built environment, this reshaping involves structural changes" (Sassen, in *Metropolis Magazine* 2000). Sassen further argues that the point of intersection between the electronic and digitalized and the physical is worth considering and exploring. The building at 333 West Wacker in many ways serves as a catalyst for its neighbors, the R. R. Donnelley and Leo Burnett buildings, which further explore this process.

The R. R. Donnelley Building—77 West Wacker
The Leo Burnett Building—35 West Wacker

Architects, Ricardo Bofill Arquitectura with DeStefano + Partners (1992)

Architects, Kevin Roche–John Dinkeloo & Associates, with Shaw and Associates (1989)

New economy businesses need quick access to digital infrastructure, transportation, and real estate. Chicagoland rates highly on the first two requirements, but must continue to develop more flexible leases and finance buildings that serve as incubators for start-ups, with space and shared infrastructure and business support services. (NEGSC, 6)

In the 1980s *postmodernism* was the broadly applied term for a style that reached into the past for inspiration. Glass-box modernism had run its course, and architects gravitated to historical roots, sometimes to a mixture of roots. Architecturally, the Donnelley and Burnett buildings reflect postmodern intentions (see Figure 20). In different ways, these two projects both reach beyond the city's borders and look within for inspiration. For the Donnelley Building, Spaniard Ricardo Bofill was brought in to direct the design for Chicago-based DeStefano + Partners, the building's architects. Bofill wanted his tower to reestablish a dialogue between the classicism of stone and the high-tech of glass, although the desired effect is of light and transparency.

In the case of the Burnett Building, Kevin Roche looked to the works of Louis Sullivan and the first-generation Chicago School. According to architectural historian Jay Pridmore: "In the Leo Burnett Building, the postmodernist gaze focuses on the old Chicago School. Kevin Roche, an Irish-born architect, conceived the structure as a classic Sullivanesque skyscraper—with base, shaft, and capital formed as three distinct elements. . . . There are also ornamental touches of Frank Lloyd Wright and the horizon-hugging architecture of the Prairie School" (Pridmore 2000, 60). The checkerboard pattern covering the entire height of the tower disrupts its verticality, visually shortening and broadening the building.

Both buildings marry materials that have come to typify Chicago architecture old and new. The Donnelley Building uses Portuguese white granite for the pilasters and arches, which are melded into the glass facade. The building's large

20—Leo Burnett (left) and
R. R. Donnelley buildings,
September 2000

marble lobby features shallow pools and bamboo hummocks. Here, giant white
marbled sculptures by Bofill are positioned alongside sculptures by Tapies and
Xavier Corbero (Sirefman 1996, 140). In the Leo Burnett Building, granite is used
to symbolize the heavy masonry walls found in the structures of the old Loop
even though this building is essentially a steel structure with a thin cladding of
stone (Sirefman 1996, 138).

Functionally, the two buildings house businesses that serve the global economy, but, Sassen notes, "Processes of economic globalization are . . . reconstituted as concrete production complexes situated in specific places containing a multiplicity of activities and interests, many unconnected to global processes." And just as focusing on cities "allows us to specify a geography of strategic places on a global scale, as well as the microgeographies and politics unfolding within these places," so, too, can focusing on the forms within them (Sassen 2000, 4). These buildings reflect Chicago's new informational economy as well as the city's established industries and businesses. Corporate headquarters, primarily for service- and information-based businesses, are increasingly dotting the Loop area. Since the Loop is a blend of old and new, finding a suitable design that fits this transition and sustains the visual coherence of the area becomes a primary concern. Efforts to achieve these objectives are evident in the designs of both these buildings, even though they are very different.

These two additions to the riverfront caught my attention when I first returned to Chicago in 1999, in part because of their prominent location and in part because of the way they engaged in conversation with the older forms, many of them iconic, along the river's main branch. The Burnett and the Donnelley buildings now have become more familiar, but they continue to engage me because of their very different responses to the river and to postmodern and postindustrial times; perhaps also because they are not iconic. In fact, both structures have generated controversy for their designs. Considering that they reside next to 333 West Wacker and across from Marina City, the IBM Building, the Merchandise Mart, and other landmarks, the standards are high. Some feel that the newer additions do not match up to the others. But considering the city's new goals, perhaps these two buildings express the newer ideology that form should not be the focal point, rather that it should take more of a backseat to the activity and connectivity generated within and among them. The Leo Burnett Building and the R. R. Donnelley Building do not turn their backs to the river. Their facades reflect the river and their neighbors in different ways—one as a fractal image and the other as a mirrored image. The older, more "established" buildings took a risk; these newcomers must do the same. They add another layer to the evolving morphology of the city and serve as reminders that it takes risk and style to make it in Chicago, much as it does for the businesses they house. In DPD member Benet Haller's opinion: "Not every building has to be a 'home run.' But glass boxes without style or substance will not cut it" (Haller 2002). Time will reveal their fate on both counts. Clearly Chicago has its share of glass and steel, but it incorporates granite and brick to counter-balance and localize, as one can see simply by looking across the river at the Merchandise Mart and the Reid-Murdoch Center.

The Retail Center of the Merchandise Mart— at the River between Wells and Orleans Streets

Architects, Graham, Anderson, Probst & White (1931) and Beyer Blinder Belle (renovation, 1991)

General recommendations for the Central Loop include: Creative reuse of existing buildings. Strike a balance between preserving a healthy office environment and meeting the housing, retail and open space needs of new residents. Focus on active retail and entertainment uses at street level. (CAP, 50)

The industries that were once the major users of the River have become less polluting or have moved away. And Chicagoans have learned to appreciate the River as a recreational destination, a place to paddle a boat or have lunch. (CAP, 63)

The Retail Center of the Merchandise Mart is significant in the way it blends past and present and opens to the public what was once a private space. The Merchandise Mart has historically been viewed as a closed building. Its retail spaces functioned primarily as service shops for the wholesale and office tenants above. Graham, Anderson, Probst & White, the firm that built the Mart in 1931, was responsible for its general renovation and cleaning that took place between 1986 and 1991. The firm of Beyer Blinder Belle (BBB) was then put in charge of converting the Mart's first and second floors into a 250,000-square-foot shopping arcade, which would be open to the public. BBB faced the challenge of creating new forms and meaning within this existing national landmark and within a space that housed service, office, and retail spaces. For the interior design and materials, BBB drew upon the Chicago School Art Deco character of the original building. The terrazzo floor patterns and the light fixtures of the new portions of the north lobby and arcade, for example, offer a more contemporary design, derived interpretively from the character of the original building. The south entrance was redesigned according to the original architectural drawings, at a scale visible across the Chicago River. This entrance, the south lobby, and arcade make strong reference to the original fabric as reflected in the storefronts' signage and graphics, in the cast ornamental entrance detailing, and in the carved stone at the south entry portal (BBB 2001).

During the renovation process, truck docks and service areas were moved from the north half of the first floor to the river level below. They were replaced by a new two-story lobby offering views to the second level above, to open the space physically. New parallel arcades were carved from existing service and tenant spaces to maximize retail frontage. A series of new escalators connect the upper and lower levels. Three new entrances along the north side open the building to the revitalized River North neighborhood. The Tenant Design Guidelines Manual requires clear glass along the ground-level exterior storefronts, offering views to the retail activity or displays within (BBB 2001).

The Merchandise Mart is energized by new landscaping and graphics as well as new lighting at the river's edge (see Plate 9). The walkway and greenspace on the lower level are especially effective in connecting and disconnecting the predominantly business space to the recreational or residential spaces. The walkway offers a fluid path to newer developments such as RiverBend and to the newly renovated Reid-Murdoch Center, which had previously been visually and physically cut off from this part of the Central Area and the main branch of the river. The walkway and greenspace also counter the scale of the Mart's massive structure. Inside the Mart, individuals are offered a unique experience in shopping as well as a glimpse into the history of Chicago. All these features could turn what previously was not a well-trafficked area into a lively thoroughfare and destination point. Originally built when the river was meant to emphasize the industrial age, the Merchandise Mart's appearance is certainly that of a space of place.

PLATE **1**—Drawn from Community Area Map (City of Chicago, 2004), Chicago Neighborhood Map (Big Stick, 2003), and 2006 real estate maps.

114

PLATE **2**—State Street kiosk and lamppost, August 2004

PLATE **3**—*(above)* Marshall Field's interior, January 2001

PLATE **4**—*(right)* Pritzker Park—State and Van Buren streets (Fischer Building in background), July 2001

116

PLATE **5**—Sears on State Street, July 2001

PLATE **6**—McCafé on North Wabash Avenue, July 2001

PLATE **7**—Harold Washington Library and Old Colony Building (1894) to the right, September 2000

PLATE **8**—Sidewalk detail on Randolph Street and State (shadow of State Street streetlights), July 2003

118

PLATE **9**—*(right)* Walkway
and green space at Merchandise Mart, July 2003

PLATE **10**—*(below)* Reid Murdoch Center, August 2004

PLATE **11**—Centennial Fountain, September 2000

PLATE **12**—(*right*) RiverView
(east tower—see plate 11),
July 2003

PLATE **13**—(*below*) River
Gateway, July 2001

PLATE **14**—Sheraton Chicago Hotel and Towers, July 2001

PLATE **15**—Navy Pier along Lake Michigan, January 2001

PLATE **16**—*(above)* Park Grill,
Millennium Park,
August 2004

PLATE **17**—*(left)* Jay Pritzker
Music Pavilion and Great
Lawn, August 2004

124

PLATE **18**—Crown
Fountain, August 2004

PLATE **19**—Lurie Garden,
August 2004

PLATE **20**—West Loop, July 2002

126

PLATE **21**—Archer Courts,
Phase I curtain wall at dusk,
2002. *Mark Ballogg*

PLATE **22**—Archer Courts
Phase II, 2002. *Peter Landon*

PLATE **23**—Rhapsody on North Wabash Avenue, July 2002

PLATE **24**—*(above)* Midway
Airport Triangle Concession,
2004. *City of Chicago,
Department of Aviation /
Matt Carmichael/
photomattic.com*

PLATE **25**—*(right)* Family
viewing part of Home Suite
Home exhibit—in front
of Wrigley Building,
July 2003

But with recent modifications to its interior and exterior connecting it with the river and with recent developments, it has made its transition to the postindustrial age both fluidly and innovatively, showing that appearance is everything. The Reid Murdoch Center provides a similar lesson.

Reid Murdoch Center—325 North LaSalle Street

Architects, George C. Nimmons (1913); renovation, 2001/2

In early 2000, the City of Chicago awarded Friedman Properties the right to redevelop the Traffic Court Building at 325 North LaSalle Street. This massive, over-340,000-square-foot Arts and Crafts–style structure fronting the Chicago River's north bank between LaSalle and Clark streets was built as a central food-processing plant for Reid, Murdoch & Co. The building was converted into the city's traffic court and was referred to as the Traffic Court Building, although its original name remained part of the riverfront facade. Designed by George C. Nimmons, a Chicago-based architect and student of Daniel Burnham, the building was one of the first structures to be erected in full accordance with Burnham's belief that the Chicago River should serve the city as much as the Seine serves Paris and the Thames serves London. Listed on the National Register of Historic Places, the building is already a Chicago landmark. Its most distinguished feature has always been a clock tower with four massive, internally illuminated, translucent glass faces. "The tower, rather than being located over its then Clark Street showroom entry or its LaSalle Street freight-loading areas, was directly in the middle of the structure on the riverfront facade" (Friedman Properties 1999, 6). When commercial river traffic was at its peak, Reid, Murdoch & Co.'s principal facade faced the river where boats and barges loaded and unloaded foodstuffs through a system of variegated chutes and lifts. On the north side, two spur rails entered the building while carts, wagons, and later trucks had access on what is now lower LaSalle Street. The city's bridge project created the current LaSalle Street and Clark Street entries, at what was originally the building's second floor.

The renovation and redevelopment of this structure are very significant for the City of Chicago and for the River North area in particular. More than just a structural restoration, this is a first step in the revitalization of the north bank of the main branch of the Chicago River, signaling a return to a different kind of around-the-clock hustle and bustle that all but disappeared with the demise of commercial river traffic. (Marina City made similar overtures in this direction decades earlier and is only several buildings away from it.) The building also creates a link between the Loop and River North at both LaSalle and Clark streets. For the first time in years, people are able to enjoy the riverfront in the heart of the business district. There is one-stop home-decor shopping at the retail level. Above the store are professional office spaces, including "high-tech" office suites. The top floors and part of the clock tower itself house luxury rental residential apartments (see Plate 10). According to the developer, Albert Friedman, the goal has been "to reshape the public image of the building from its recent past as a governmental office building and courthouse to its future as a shining example of its Prairie-style architectural heritage (Friedman Properties 1999, 7). Former DPD commissioner Christopher Hill chose Friedman's firm because his plan had "a mix of uses that the other proposals didn't have. This proposal has a very active river presence: walkways, boat docks, exterior eating areas. We want people to enjoy the river" (in Spielman 1999a). This includes nonresidents as well as residents.

A new river-edge veranda and dock area receives a Mercury Cruise Lines executive cruise boat, newly commissioned exclusively for this redevelopment. The Reid Murdoch Center also joins a growing number of buildings on the riverfront that have incorporated restaurants—in this case, Fulton's on the River—as part of their mix. These restaurants provide a way to turn back to the river, to reinforce the physical and social connectivity that is now a more desirable stance for these sites.

The Reid Murdoch project has not been without controversy, however. Concerns include the aesthetics of the alteration of the river's edge, rights of ownership, questions of use, and compensation for this space and for build-outs or expansions (von Klan 1999). River protectionists such as Friends of the River were uneasy about the effect that a thirty-foot build-out here and at similar sites would have on the appearance of the river. The Friends' president asks: "Will [the build-outs] result in an unsightly, cramped or jagged River edge? What provisions for preserving the aesthetic value of the River need to be made? Would tapered edges on each end of the build-out help counteract a potential lack of visual continuity along the river?" (von Klan 1999). The Reid Murdoch Center is working to address environmental issues and to keep the dialogue of old and new, the zig and the zag, alive along this part of the river. A project in the making with similar goals is the Trump International Hotel & Tower.

Trump International Hotel & Tower

Architects, Skidmore, Owings & Merrill (2007)

Given its prominent location and proximity to the vibrant River North and North Michigan Avenue districts, the Sun-Times redevelopment site presents a unique opportunity to create a significant public space, with riverside walkways, retail and restaurants. (CRCD 1999, 58)

This fourth population [Metropolitan businesspeople] . . . is characterized by having a considerable availability of both private and corporate money. It typically stays for a few days, but sometimes for more extended periods, but it is not a permanent population. . . . This is a population of expert urbanites, individuals composing it tend to know their way around, be very selective in terms of shopping and hotel and restaurant use, as well as in the use of top cultural amenities. (Martinotti 1994)

In what will occupy most of the current "footprint" of the Sun-Times building, Trump International Hotel and Tower was originally designed to be the world's tallest building at 120 stories. After September 11, 2001, however, Trump decided "now is not the time" to go for the world's tallest. Instead, he adopted a downsized plan calling for a ninety-story, 1,125-foot hotel and luxury condominium tower of 2.4 million gsf, which will be the fourth-tallest building in Chicago. Designed by Adrian Smith of Skidmore, Owings & Merrill, the mixed-use high-rise responds to the unique oblong shape of the site along a bend in the

Chicago River between Wabash Avenue and Rush Street (see Figure 21). Smith designed the glass-and-steel building as a parallelogram whose north and south fronts slice diagonally, following the river bend. The flat-topped tower steps back as it rises, its notches acknowledging the profile of the Wrigley Building to the east and the IBM Building to the west.

As indicated in the plans, the residential component contains 461 luxury condominiums. The hotel component offers 200 condominium guest rooms, a health club and spa, restaurants, grand and junior ballrooms, a conference center, and an executive lounge. At street level, plans call for ninety thousand square feet of retail space for boutique shopping and dining venues. A garage below street level will accommodate eleven hundred vehicles. The hotel condominiums provide the opportunity to own a hotel guest room through a fee-simple purchase of a deeded unit, which can either be used by owners or their guests or be rented through the hotel's rental program. Like the residences, these units can be sold at any time. The complex serves both traditional residents and the new city user, that is, the transnational businessperson and tourist, who is an expert urbanite living between cities (Martinotti 1994).

While the design is clearly geared for high-end tenants, the complex offers something for the public as well. The main public amenity will be a three-tiered riverwalk on the building's south side, with one level outdoors and the other two covered to permit shoreline strolling even in bad weather (Kamin 2001j; Roeder 2001g). The building will include ample plaza space along the Chicago River, meeting Mayor Daley's insistence on plenty of greenery. A small public plaza to the east of the building will also be retained. At the ground floor, there will be a walkway through the building that will permit views of the Chicago River. A restaurant space on the sixteenth floor in the hotel section will afford spectacular views of the city. From the outside, views of this part of the city will be facilitated by the building's setbacks, which will be placed on both the river and the Wabash Avenue sides. On the Wabash side, setbacks will begin on the twenty-ninth floor and extend the entire length of the tower. On the river side, setbacks will occur at the sixteenth and fifty-fourth floors (Cremer 2005).

21—Rendering of Trump International Hotel & Tower.

© *Skidmore, Owings & Merrill LLP*

Benet Haller believes: "The most encouraging thing about this project is the possibilities afforded by the walkway." The ability to connect Michigan Avenue to State Street in a more fluid way will help the realization of a riverwalk and space of flows along the river. "Corridors that connect, especially along the river are vital in the Central Area. Some spaces make that less feasible. . . . But where it can be facilitated, efforts should be made to foster pedestrian paths" (Haller 2002). The Trump Organization has worked with the city and with the Friends of the River to ensure that accommodations for the walkway as well as environmental concerns are made. Russell Flicker, a former representative for the Trump Organization, noted that the collaboration has been helpful and has gone well (Flicker 2004).

When Trump first announced the mixed-use project, he pledged to deliver quality architecture. Selecting a well-respected Chicago architect and firm seemed to indicate he would keep his promise. The plans won favorable notices from city officials, who say that Trump's building will be well suited to Chicago's tradition of distinguished architecture. Others are not as satisfied. Architectural critic Blair Kamin claims that the design "fails to live up to the skyline standard set by its neighbors, including the Wrigley Building and the rest of the great ensemble of 1920s skyscrapers that flank the Michigan Avenue Bridge" (Kamin 2001k). Other critics focus on the quality of the public space, and calling the building a "skyblocker," they express concern about its potential impact on the view along the river.

What is significant about the plans for the project so far is the dialogue that it has generated and that it continues to generate. Architecture is serious business for Chicago residents, as is demonstrated by the intense deliberations concerning the Trump building's relation to the site and to the larger urban landscape. Kamin notes: "In any tall building, to be sure, there is a tug between designing from the inside in order to snare tenants and designing from the outside in order to make the building sympathetic to its surroundings. Yet the best skyscrapers resolve the demands of art and economics, form and function" (Kamin 2001k).

Kamin's view is guided, however, by the traditional way of framing the city, from the lake. Perhaps more attention will be paid to river views as the river rises in prominence. And perhaps more diversity of materials will be engaged in order to sustain diversity over monologue. As Haller explains: "Important to Chicago's vision for itself is that the new buildings don't all be glass boxes. Chicago has a tradition and desire to use real materials, granite, limestone, and brick. . . . The use of substantive materials, used in a creative and functional way is important and planning boards and committees have tried to reinforce this in deciding what plans and designs will fly" (Haller 2002). As with all building after September 11, 2001, design will take on additional importance—not just in terms of safety, security, and finances but also in respect for history and spaces of place. The Sun-Times site is among the most strategic for Chicago's Central Area. In a city that has always scrutinized design as a statement of essence, it will be interesting to see what comes to be built here (and how it is received) as notions of public space, security, and imageability take on more profound meanings.

On a more functional level, the Trump building is replacing the former home of an entity that sociologist Robert Park considered vital to the working of a city: a newspaper. "The newspaper is not merely printed," he believed. "It is circulated and read. Otherwise it is not a newspaper. By making information about our community life accessible to every individual at less than the price of a telephone call we are to regain . . . even in the complicated age . . . of the Great Society some sort of working democracy" (Park 1967, 82, 80). Circulation is as much about information as it is about material goods. The site shows signs of making the transition from serving local residents to serving the new city user. As information gains in importance economically, politically, and socially, information technologies are also changing. What replaces this entity physically, but more important, what replaces it in the social realm, should, as Park noted, reflect the public realm and foster the life of the city. In the Trump International Hotel and Tower we find circulation of information coming from the transnational business person and tourist intersecting and interacting with residents and workers at this very vital and busy intersection of the city. The Trump Organization is making many efforts to incorporate all user types. In addition to hiring a local firm, they are seeking local as well as national and international firms for retail and restaurant space (Cremer 2005). There is a strong desire to have the Trump complex be a good neighbor to local venues as well as to have it attract users from the outside.

New structures and uses can alter perception and recenter perspective visually and functionally. As Kamin notes: a successful outcome "still could happen here if there is the right sort of encouragement from city officials and the right kind of accommodation from the developer" (Kamin 2001k). If the Trump building indeed creates a dialogue with its surroundings and users and has us rethink what the order should be, it is indeed informing in the way Park intends. An informational city must reflect this and, more important, must work to provide the opportunities and space for such dialogue to occur.

Michigan Avenue Bridgehouse Museum and River Center

Architect, Edward H. Bennett, and engineer, Hugh Young (1920); renovation, 2005/6

The education sector is a growing presence in the Central Area. (CAP, 1)

The river and Chicago's manmade geography come together here. It is the perfect place to consider what the river means to Chicago and the region. (*River Reporter* 2003, 5)

The city and the environmental group the Friends of the River successfully negotiated a lease for the two bridgehouses on the bridge at Michigan Avenue and Wacker Drive. The Michigan Avenue Bridge opened on May 14, 1920. Built to ease traffic flows by extending Michigan Avenue north of the river, it later became the gateway to the Magnificent Mile. Today, it is one of the busiest and most recognized places in Chicago (*River Reporter* 2003, 1). Tourists, shoppers, downtown workers, and residents move across the bridge every day.

The northeast bridgehouse will be transformed into a River Center and the southwest bridgehouse will house a museum, slated for completion in 2006 (see

Figure 22). Truly a working or living museum, it will utilize all five floors of the bridgehouse to educate visitors about the river's history, its value to the Chicago area, and visions for the future. An important feature of the museum will be the historic interpretation of the river's bridges, particularly the Michigan Avenue Bridge.

The Michigan Avenue Bridge was the first double-deck, double-leaf, trunnion bascule bridge ever built. The bridge operates in seesaw fashion (*bascule* is French for seesaw). As each leaf tips up on its fulcrum or trunnion, the short end is carefully counterweighted so that a relatively small electric motor can lift the span (Pridmore 2000, 18). Since its development, all but one of the bridges built over the city's waterways since 1903 have been of this type. The bascule bridge is now also widely used around the world (Schulze and Harrington 1993, 127; *River Reporter* 2003, 5).

22—Michigan Avenue

Bridge, August 2004

When it was built, the bridge linked Michigan Avenue facing Grant Park to the commercially growing portion of the avenue north to Oak Street and Lake Michigan. The double deck allows traffic to serve both the upper and the lower levels of the avenue and provides access on the lower level to Wacker Drive. When the bridge was sited, the angle of the roads it connected created opportunities for high levels of use at its northwest and southwest corners and for visibility at its other two corners (Schulze and Harrington 1993, 128). It seems fitting that the bridge physically reflects a duality. It is also fitting that the bridge be transformed into one serving double duty. The city will benefit from having the bridgehouses occupied, which will reduce the costs of upkeep and maintenance. Friends of the River negotiated a ten-year renewable lease, with two renewable ten-year terms at one dollar per year.

The area around the Michigan Avenue Bridge is among the most significant in the city. Structures such as the Wrigley Building (Graham, Anderson, Probst &

White, 1921), the Tribune Tower (Howels & Hood, architects, 1925), and the Jewelers Building (Giaver & Dinkenberge with Theilbar & Fugard, architects, 1926) as well as the bridge itself are part of Chicago's heritage. Consequently, any new development here is bound to raise especially high levels of concern about design. And to this, concerns have now been added about the environmental impact on the river and on the direction that new development will take in the area. The Trump Tower and the Bridgehouse Museum could not be more different in design and purpose. Their juxtaposition reifies the character of the river today, that is, the importance of looking at what appears on the surface of the river, and what appears above and below. To that end the river must be viewed and understood from a variety of vantage points. Not only is this intersection a space of place, it is most certainly a space of flows, with multiple bridges to connect time, place, and use well into the twenty-first century. Another structure that invites this multiplicity and juxtaposition of views is Wacker Drive.

Revive Wacker Drive Project (2001–2002)

Roadway improvements should be completed and their quality upgraded in the Central Area to support accessibility and pedestrian quality. (CAP, 78)

In improving the means of transportation [new technology] has progressively extended the limits of the world market and of economic society. (Park 1974, 2:121)

Today, Wacker Drive is a national landmark candidate, but it has long been a local landmark for the city's residents and commuters. When the street was first conceived, people thought it was a dream; when the redevelopment plan was unveiled, people thought it could not be done (see Figure 23). Chicago has proved skeptics wrong, both then and now.

23—Vietnam Memorial on the revived Wacker Drive, 2003.

The reconstruction section of Wacker Drive along the main branch of the river began in February 2001 and was completed in November 2002, earlier than projected. It was the first time that the road has been renovated since it opened in 1926. The project rebuilt the oldest and most deteriorated segment of this historic thoroughfare at a cost of $200 million. The goal of this revitalization and rehabilitation project has been to "marry the historic fabric of the past to the ideals and needs of the future to ensure a great urban amenity for generations to come" (Revive Wacker Drive Project [b]). Project objectives included rebuilding and restoring the Wacker Drive structure, easing the flow of traffic on adjacent streets, enhancing the streetscape to improve safety and operations of the roadway, improving both access to and safety on lower Wacker Drive for deliveries, and expanding development of a riverwalk using the original material—Indiana limestone—to restore the facade (Revive Wacker Drive Project [b]).

Wacker Drive was a cornerstone of the Chicago Plan of 1909. Designed with an upper and a lower level running in all directions (north, east, south, west), the roadway was created as a distributive artery for seven major north–south streets and nine east–west streets. It was a radical departure, both in purpose and in construction, from any work previously undertaken by the Chicago Plan Commission and its chair, Charles H. Wacker. Wacker Drive combined advanced architecture and engineering design. The octagonal columns supporting the drive—resembling Atlas supporting the roadway—were a notable innovation providing both beauty and enormous strength. One of the first streets to allow intermodal freight transfer, Lower Wacker Drive served as a dock for boats that unloaded cargo to waiting trucks. On the lower level, electric light fixtures were concealed in the top of the columns so that the radius of illumination from each lamp overlapped the illumination of the next, thereby avoiding "black spots" (Revive Wacker Drive Project [c]).

Wacker Drive continues to break ground and light the way for the city's Central Area. It serves as an important roadway for distributing traffic within the CBD—as many as sixty thousand cars and thousands of pedestrians use it daily. Without it, other streets in the downtown area would be overwhelmed. Lower Wacker Drive facilitates parking, major deliveries, and refuse pick-up from fifty-seven high-rise buildings while also relieving traffic congestion. As the Central Area is redefined, the importance of Wacker Drive increases, because it connects areas west and south of the Loop that were once considered marginal and thus furthers their potential development and viability. In the process, the peripherals enhance the center and the outer layers enhance and reform the core.

Literally and symbolically, Wacker Drive reconnects Chicago's past with its future. Barely more than a mile long, the drive merges water, road, mass transit, and pedestrian traffic. Currently a space of place and destined to become a space of flows once again, Wacker Drive will fulfill Burnham's vision of a main artery of the city. It will also fulfill his vision of providing greenspace in the city. Wacker Drive exemplifies the Chicago tradition of bringing together architecture and engineering and, in the process, offering users functional, aesthetically appealing, and innovative structures. The buildings that hug this road are enhanced by its presence. Now as in the past, and hopefully for many years to come, it will contribute to the new Central Area's visual and social viability.

Gleacher Center

Architects, Lohan Associates (1994)

Chicago will be an American model for what is possible when business, educational, and public institutions unite to provide the technology that supports opportunities Chicago citizens deserve. (Chicago, Office of the Mayor 2000, 306)

With the exception of the University of Chicago, which has had a technology transfer program for many years, the region's major research universities license fewer technologies (0.5 versus 2), start up fewer businesses (1.3 versus 2), and assist less in building businesses (8.3 versus 16) than the national average. (NEGSC, 8)

It seems fitting to have a branch of the University of Chicago in the city's central area and on the river's main branch, as so much of urban sociology and progressive education had its roots at this university. The idea that social distance is as much about relationships as it is about physical position also has relevance here because Gleacher is located in one of the more gentrified areas, Streeterville (in the Near North). The Gleacher Center houses the University of Chicago's Graduate School of Business and School for Continuing Education (see Figure 24). One goal of the center's design was to create a downtown identity for the university. Another goal was to improve the area along this stretch of riverfront for pedestrians. The Gleacher Center is a composite of several architectural styles. Its masonry facade echoes the Gothic-revival buildings of the University of Chicago's Hyde Park campus. "Its expansive walls of glass and steel evoke the modernism of Mies van der Rohe, who was Lohan's grandfather, and the five-story atrium recalls the great central atriums of the [first-generation] Chicago School, which valued natural light almost as much as rentable space" (Pridmore 2000, 80).

The significance of the Gleacher Center goes beyond its architectural impact. Bringing part of the University of Chicago to this part of the city offers a new role for the city's CBD as well as for the university. As an educational facility, the Gleacher Center creates another function for this part of the city; it encourages a more diverse population to enter the Central Area and use it in the evening as well as during the day. As part of the University of Chicago, the campus not only reflects its primary subject matter (a Graduate School of Business and Continuing Education Center in the midst of the city's CBD) but provides a way for the university to expand its role in the city from which it draws sustenance. The feeling of the Gleacher Center is quite sociable; yet it is situated in a part of the city and riverfront where the

24—Gleacher Center,

August 2004

local aspects of work and living reside alongside the more global ones, e.g, hotels, NBC Chicago headquarters. It has been the view of some that "Sociology today bears a surface resemblance to many of the dominant ideals of modern America. It is hard-nosed, quantitative, scientific, and practical minded. Like technical experts . . . sociologists seem immersed in their statistics and their computer programs, oblivious to human realities behind numbers and abstractions" (Collins and Makowsky 1978, 225).

From the outset, social sciences at the University of Chicago, including the sociology and economic departments, took great pains to humanize the study of people and institutions. The Gleacher Center reifies this legacy. In doing so, it strengthens its impact in the city's center, diversifying and softening an area that was once dedicated almost solely to commerce. During my many visits to the Gleacher Center "campus," it was not uncommon to see students reading and relaxing alone, or with others while they ate food from nearby restaurants. They were often joined by people who worked in the nearby offices. The presence of a new center for learning makes sense at this point in the realigning downtown area. And the river and riverwalk, as part of this new campus, offer ideal vantage points from which to observe and reflect on the issues at hand, or to find temporary respite from them.

Architects, Lohan Associates
(1989)

Centennial Fountain

General recommendations for the river: Develop the Chicago River as Chicago's second premier waterfront, a shared amenity with public access, promenades, parks, outdoor cafés, and high-quality mixed use buildings. Elevate the River as a civic corridor and primary open space focus. Develop the River as an environmental corridor. (CAP, 64)

The water is carefully controlled; its movement across the top of the table slowed to an almost imperceptible rate: it appears still until a visitor touches the surface—interacting with the piece—or until the water reaches the edge and turns, appearing to flow almost upside down. . . . I wanted to completely capture the power of the water—keeping its flow in careful check so that its energy seems to emanate from within the stone. (Lin 2000, 4:29)

Lohan Associates, the firm that designed Gleacher Center, also designed the Vermont granite fountain and water cannon across the river to celebrate the centennial of the founding of the Chicago Sanitary District, the governmental body that succeeded in reversing the flow of the river. Architect Dirk Lohan "wanted to symbolize the natural phenomenon of water, how it comes from one source, spreads, and goes back to another" (Lohan, in Pridmore 2000, 78). The Centennial Fountain project is part of the Cityfront Center Master Plan, a plan intended to create a "community of humane and urbane ambiance" for forty acres of land lying at the mouth of the Chicago River on Lake Michigan by emphasizing the quality and character of ground-level pedestrian spaces in order to define and unite public spaces and the spatial systems uniting them (Centennial Fountain 2001). Providing the last prime space available for mixed-use development adjacent to Chicago's CBD, this site includes River Esplanade, the Ogden Slip Promenade, Mayor Ogden Park, and the Centennial Fountain.

The Centennial Fountain serves as a landmark and gathering place. But its rhythm does much more for the surrounding area. It moves the eye from the land to the river, and to the lake. The eighty-foot arc spouting into the river offers an ephemeral sculpture. It injects one form of flow (the natural) into another (the man-made), thereby weaving back and forth between actual and virtual space.

Development along the riverfront today suggests consideration of the river's natural character and attention to its past, so that "vestiges of Chicago history along the river are recognized, and if possible saved" (von Klan, in Finley 2002). Centennial Fountain satisfies both concerns with grace and style. Spurting and spilling into the river, it breaks the rhythm of a steady flow of the river or the grid of the street to introduce spontaneity and temporal asymmetry. In its emphasis on asymmetry, Lohan's design conveys Lin's simple conceptual message that things do not have to be or look identical in order to be balanced or equal (see Plate 11). This statement has tremendous significance at the site that intersects Chicago's two primary waterways and for a city moving toward duality or multiplicity in more equitable ways than in the past, when centrality defined and overshadowed all else. It is also a playful reminder of the many ways in which water can engage and be engaged by people.

RiverView

Architects, DeStefano + Partners (2000–2001, 2003–2005)

Today's educated and often high-income workers are footloose, choosing among cities for their amenities and quality of life—safety, recreation and entertainment, personal mobility, and architectural aesthetics. Chicago has historically had a strong residential base and is currently desirable for residential construction. (Krontoft, McMillen, and Testa 2001)

While rental housing development was predominant in the 1980s, for-sale housing became the product of choice in the 1990s. Despite achievable rents of about $2.25 per square foot and high occupancy rates, project economics favor condominium developments. (CAP, 13)

Just east of Michigan Avenue lies RiverView, the first project built in the new River East neighborhood. The first phase of the brick-and-limestone development includes a thirty-story tower and eight three- and four-bedroom townhouses at the base of a five-story parking structure (see Plate 12). The second stage of RiverView, under construction in late 2005, adds a second tower and eleven more townhouses.

RiverView makes a statement about living the good life in the heart of the city. Both phases of RiverView feature units with gourmet kitchens, master baths, and hardwood floors in living and dining rooms. Amenities within the complex include a private health club with an indoor swimming pool, a private rooftop sundeck, indoor parking, conference facilities, and access to the landscaped Riverwalk (DeStefano + Partners 2001b). Walkways are scaled for easy movement and interaction. An effort has been made to provide a sense of privacy for residents yet still allow public access.

In many ways, RiverView continues to break social and architectural ground in much the same way as Marina City and River City did when they were first built. Like these and like DeStefano's RiverBend Planned Development,

RiverView has been designed to harmonize with its surroundings. Yet it evokes a stronger visual presence as a residential space than these structures do, thanks to its form, materials, and colors. Its teal blue glass, white limestone, and terra-cotta brick complement the water and the greenery. The colors also have a contemporary feel. Furniture designer Karim Rashid believes that "the aesthetics of the digital age have had a huge impact on the physical world." He cites as examples the colors inspired by computers and the "very analog tendency toward the tactile and highly sensorial, like the rubbery Blob object containers" (Rashid, in *Metropolis Magazine* 2000). Objects with amorphous shapes and vivid colors such as Apple computers and ipods, for example, counter the more traditional, bland-looking containers for such appliances. In essence they soften the "hardware," making it more human, more fun, more moving. There is something to be said for computer-generated influences if they can be integrated into a site in this way. At this section of the river corridor, the colors used for RiverView have also been adopted for the street fixtures, the riverwalk, and the gateway connecting RiverView to the lakefront. The teal or blue-green, white, and terra-cotta signify that this area is a space of flows, in contrast to the dark traditional green, grey, and rose that once defined State Street as a space of place. It is a small, perhaps subtle gesture, but it helps to unify the area, enhance the connection with the water, and give the site a vibrant, fanciful, and contemporary feel.

Architects, Solomon Cordwell Buenz & Associates (1992)

Sheraton Chicago Hotel and Towers

Increasingly, business and top level tourism go together. . . . The fourth population is increasingly constituting a transnational middle-class, living not in a city, but in cities, or better between cities and it affects the morphology and functions of all large urban centers. Hotels, offices and commercial centers built by the same companies in many cities, go together with the standardization of local shops interested to cater to an increasingly homogeneous transnational population of urban travellers. (Martinotti 1994)

Chicago has its share of cookie-cutter hotels, but many resist standardization and emphasize their locality by finding continuity and identity from within in order to meet more global or externally generated needs. Sheraton Chicago Hotel and Towers is one such structure. The Sheraton reflects the growing importance of tourists and professionals as city users who want easy access to specific areas of Chicago. Michigan Avenue and the south side of this corridor of the river are already home to numerous hotels. The siting of the Sheraton on the north side is slightly different because, although forming part of the agglomeration of hotels found here, it adds to the critical mass of people using this space by joining the expanding and increasingly diverse mix of residential, retail, educational, and recreational facilities.

Functionally keyed to the city's present and future, its design was nonetheless inspired by the city's architectural past, specifically by Louis Sullivan's Carson Pirie Scott Building (see Plate 14). Like Carson Pirie Scott, the Sheraton's corner towers are curved, giving the building a strong vertical presence, but its strong horizontal lines play off the new riverwalk, which runs the length of the hotel (Pridmore 2000, 74). This horizontality helps sustain the human scale, as does the riverwalk and the stream of restaurants drawing people from nearby office buildings and hotels during lunch and after hours. The mix afforded by hotels, schools, and residences along with the fluid path of the riverwalk will make this a twenty-four-hour, seven-days-a-week area for residents, commuters, and visitors.

Solomon Cordwell Buenz & Associates (SCB), the local architectural business responsible for the Sheraton's design, is making its mark on the city's landscape. Its portfolio for this area includes other hotels, commercial spaces such as the Crate and Barrel flagship store on North Michigan Avenue, and residences such as The Heritage at Millennium Park. These buildings represent an important part of Chicago's present and future image. At the same time, SCB blends past and present in ways that perhaps only an indigenous firm could.

Riverwalk Gateway

Architects, Skidmore, Owings & Merrill (1999)

Recommendations for the riverfront: Achieve continuous public access where possible. Create new opportunities for varied experiences along the River. Enhance the network of parks and special places. Create a continuous system of riverfront parks. Create better connections over the River for pedestrians and cyclists. Improve the environmental quality of the River. (CAP, 64)

The Riverwalk Gateway is proposed as a welcoming connection between lakefront attractions and the downtown riverwalk. It will be an important addition to the roster of improvements to the mouth of the river. (CRCD 1999, 56)

Plans for the Central Area, beginning in the 1980s, called for a series of continuous walkways along the riverfront, walkways that would begin at Roosevelt Road at the southern end and proceed along the lakefront to Navy Pier. In spite of logistical and technical problems, architects and planners succeeded in creating part of this with Riverwalk (Pridmore 2000, 13).

The new Riverwalk Gateway serves as a bicycle and pedestrian connection between the Chicago Riverwalk and the Lake Michigan bike path in downtown Chicago (see Plate 13). Commissioned by Mayor Daley and the CDOT as part of the larger Chicago River Master Plan, the 220-foot-long passageway running beneath an elevated section of Lake Shore Drive provides a safe and comfortable link for pedestrians and bicyclists. A sharp contrast to what was previously an impassable, gritty space, the steel-and-cast-concrete structure offers brightness and light as it beckons the user toward panoramic river and lake views. SOM's design pays reverence to the materials and style of the 1930s Art Deco bridge above the passageway. The series of steel arches spanning the walkway reflect the shape of the bridge, while lanterns bracketing each end of the structure recall the architecture of the bridgehouses (see Figures 25 and 26).

Along the interior walls, ceramic-tile panels installed in the spring of 2000 bear murals reflecting waterfront themes, local figures, events, and sights. A dynamic lighting scheme provides both safety and beauty. Ornamental lights

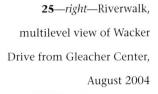

25—*right*—Riverwalk,
multilevel view of Wacker
Drive from Gleacher Center,
August 2004

26—*below*—Riverwalk, lower
level looking west toward
Michigan Avenue Bridge,
January 2005

adorn the steel arches while a series of brilliant wall washers illuminate the murals. The colors are contemporary and reflective of water—both of the river and of the lake, which this gateway connects. The gateway, completed in 1999, succeeded in turning a negative urban space into a positive public one, yet it managed to stay within a limited budget (SOM text, van Vechten e-mail, January 16, 2002). Indeed, the gateway acts as a Wide Area Network (WAN) for the Central Area. As a result, the movement of people and boats along this corridor really connects what were once disparate parts of the Central Area into a more fluid whole.

North Pier Terminal

Architects, Christian Eckstorm (1905–1920) and Booth/Hansen & Associates (renovation, 1990)

Chicagoland, with many features necessary to attract new economy businesses, has an opportunity to create a more vibrant entrepreneurial community. Residents enjoy an enviable quality of life. (NEGSC, 9)

From the exterior, the North Pier Terminal is rather unremarkable. Featuring brick walls, rows of windows, and pyramidal towers, which enliven it to some extent, the building can easily slip under the radar. The interior, however, offered an abundance of open space well suited for venues such as large furniture showrooms and warehouses, so when the building was renovated for commercial and retail use, "architects took advantage of this openness to create a series of flowing spaces that open out onto the Ogden Slip wharf" (Pridmore 2000, 67). Today, it sits opposite the back side of RiverView and other residential housing. Its low-rise scale in comparison to the residences and commercial buildings deemphasizes the structure and focuses attention on function instead of place. Retail in the North Pier Terminal, from gourmet food shops to restaurants, caters to upscale customers; landscaping and outdoor sculpture enhance the site. Boat slips and the dock, which offers eateries in season, further promote multipurpose use of both river and structures. The pier complements the river, the riverwalk, and the new residences springing up nearby; it seems dedicated to serving local residents, an especially important duty because this is in an area that could be overwhelmed by new city users.

Sustaining neighborhoods that cater to residents without much concern for other city users is a significant ramification of the new alignment that preserves the distinction between public and private spaces. Benet Haller observes: "heading further along the North fork of the river there are places—Ohio, Chicago Streets—where it might be harder for tourists to find. . . . Maybe it will become an area that residents or locals know about and use" (Haller 2002).

As the Central Area is reshaped and new neighborhoods develop, some may indeed serve more local residents than visitors. Such an outcome will ensure the stability and critical mass needed for neighborhoods to thrive. The North Pier Terminal is likely to become such a neighborhood because residential-appropriate activity is turned inward, facing the slip, whereas commercial activity faces the street and the grid. Here the water quiets and calms, while the

street energizes. Paths move people fluidly in and out without ever totally closing off the space. At the same time, benches, wide steps, and sculptures along
the wharf invite a person to stop and sit. The duality of the terminal and the
adjacent features is fitting for a place that needs to accommodate not only new
city users but also people looking to make this part of the city their home.

Navy Pier

Architects, Charles Frost
(1916) and Benjamin
Thompson and VOA
Associates (renovation,
1990–1994)

Something special had to be erected here, where the activities determine the form and the
form influences the activities—flexible enough to be used in foreseen as well as in yet unfore-
seen ways. . . . Actually, Navy Pier is not a single building, but a flexible arrangement of
structures that allow a variety of different activities. (Jahn 2001)

Chicago began on the water at the place where Lake Michigan and the Chicago River meet.
In its early days, Chicago had a working waterfront, delivering the raw materials of a manufacturing economy, carrying away finished goods to a vast region. . . . Together, Chicago's
waterfronts constitute the City's grand civic spaces, where people can come together and
celebrate. (CAP, 63)

27—Navy Pier,

September 2000

Navy Pier is located where the river flows into the lake. As time and need have dictated, its design and use have changed. All three plans (that is, the CAP, NEGSC, and the CRCD plans) call for recreational facilities along the waterways to serve residents and visitors, and once again Navy Pier has responded, but this time in twenty-first-century style. Navy Pier was inspired by the *Plan of Chicago* (1909), which called for two long piers as part of a grand symmetrical design for the lakefront. Only Municipal Pier was constructed. Designed by the Beaux Arts architect, Charles Frost, three-thousand-foot-long Navy Pier rests upon timber pilings, steel tie rods, and concrete walls, all of which are invisible. When it was first built, it had freight facilities as well as a dance and modern music pavilion at its far end. Renamed Navy Pier in 1927 to honor World War I veterans, it served pleasure steamers and hosted trade shows. During World War II, it was a training center for the U.S. Navy. From 1946 until 1965, it functioned as the Chicago campus of the University of Illinois. When the university moved out, the structure fell into disrepair until the city began renovating it in 1976.

Today, the Pier houses a number of elements. A concert hall, with a domed one-hundred-foot-high ceiling, is supported with exposed, half-arched radial steel trusses; the Crystal Garden, added as part of the recent renovation, is inspired by the vast glass exposition halls erected in London and Paris in the mid-nineteenth century; the new Ferris wheel evokes memories of the World's Columbian Exposition of 1893; and the Skyline Stage, with a fabric roof wrapped over a steel superstructure, is a unique space in the city. Stores, booths, boat and bicycle rentals, many restaurants, a Shakespeare theater, a seasonal skating rink, a children's museum, and park space dedicated to children also occupy the pier. One might argue it is too commercial—in the way airports, museums, and many other facilities have become. Koolhaas observes: "What we've seen in the past 20 years is that shopping has begun to connect itself to almost every activity known to man. . . . Museums have shopping, Churches have shopping—and are dependent on them" (Koolhaas 2002, 9). But the design of Navy Pier commands the would-be shopper's attention at certain places, particularly at the Shakespeare Theater and in the Crystal Garden, where there are spectacular views of the city's skyline, the lake, and ribbons of street life that now surround the Pier.

The Pier's location—at the intersection of the lake and the river and at the nexus of Lake Shore Drive and the new Riverwalk—connects this otherwise removed section to the Central Area more fluidly. This makes Navy Pier an LAN more than an intrusion or extrusion (see Plate 15). It also bridges areas north, south, and east, much as RiverBend does. Together, the two form the east–west bracket of the river's main branch. And the multimodal ways in which one can arrive at Navy Pier fosters the sense of flow—in a contemporary way. Here, the river and riverwalk combine, working in tandem to bring to this area an energy and rhythm that is unique to waterfronts. This powerful combination of river and riverwalk culminates at and intersects with another waterfront: the lake. This merger further enhances the role of these conduits. What might have been a solitary path, in essence, becomes a powerful and encircling network of movement and connectivity culminating at a space of diversity and presence.

PART

Millennium Park (1999–2004)

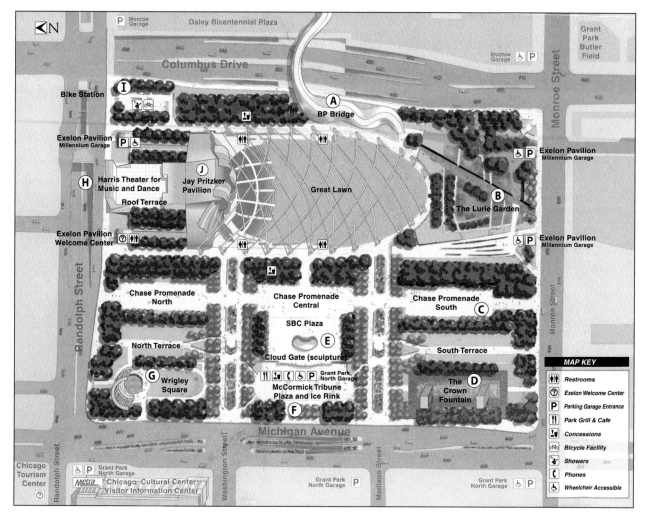

N

Monroe Garage

Daley Bicentennial Plaza

Grant Park Butler Field

Columbus Drive

Monroe Garage

Bike Station

I

A

BP Bridge

Monroe Street

Exelon Pavilion
Millennium Garage

P

Exelon Pavilion
Millennium Garage

P

Harris Theater for
Music and Dance

H

J

Jay Pritzker
Pavilion

Great Lawn

Roof Terrace

B

The Lurie Garden

Exelon Pavilion
Welcome Center

Exelon Pavilion
Millennium Garage

P

Chase Promenade
North

Chase Promenade
Central

Chase Promenade
South

SBC Plaza

C

Randolph Street

North Terrace

E

South Terrace

Monroe Street

Cloud Gate (sculpture)

G

Wrigley
Square

Grant Park
North Garage

D

The
Crown
Fountain

P

McCormick Tribune
Plaza and Ice Rink

F

Michigan Avenue

Chicago
Tourism
Center

P

Grant Park
North Garage

Washington Street

Metra Chicago Cultural Center
Visitor Information Center

Grant Park
North Garage

P

Madison Street

Grant Park
North Garage

P

MAP KEY	
	Restrooms
	Exelon Welcome Center
P	Parking Garage Entrance
	Park Grill & Cafe
	Concessions
	Bicycle Facility
	Showers
	Phones
	Wheelchair Accessible

Much of Chicago's image is derived from engineering and architectural feats, and rightly so, but there is also a formidable legacy arising from its landscape architecture. Here the character of the city can be felt as well as seen. In 2001 Mayor Daley held the city's first greening symposium, in which he recommitted himself and the city to the integration of more landscaping, in small and large gestures and throughout the city. From sidewalk planters to roof gardens, to what is perhaps the city's most ambitious project, Millennium Park, Chicago is breaking new ground in the design and the use of landscaping, just as it has done in architecture and sociology. Millennium Park is an example of the city's recent efforts to make landscape architecture a prominent feature of this postindustrial city.

Millennium Park is comprised of 16.5 acres of former railroad right-of-way and 8.1 acres of former historic parkland at the northwest corner of Grant Park. It is bounded west to east by Michigan Avenue and Columbus Drive, and north to south by Randolph Street and Monroe Street. Its one-million-square-foot space sits above a new underground garage and the reconstructed Grant Park North Garage (Millennium Park Project, 1999–2000).

By reclaiming the last unplanned parcel of land adjacent to the Grant Park complex, Millennium Park is positioned to complete the physical and symbolic centerpiece of the Plan of Chicago (1909) (Millennium Park Project, 2002). But the park is intended to be much more. While Millennium Park may be viewed as an addition to the Grant Park complex or a bridge between the old and new Central Area, it can also be understood as an ingenious complex in its own right. Millennium Park fuses and is infused by Chicago's enduring natural features and the changing currents of technological innovation. Millennium Park's creations transport people to and from a variety of visual and auditory spaces. Some connect to the larger surroundings while others turn inward, away from the surroundings, offering respite from cues usually associated with the built environment. The park fulfills the two primary considerations for every large city as articulated in the 1909 plan: "an adequate means of circulation; and . . . a sufficient park area to insure good health and good order" (Burnham and Bennett 1970, 80). Millennium Park is also helping to redefine the Central Area's landscape, and this time with an eye to the environment as much as to economics. The whole of the composition celebrates greenspace and recreation within the context of an enlightened twenty-first-century city. For all these reasons, the park is worthy of closer examination.

29—Site of Pritzker Music Pavilion and Harris Theater overlooking Michigan Avenue streetwall, July 2001

Already the prairie state of Illinois is nearly one-half urban, and the tendency towards city life is fast increasing. At the same time the need for breathing spaces and recreation grounds is being forced upon the attention of practical men, who are learning to appreciate the fact that a city, in order to be a good labor-market, must provide for the health and pleasure of the great body of workers. (Burnham and Bennett 1970, 47–48)

[T]here is a growing sense that open land must be preserved as an integral part of the landscape, through regional land use plans, purchases for parklands, and tax abatements for working farms. . . . An increased understanding and respect for the landscape of each region could lead to a growing rejection of a mass culture that erases all such distinctions. (Fishman 1996, 492)

When Chicago became a city in 1831, it chose for its motto "Urbs in horto" (city in a garden). Perhaps even then, those involved in shaping the city understood the importance of balancing nature and built forms, in order to create a place where people would live and work. This vision was quickly tested, however, as the city grew and industrialized with unprecedented speed. Nature, it seemed, gave way to built forms. In 1869 a movement was started to revive the half-forgotten and wholly disregarded motto by proposing plans for city gardens and parks, but it did not garner the momentum needed to counter the forces of development. When Danish landscape architect Jens Jensen arrived in Chicago in 1886, he noted: "Chicago was once called a garden city. What has become of the gardens? What has happened in Chicago has happened in many other large cities where speculation has been the guiding force" (Jensen 1990, 94).

Jensen served the City of Chicago as general superintendent and landscape architect for the West Chicago Park District from 1894 to 1900 and again from 1906 from 1920. He left to establish an independent design firm in Ravinia, Illinois (Jensen 1990, xiii). His greatest work for the city treated the land as an equal partner in his horticultural decisions. In the parks he designed, nature was the pervasive background for all outdoor activities, reinforcing a view of the land as part of an economic community (Grese 1992, 191). Jensen wanted his designs, "fleeting thought[s] that must be caught on their wings," to reconnect urban dwellers to the natural landscape and its cycles and to bring users into an intimate relationship with the compelling but harsh landscape (Grese 1992, 190). Jensen designed sensual spaces that were deliberately open-ended but which fostered a sense of enclosure as well as mystery (Grese 1992, 193). They quietly infused emotion and spontaneity into what was increasingly becoming a highly rational and ordered terrain.

Jensen's parks and gardens reflect the debate regarding what landscaping should look like and what it should evoke. He acknowledged: "The parks to which I was now attached, and with which I was to remain for a good many years, represented two definite ideas that had become a conflict within me, a conflict which was now raging—the natural or architectural" (Jensen 1990, 34). He was referring in part to the more formal, controlled approach to gardens and parks as exemplified by the gardens at Versailles, which had inspired designers for Chicago's Grant Park. "These gardens" he wrote, "were a good example of French garden architecture of a time when the ruling forces spent public money so lavishly that it continually brought into poverty the people who had to pay the upkeep. . . . These gardens were connected with a pompous boulevard which was used for army parades, exhibiting glorious military uniforms, or royalty parading under the long rows of stately trees—trees as pompous as the display that took place under their arching boughs" (Jensen 1990, 35).

Jensen instead favored parks and gardens that took a more informal and contextual approach: "For true expression, you must look in the simple gardens of common folk. Here is found a true art that has grown out of the soil and out of the heart of those people. They belong!" (Jensen 1990, 4–5). Rather than seek resolution, Jensen instead chose to sustain the tension and use it as a source of energy and a presence in his work. "Tension" and "contrast" became tools rather than problems needing elimination, and using these tools, landscape architecture would heighten and be heightened by built forms—that is, rather than landscaping serving or embellishing built forms, the two would work together to heighten one another and attend to the user. As Jensen's work evolved, it demonstrated a growing sense of stewardship toward the natural environment, which he hoped to awaken in others (Grese 1992, 195). Jensen believed it was the job of the landscaper to give "humanity the blessing of spiritual values as they are interpreted in his art" (Jensen 1990, 105). It would be left to the individual and the community to interpret from nature, which Jensen believed inspired all but could not and therefore should not be imitated, and ideally to create "compositions of living tones," which grew from the beauty of the region and the creativity of people (Jensen 1990, 105).

Jensen's work has found renewed recognition thanks to recent interest in landscaping that seeks to promote environmental as well as aesthetic integration in new urban designs. These efforts are framed around the notion of "sustainability," that is, "conservation and improvement of a community's resource base (its natural wealth of people, animals, land and environmental systems) to improve the quality of life for this and future generations" (Jencks 1993, 135). Designers committed to sustainability seek to provide

an increase of open space, including urban forests, parks and community gardens; the combining of trees and other greenery for a cooling effect in urban design, and to increase planting of trees overall; pedestrian-oriented, human scale urban design; increased bike usability; mixed use planning to decrease commuting; timely, convenient and affordable public transportation; efficient water use and water recycling and encourage drought resistant landscaping, and a community process to plan transportation routes that do not disrupt traditional neighborhoods. (Jencks 1993, 138).

Millennium Park addresses many of these concerns as well as the need for health, pleasure, and order voiced earlier by Jensen and by Burnham and Bennett. The use of landscaping in this park, in conjunction with built forms, raises the bar for architecture and design.

The design for Millennium Park was relatively modest when the project was first announced in early 1998. The first plan, which called for the new park and garage by Skidmore, Owings & Merrill (SOM), was essentially an extension of Edward Bennett's French Beaux Arts plan for the rest of Grant Park (Millennium Park Project 1999–2000, 1). This was significantly revised when Teng Associates included an underground garage at the reconstructed northern portion of Grant Park. This redesign, along with successful efforts to raise private donations for the park, enabled the city to expand its designs to include an outdoor music pavilion and a pedestrian bridge designed by Frank Gehry, a music and dance theater, a plaza featuring a sculpture by Anish Kappor, the reconstructed and relocated Peristyle, an ice rink, a full-service restaurant, a three-block-long promenade for arts fairs and other temporary attractions, a two-and-a-half-acre garden in the southeast corner of the park whose design was the object of an international competition, and an interactive fountain designed by Jaume Plensa. In addition, the new design provides for an underground parking garage for forty-three hundred cars and a heated indoor parking space for four hundred bicycles, complete with lockers, showers, and bike-repair facilities (Millennium Park Project 1999–2000, 1).

Funding for the park comes from public and private sources. This partnership reminds us that one criteria of community is the combining of systems and institutions in order to perform major social functions having local relevance (City of Chicago DPD 1966, 9). The city's contribution of approximately $270 million is generated by the garage parking revenues and TIF bonds ($35 million) dedicated to downtown improvements (Millennium Park Project 1999–2000). Park enhancements have been funded by private donations totaling $205 million, which include an endowment of $30 million set aside for the park's maintenance (Uhlir 2002; Herrmann 2004).

Aside from generating revenue for the city, Millennium Park's siting above garage space in the Loop is significant for other reasons. The 1966 *Comprehensive Plan of Chicago* recognized that, "The transportation network, which provides for access and communication among the interrelated functional systems of the city, has been and will continue to be the single most important influence over the city's structure" (City of Chicago DPD 1966, 31). This observation has even greater validity and urgency in the new global terrain where connections and ties to peripheral areas are intensified. To this end, Millennium Park's location and design make accessibility to the Loop through multimodal forms of transportation among its top priorities.

The amount of vehicle parking space adjacent to the CBD is critical to the retail and commercial viability of the area. On weekdays, the garage serves the business commuter shoppers and tourists. In the evenings and on weekends, it serves the Harris Theater for Dance and Music, the restaurants, the Randolph Street Theater District, and year-round events in the vicinity, helping to make the Central Area a vibrant and viable place twenty-four hours a day, seven days a week. In addition to automobile traffic, Millennium Park makes provisions for pedestrians, bicycles, buses, and trains. The city is expanding and enhancing the two existing commuter rail lines with the construction of two new train platforms and a new entry pavilion. The underground "pedway" system will be extended into the park site, thus connecting to the garages and to the rail terminal, and the CTA mass transit lines. A new private roadway beginning at Millennium Park and running north and south below street level provides quick and efficient charter-bus service connecting the North Loop hotels with the McCormick Place Convention Center (currently undergoing expansion) and the newly renovated Soldier Field Stadium (Uhlir 2002). All of these efforts reflect the increased hypermobility and hyperconnectivity required for dual cities. The park is a hybrid space, comprised of public and private, visible and invisible alliances and connections from within the community.

At the same time, the park is opening corridors in order to reach out to what were once considered peripheral regions and to move beyond city center and the city to the regional level. As noted in the 1966 *Comprehensive Plan of Chicago*, "[R]egional scale is composed of design elements which are generally associated with the city or the metropolitan area as a whole, rather than with the particular place where a person lives or works. The regional scale of the environment consists of buildings, monuments, shopping streets, amusement areas, landmarks, and scenic attractions which make a great city unique. These are the features that tourists are most likely to visit and that residents mention most often when they are asked what things about their city are most important or recognizable." Shifting to a regional scale realigns the frame from which to view city center and its components and their impact on a more expansive (and diverse) surrounding area. This move requires "the individual to relate himself to a vast and complex metropolis, . . . knowing what kind of an area he is in, what he is approaching and where he is relative to the total area" (City of Chicago DPD 1966, 18). While legibility is clearly important for residents and commuters, it has even greater significance for tourists or visitors. How can the city design for local users' needs while also encouraging and building for visitors? Can design sustain its localism while also attracting outside users? This is one subtext of the larger issues arising from Chicago's shift from an industrial to a postindustrial city.

The transition is not merely economic; it is also socially driven. Sociologist Guido Martinotti describes the transformation in terms of first-and second-generation metropolises (Martinotti 1994). The pivotal differences arise from who the significant or dominant city users are. The first-generation (or early) metropolis consisted of inhabitants and workers who, over time, grew apart until the workers became commuters. The commuter population spent most of the time in the central city secluded in working organizations and largely separated from the rest of the city population. Increased mobility, combined with greater income and leisure, has created a new population of city users who move to a city in order to use its private and public services for various purposes, ranging from shopping to seeing movies, visiting museums, or eating at restaurants. Martinotti describes the resulting metropolis as a second-generation (or mature) metropolis.

The second-generation metropolis is very different from the first generation in form and intention; in many ways it is a network city or city of networks, real and virtual. At the same time, a very specialized population—made up of metropolitan business people—is emerging, which includes convention-goers, executives, professionals, consultants, and international managers, all of whom go to central cities to do business and establish contacts. Although small, this population is growing, and, perhaps more important, it has a considerable amount of both private and corporate money. Residents and metropolitan business people have an increasing effect on the structure of cities. This has most clearly been seen in global cities such as New York, Tokyo, London, and more recently in the United States, in cities such as Miami, Los Angeles, and Chicago. Large metropolitan centers and their economic functions are affected more and more by growing populations of city users. This population constitutes what Martinotti calls the "transnational middle class," living not in any one city, but in cities, or more accurately between cities, which affects the morphology and functions of all large urban centers.

Cities are increasingly the product not so much of national economies but, rather, of a segmental unit of a larger entity. Furthermore, business and top-level tourism increasingly go together. And the growth of the metropolitan-business-people population creates another important phenomenon, namely, the internationalization or globalization of metropolitan centers. Hotels, offices, and commercial centers—often built by the same companies but in many different cities—go together with the standardization of local shops interested in catering to an increasingly homogeneous transnational population of urban travelers. No longer primarily for local inhabitants, cities are growing increasingly to be structured for guests and visitors (Martinotti 1994).

Millennium Park has drawn criticism on the grounds that it caters more to visitors than to residents of the city. Mayor Daley has adamantly denied this claim, asserting: "I want to emphasize that we are doing all these things for the people of Chicago, and not just to attract tourists or conventioneers or suburbanites or new businesses. . . . [The] same amenities that draw suburbanites and residents also attract tourists and conventioneers" (Office of the Mayor 2002c).

Millennium Park has already encouraged the expansion of residential—especially upscale residential—development in the central district. Its project director, Ed Uhlir, believes that "the park is meant to draw tourists, but is also very much the people's park" (Uhlir 2002).

Framing the intended use of the park as either for residents or for visitors exclusively is unrealistic. In truth, the city needs both populations. This framing also runs counter to the city's vision for the Central Area. A more useful frame from which to view the needed diversity of uses and users should begin, as suggested by Charles Taylor, "with the presumption of equal worth, but not with one's mind made up that they are the same, or of equal value, in all respects." Here, "one has to be prepared for judgements of inequality, the constant give and take of dialogue which presumes a generalized respect but also an indeterminate outcome" (Taylor, in Jencks 1993, 118). So, although not all groups can be treated with equal weight at any given time, they are given voice and identity. According to Taylor, this frame helps avoid the trap of falling into a form of inverted cultural condescension, which is as bad as the old notion of multiculturalism. Both frames, in Taylor's view, lead to the dissolution or devalorization of differences.

Architect and critic Charles Jencks uses the term *heteropolis* to refer to a terrain that embraces rather than excludes or absorbs diversity. In designing for a heteropolis, one "assumes the conflict of at least two major languages: the local and the universal, the particular and the technological, the historical and modern" (Jencks 1993, 118). "In order to survive, the heteropolis has to comprehend more fully the two conflicting modes of justice—the politics of universalism and of difference—and to engage their values more deeply in a new set of relationships. . . . As the hetero-architecture of Los Angeles, for example, shows, there is a great virtue, and pleasure, to be had in mixing categories, transgressing boundaries, inverting custom and adopting the marginal usage" (Jencks 1993, 122–23). Hetero-architecture overcomes the prevalent tendency to see things in "either-or" terms, just as the heteropolis does. The defining goal of the heteropolis is not only to sustain itself as a viable economic and ecological entity but to further "a slow, peaceful interweaving of world-views" (Jencks 1993, 123, 121).

Millennium Park embraces the spirit of a heteropolis in many respects. Both built and unbuilt forms are infused with this sense of the diversity of uses and users. Simultaneously, the park promotes a more environmentally responsive urban landscape. Here "the land" is viewed as a terrain whose presence needs to be recognized in relation to built forms. In Millennium Park, landscaping and situational (natural) forms are used as sources of design inspiration. In some cases they serve as solutions to design and spatial problems; in others, they ask for design solutions that respect their presence—moving them from the periphery to the center of urban design or city morphology. In architect Maya Lin's view: "Landscape can make its own sense of place without using an architectural language. This gives one the chance to create landscape works within an urban or architectural context" (Lin 2000, 6:17), further realigning center with periphery. The park can therefore serve as a site from which to consider how nondominant cultures and peripheral spaces can successfully reside alongside the dominant ones. More strongly, the park offers a frame from which to realign the whole and its parts.

As a corridor to and nexus for many kinds of activities, Millennium Park, along with Grant Park, opens a new set of possibilities for hubs, paths, and gathering places in much the same manner as a WAN or multiple LANs operate in technological (infra)structures. In this case each and all the creations are dedicated to some notion of recreation. Each feature keeps alive, perhaps more than ever, "A love for the garden [as] a vital factor in human civilization" (Jensen 1990, 102) while using cutting-edge technology to create the forms, and the pathways that connect them. Together, nature and human invention produce a dynamic and unique composition, created by the synergy of diverse interpretations of what recreation might mean for Chicago in the twenty-first century, that is, a park for this millennium—Millennium Park. The synergy is also derived from a reconsideration of what the term *boundary* means, both physically and cognitively. In some cases, the boundaries created in and by the park are meant to clearly and strongly define and separate spaces; in other cases, boundaries offer transitions. In still other cases, boundaries are dissolved while opening up the space to the larger whole. Consequently, the park is composed of spaces that are introverted and spaces that are extroverted; a consequence of lines and many curves. From these, multiple possibilities of form and use arise. The park is at once a site of creation and re-creation, synergized into a site of recreation. It is in this sense that the park is viewed and analyzed here.

The Great Lawn

Designers, Gehry
Partners, LLP (2004)

The prairies, too, have mystery. They, too have a horizon that calls. Early treks across the Great Plains, they become a sea indeed. However, the prairies give a far more secure feeling than the sea. The prairies are inhabited; they are human. . . . The plains speak of freedom—earth and sky meet on the far horizon. There is nothing to intercept the vision from the infinite. (Jensen 1990, 21, 28)

CREATION—Jensen viewed the Midwest through the prism of its natural features, especially the prairies. In many ways, the Great Lawn evokes a sense of this Midwestern terrain and spirit. Gently sloping up from the north to the south, it offers four thousand fixed seats in the main music pavilion area and an additional six or seven thousand informal seats on the surrounding lawn, on an expanse of site measuring 580 feet north to south by 320 feet east to west (Millennium Park Project 2002). The Great Lawn is a naturalistic essay, although not natural by nature-plant purists' standards, in that it utilizes high-tech "grass" and man-made slopes.

RE-CREATION—The Great Lawn reconciles natural and architectural forms with human experiences. The lawn is intended as a place to listen to music emanating from the music pavilion or from the urban or natural surroundings (see Plate 17). Thus, the Great Lawn is a place whose meaning is derived from the experiences of each individual and the experiences of the collective as they come together for a memorable event. It is a soft boundary—a space of transition. Its slopes offer curves that for Jensen "are always new, always revealing new thoughts and new interests in life" (Jencks 1993, 38). According to land-scape architect Thomas Christopher: "What we learn from our surroundings when we watch and listen carefully and patiently is invaluable. [A] solution to questions about how to deal with the landscape within or outside the garden will reveal itself" (Christopher 2002, 180). To access these revelations, we are re-quired to make reconciliation with Nature and with our nature. We must sur-render to natural time and intuition, shut out the external distractions, and lis-ten to what lies within. The Lawn offers a place to pause, to reconnect with nature, with others, or with oneself. The Great Lawn also connects two of the most remarkable creations in the park: the Lurie Garden and the Jay Pritzker Music Pavilion. The garden creates space from natural forms, and the pavilion unbuilds the built as we know it.

The Jay Pritzker Pavilion

Architects, Gehry Partners, LLP (2004)

CREATION—An open-air venue that frequently features the Grant Park Sym-phony Orchestra as well as jazz, blues, and other world music performances, the Pritzker Pavilion is sited above a three-level underground parking structure (see Figure 30). A busway and metro-rail tracks, running adjacent to Grant Park, pass beneath the pavilion and the Great Lawn at the lowest level. Even before it was completed, the "crown" of the pavilion, visible from surrounding city streets, made the pavilion a part of the skyline of the newly defined Cen-tral Area and a focal point for the city's new park. The pavilion's sculptured ex-terior wraps the stage with fifty-two hundred interlocking stainless-steel sheets, which cover ribbon-like panels that blossom like petals of a flower across the expanse of the structure. As with the petals of real flowers, no two panels of this flower are exactly alike in size or shape.

A key challenge for designing this structure was how to provide uniform sound distribution to ten thousand patrons over a four-acre area without visual obstructions. The answer resulted in audio innovations incorporating natural and technological features. Gehry designed a distributed reinforcement and en-hancement sound system suspended from a trellis, which spans the entire six-hundred-foot length and three-hundred-foot width of the Great Lawn. The trel-lis, in the shape of a flattened dome, is constructed of curved steel pipes typically spaced sixty-five feet apart. It is supported by cylindrical concrete pylons clad in stainless steel panels. The trellis complements the canopies created by trees and plantings in the garden and fits the pavilion to both the verticality of the city's skyline and the horizontality of its expanse. The pavilion's balance is not sym-metrical or traditional but, rather, organic and asymmetrical.

The elegance and simplicity of the trellis belies the cutting-edge technology it supports. The acoustic enhancement system was designed by the Talaske Group, located in nearby Oak Brook, Illinois, to work in conjunction with the sound rein-forcement system at Millennium Park. Talaske utilized cutting-edge computer-modeling software (Catt-Acoustic) from Sweden, to evaluate and optimize the acoustic design of the pavilion. This sound system gives the audience a fuller sense of the onstage sound and controls the volume in the surrounding neighborhood.

As an outdoor environment, the site is exposed to noise from traffic and trains, but coordination of landscape elements offers some relief. More important, the acoustic enhancement audio system masks peripheral city noises and minimizes weather-related effects on the sound (Talaske Group 2002).

During evening performances, a decorative lighting system of colored light washes and projections is used to enhance the tone of the performance at the pavilion. This is one of the few structures that Gehry granted permission to light in this way. Ordinarily Gehry does not permit lighting a structure, but, because of the diversity of venues planned for the pavilion, he felt in this case that lighting could be understood as part of the aura of the musical performance. In this way, the pavilion can recede from the focus of attention and empowers the music.

When lighting is treated as an element of the structure, it appears as a light from within rather than an external or alien feature. Nature is a master of this effect. As Jensen noted in his observations of light on birch trees: "The reflected light of moonbeams playing on the white bark of the birches illuminates the woodlands with surprising clearness. . . . To see the fleeting white blossoms of the shad entwined with the white bark of the birch trees was a sermon we were willing to go more than one hundred miles to listen to. . . . In groups upon the woodland border, [the aspen] gives the landscape a decided musical note" (Jensen 1990, 47, 46). Architect Santiago Calatrava describes the impact of lighting on built forms in a slightly different way. For him, lighting also adds the qualities of movement and change: "[For] centuries and millenniums, people understood architecture as something static. But in fact architecture changes. When the sun moves around, you see the shadows. The day, the night, the buildings change. So there is a movement, a kind of life in the building. And today, it is possible to express that and emphasize not only the functional needs of the building but also to emphasize this metamorphic character that architecture can have" (Calatrava 2002, 3). The Pritzker Pavilion works to marry nature and cutting-edge technology in this way.

Certain works blur the boundaries between architecture and sculpture; and, according to Maya Lin, "Frank Gehry is the only architect who has successfully merged the two disciplines" (Lin 2002, 4:45). In fact, Gehry often refers to his works as "sculptures," revealing not only how he views his work but how he understands the goals of the architectural process. "I approach each building as a sculptural object, a spatial container, a space with light and air, a response to context and appropriateness of feeling and spirit," he explains. "To this container, this sculpture, the user brings his baggage, his program, and interacts with it to accommodate his needs. If he can't do that, I've failed" (Gehry 1989). Gehry's building consists of juxtaposed collages of spaces and materials that make users appreciative of both the theater and the backstage, which are simultaneously revealed. He is quite aware of the possibility afforded by the fluidity of and respect between the frame and the framed, and of the role played by the user. Here the natural (or wild) justifies the built (or ordered) by merging the structures with the landscape, rather than, as Jensen noted, "having them stand alone as exclamation points" (Jensen 1990, 100).

RE-CREATION—Nowhere is this relationship more apparent than when viewing the Pritzker Pavilion in relation to both its immediate surroundings and the larger landscape—both built and natural, especially the waterways. Gehry has stated that his source of inspiration for the design of the pavilion came from the river and the architecture along and around it, especially the works of Mies van der Rohe. Gehry originally conceived of a dome that was flatter or more square as a nod to Mies, but officials rejected this design. Gehry also understood that the "sculpture," as he refers to it, had to fit into what was already a strategic and transforming space in the city. The design most clearly had to offer a "worthy structure to showcase the city's established enthusiasm for good music" (Gehry 2002a).

No stranger to creating venues for musical performances, Gehry has a deep understanding of the technical as well as the aesthetic parameters of music as it relates to architectural design. Music has often been compared with architecture, and while some, like Goethe, may view architecture as music frozen in time, architects such as Gehry emphasize the movement and flow in the structures they design. As a result, the designs deepen the formality as well as the asymmetry, ideas that resonate with the conceptualization of Millennium Park as the link between the lakefront and the Central Area by decentering the old focal points of the CBD. Spaces of place give way to spaces of flows through visual and auditory cues. The spaces move people along, shift them from one space and experience to another, spatially and temporally, in much the way music does.

Gehry makes the "sculpture" dance in a way that is quite fitting for this project. Sound, light, and movement help the pavilion achieve its dynamic personality. It is a multisensory construct, interpreting rather than imitating a natural one. What could have been a space of place—a deliberate attempt to build a monument in static terms—is now a space desiring to create new and unique memories for each individual who experiences it. Formally, the pavilion is designed to include a variety of performance types, so it needs to be flexible. This is achieved, in large part, by the melding of architecture and sculpture in the form, and by integrating human interaction in the design as well, thus unfreezing the music, as it were. So while the pavilion overwhelms the senses, it does not dictate the performance within because it makes space for the input of the user. The pavilion indeed enlists the user as part of the design and the experience, thus eliminating the boundary between the two.

In conjunction with the Great Lawn, the pavilion also blurs boundaries between inside and out; it engages Eastern and Western notions of space, so that there is a sense that "You are standing still and moving at the same time" (Oudolf 2002a). The pavilion acts as screen rather than wall, bridge rather than boundary. And as Calatrava observes: "Everybody understands the relation between nature and the artificial work of the engineers" (Calatrava 2002, 2). The pavilion is built as precisely and innovatively as were the works by the early Chicago architects who were inspired by engineering but who connected engineering with art to inform their interpretation of architecture. To further reify this sense of connectivity, Gehry has included a Pedestrian Bridge.

Architects, Gehry Partners, LLP (2004)

The BP Pedestrian Bridge

CREATION—The pedestrian bridge extends from Daley Bicentennial Plaza just off the Lakefront to the Music Pavilion and the Lurie Garden (see Figure 31). Columbus Drive, a multiple-lane, high-speed, grade-separated thoroughfare, is a significant physical barrier between the eastern and western areas of Grant Park and between the Lakefront and the Loop. The new pedestrian bridge creates a path linking these four areas of the cityscape. As pedestrians traverse the bridge, they gently rise above street level and the tree canopy and can experience changing views of the park and the city as they cross Columbus Drive.

Composed of cladded stainless steel panels, similar to those of the Pritzker Pavilion, and a boardwalk of Brazilian teak, the bridge presents a thin profile as it ascends above Columbus Drive. The sloped sides of the bridge on either side of the pavilion and lawn form a berm, designed to lower substantially the level of road noise entering the seating and stage areas. The serpentine shape of the bridge evokes the feel of a natural (nonlinear) path and also echoes the river and the design of River City, although these references were probably not intentional.

RE-CREATION—A bridge can be as significant as a building in creating and defining places. It is both a conduit for other places and a presence in itself. According to Calatrava: "A bridge has an impact, . . . and a presence, and dignifies the landscape in a way, or it potentially enhances places that don't have a quality. Once a bridge is there, it can give them something because it spans and adds to what they project to the community. Once the bridge has been put there, it makes [the space] unique" (Calatrava 2002, 1–2).

The presence of the bridge reminds us of the connection between art and architecture: "The Music Pavilion and the Pedestrian Bridge respond to one an-

other sculpturally within the landscape of the park, allowing the bridge to function as a key link in the spatial sequence connecting the tight urban fabric of Chicago directly to the Lakefront" (Millennium Park Project 1999–2000). But the bridge also reminds us of the connection between architecture and engineering. In this sense, Gehry's creation pays homage to the legacy of the engineers who inspired architects in Chicago while moving the city into the new informational, virtual, and high-tech culture. As architectural historian Carl Condit reminds us:

It was engineers who first pointed the way in which a new structural art would have to take. They built primarily for use . . . expressing directly, simply and honestly, the system of construction they employed. . . . Early in the 19th Century some of the bridge engineers, imbued with a sense of harmony and proportion characteristic of the best of the architects developed a new aesthetic of construction that pointed clearly to an organic architecture appropriate to a mechanized-industrial culture. (Condit 1952, 4)

Gehry's bridge points clearly to an organic architecture appropriate to a computer-based, telematically linked culture through computer-generated designs that merge state-of-the-art materials such as stainless steel with natural ones such as wood. In scale, shape, and use Gehry has also imbued the bridge with a strong sense of its local siting while inviting peripherals in. Most important, the bridge invites people to traverse from one part of the cityscape to another. The bridge is a paradox and a wonder, just like the city within which it resides.

The symbolism and significance of the pedway for this part of the city is multifold. It does not attempt to blur or obliterate the boundaries of terrains it spans. Instead it gives voice to both and to itself. The bridge, an act of engineering and art, has transformed a natural obstacle into an asset. As with the river, perspective and (pedestrian) flow have been channeled in a new direction, in this case, to an expanse that includes the Lakefront and the city's old center. This shift reminds users that, while the Lakefront is one of Chicago's gems, it is not the only one. And because the shape and flow of the bridge mimic the river more than the lake, we are offered a new perspective and vocabulary from which to generate the city's future. In this way, the pedestrian bridge spans time as well as space. The pedway reshapes the relationship of center and periphery in a mobile, virtual way. Movement or flow, rather than static features or boundaries, re-creates these terrains. Functionally, the bridge is intended to facilitate circulation. Now, however, the flow is two-way, from periphery to center and from center to periphery.

The bridge validates two of the city's nondominant cultures: the pedestrians and the disabled. The conflict between automobiles and mass transit in urban planning is an ongoing issue of debate. In 1939 Jensen wrote: "Today the automobile rules, and it destroys the parks as gathering places for the multitudes. Urban travel to the downtown areas of the large metropolis will be taken care of by public conveyance, and the art of walking will come back as a healthy necessity" (Jensen 1990, 91). At about the same time, Frank Lloyd Wright argued for "taking pedestrians off the road bed so widening it. The upper sidewalks might be made slightly architectural features of the city" (Wright 1931, 93). Gehry's bridge responds well to both Jensen and Wright, as well as to the goal of the Central Area Plan to encourage and accommodate all modes of transportation. The street level is given to automobiles while the bridge literally and symbolically elevates pedestrians and bicycle users. Human scale is honored spatially and temporally.

All the features within the park were designed to be fully accessible to people with disabilities. There are a few places in the park with steps, but they are kept to a minimum. Wheelchair ramps are located at the same place and level as the stairs so that the disabled will not feel as though they are second-class citizens who must enter from the side or at a different level (Uhlir 2002). As a result, the park is a place where dominant and nondominant cultures are given equal voice.

The BP Pedestrian Bridge valorizes real time by building for a human pace (walking) rather than a mechanical one. It also acknowledges the tension between nature and built form—which Jensen articulated in his work and to which Wright alludes—in a fluid and graceful, yet cutting edge and playful way. So what might have been a disjunctive area between the Lakefront (nature) and the Loop (built form), between center and periphery, is, in Calatrava's terms, "justified" through Gehry's bridge.

Today, understanding and working with the imagery afforded by a bridge is perhaps more essential than ever. The events of September 11, 2001, and its aftermath are redefining architecture and engineering. There is more clarity and urgency for linking East and West, dominant and nondominant, developed and developing areas, in ways that are fluid rather than rigid, dynamic rather than static, and unimposing rather than domineering. Many architectural proposals now involve curtailment and limitation. Perhaps post-September-11 bridges can offer more unifying and liberating aspirations, as is the case in this concise and innovative feature of Millennium Park. As Calatrava notes, bridges can be worthy forms for the fusion of architecture, art, and engineering. The pedway offers itself as yet another Chicago landmark—one that bridges, both literally and symbolically, many times, places, and technologies.

The Joan W. and Irving B. Harris Theater for Music and Dance

Architects, Beeby Rupert Ainge (2003)

CREATION—The Harris Theater for Music and Dance shares common lower-level loading docks with the Pritzker Pavilion. Planned originally as an auditorium to hold five hundred people, the indoor theater now offers a fifteen-hundred-seat performance space. White in color and flush with Randolph Street, the theater's exterior is rather nondescript. The only attention-grabbing feature is the signage indicating its name, which appears in simple silver letters on the side of the building. The street-level entrance and lobby are also subdued. There are staffed information desks for questions about performances and tickets, and a kiosk offering printed information. What does stand out are the interior multi-colored light strips that direct users to the stairways leading below street level to the theater. During the day the lights are barely visible from the outside, but in the evening they enliven this part of Randolph Street and the boundary of the park. The theater's lighting helps the theater to connect the structure to Randolph Street as pathway but also makes it something more; softening the hard edges of the street and the building helps the theater to become a destination or node in its own right. The theater stage and seating are built down to forty feet below the level of lower Randolph Street. An upper-level terrace behind the theater entrance provides space for seasonal outdoor dining. Among the twelve nonprofit performing art groups represented are Ballet Chicago, Chicago Sinfonietta, Joffrey Ballet of Chicago, Mexican Fine Arts Center Museum, Munto Dance Theater of Chicago, Old Town School of Folk Music and Music of the Baroque (Office of the Mayor 2002b; Mauman 2002; Uhlir 2002). The Music and Dance indoor auditorium is the Loop's only mid-sized theater.

Located several blocks east of the city's main theater district and just east of Michigan Avenue, the Harris Theater on Randolph Street sustains and expands the physical and cognitive connections of this street and the venues associated with it. But Randolph Street is also an important connector in its function as pathway on and below street level, from Lakefront to Loop.

RE-CREATION—By creating space for smaller performance-art groups, the theater gives voice to the nondominant artistic communities, which would otherwise not have a space to call their own. By making music and dance performances accessible to a broader, more diverse audience, the theater welcomes nondominant users who might not ordinarily attend performances. The impact is reflexive. The theater grants performers exposure and grants users access, thus bringing together groups that are too often isolated from one another as well as from the mainstream.

32—*above*—Michigan
Avenue and Randolph
Street, August 2004

33—*right*—Harris Theater on
Randolph, July 2003

Few spaces are being designed for the mid-sized audience. Perhaps the term *mid-sized* can be understood as analogous to the notion of *middle class*. If this parallel can be entertained, the relevance of design and impact can go further. Current economic trends have led designers and planners to think in terms of either small niches or very large markets. This accommodation to a mid-sized market further democratizes the park in terms of what it can be used for and who can use it. It helps reshape and redefine "the middle" in terms of the most popular rather than the least common denominator. The Harris Theater is a space in its own right, but it is connected to what surrounds it physically and figuratively.

While the theater is a space of place in one sense, it is designed to be a multipurpose facility that can be used year-round, making it a space of flows as well. The theater also shares facilities with the Music Pavilion. It is a hybrid space. In its design, function, and user base, it accurately depicts how dominant and nondominant cultures cohabit the urban terrain—not as equals but as cultures very much dependent on one another. In Jencks's terms: "In a respectful meeting of unequals both sides will gain and lose and be changed. . . . [I]n the best cases, a 'fusion of horizons' will prevail, an unforced synthesis. The architect's obligation is to set the precondition for this synthesis, not assume it has occurred, and this means honoring and representing the two discourses on their own terms" (Jencks 1993, 118). Periphery can become part of the center. The Harris, in concert with the Music Pavilion, becomes a hybrid space. Further, the theater's multiple levels offer innovative points of view, leading the visitor down, then up and out of the center.

The SBC Plaza and Cloud Gate ("The Bean")

Sculptor, Anish Kapoor (2004)

CREATION—The SBC Plaza is sited above the McCormick-Tribune ice-skating rink on South Michigan, between Washington and Madison streets. The landmark of this plaza is a sculpture by Indian-born Anish Kapoor entitled Cloud Gate, fondly referred to as "The Bean" (see Figure 34). The SBC Corporation donated $3 million to help underwrite the costs of the sculpture's construction and installation. Kapoor designed "the seamless, polished steel elliptical construction" to reflect Millennium Park's landscape and the dynamic Chicago skyline while keeping the viewer in mind as well. Kapoor wanted the design "to have a classical feel yet to still be very contemporary" (City of Chicago PBC 2004). Measuring sixty-five feet long by thirty-five feet wide, and rising twenty-eight feet high, Cloud Gate appears to envelop viewers as they pass under it. The sculpture is the first Kapoor public work to be installed in the United States. According to Mayor Daley: "The Kapoor sculpture adds to the city's rich public art tradition and will join the Picasso, the Chagall and the Dubuffet as a new Chicago icon. It will be the first major addition to Chicago's outdoor public art in six years" (Millennium Park Project, 4).

RE-CREATION—Kapoor, like Gehry, blurs sculpture and architecture. Interestingly, in his comments on this relationship between the two art forms, Calatrava also mentions one of the sculptors noted by Mayor Daley. Calatrava compares sculpture and architecture by highlighting their contraposition: "Effectively, sculpture—when it is working, it can be much freer because it can work with a very high sense of abstraction, just following the rules of the material. . . . An architect has to follow function. . . . Sculpture is also superior in the scale because you can penetrate [it]; because you can go in, and the sculptors like Moore, Chillida, Dubuffet and others they seem just dreaming to do sculptures which involve you, . . . which you can go in" (Calatrava 2002, 2).

Whereas Cloud Gate does not house space the way a building or an open-aired structure such as the music pavilion does, it does achieve architectural status through users' interaction with it. More specifically, the sculpture encourages users to move under it and around it. Even when viewers stand still, its skin reflects various perspectives of the cityscape in less than "realistic" form, thus bending traditional spatial parameters even further. There is a sort of unreal reality, a materiality embedded in the virtuality of the space Cloud Gate creates as a result of the combination of the materials it uses and the users' perspective. Placing the creations of Kapoor and Gehry, two artists who ride the line between the two disciplines of architecture and sculpture, adjacent to each other in the park, advances Chicago's goal of making art a feature of both the cityscape and the

34—Cloud Gate,

May 2006

natural landscape. Cloud Gate and the Pritzker Pavilion also offer an example of how art, architecture, and nature can all interact in synergistic ways by staging a new interplay of light and reflection upon built forms.

The notion of reflection is particularly interesting because parks and gardens often invite inner reflection. Cloud Gate turns reflection outward and then inward again, evoking sociological parallels as well. The imagery of the "looking-glass" self is significant in the tradition of sociology emerging from the University of Chicago. Sociologists Herbert Blumer, Charles H. Cooley, George Mead, and Erving Goffman employ this metaphor of self as the interpretation and reaction people have to the way in which they believe others perceive them. While perhaps not intended or considered, the experience of reflection reifies the interactive quality generated by the material and design of the sculpture.

Two other observations about Cloud Gate warrant mention. First, it is significant that the sculptor is Indian, even though he now resides in Great Britain. Including Eastern as well as Western notions of art and recreation seems warranted in a city such as Chicago, determined to enter the global terrain. And while the artist may be well known, exposure in an open public space elevates his work to act as a bridge between cultures and classes that are not normally exposed to one another's point of view. Fostering culture is what cities do best.

But whose culture? As a contribution to public art, Cloud Gate diversifies the image of the city and offers an expanded window into its soul. How the sculpture has been embraced by the city's residents was perhaps somewhat unexpected. Almost from the moment the sculpture was revealed, it has been recognized as a new landmark. More important, it was immediately embraced by residents as being theirs, as being part of their collective identity. This is reflected in its informal name, and in the pride with which people refer to it. This identification with the sculpture helps abate concerns regarding whom the park was built for or whom it would appeal to. The commissioning of Cloud Gate continues the city's legacy of having works by prominent artists sited in public spaces, to soften, if not dissolve, boundaries between high culture and popular culture, in this one reflective gesture.

At a time when less and less is available in the public realm, it is significant that private funding has been used to give the city an important piece of art for users to enjoy. Architect Rem Koolhaas offers some hope that the tide is turning toward empowerment of the public realm: "Where the city used to be public and free, the city is now private, and you have to pay for it. . . . I think my instinct is that it is likely that there will be a shift back to some kind of public body and presence. And that the dominance of the market in terms of lost visions is going to shift slightly back to a situation where there is going to be a combination of public pride" (Koolhaas 2002, 9, 5). Jane Jacobs observed: "The difference between public and extended private life [space] is subtle but city design needs public space" (Jacobs 1961, 64). Mayor Daley has acted upon these observations and concerns in creating his economic strategy for the city. He states: "Chicago needs to strengthen the linkages that will retain, cultivate, and attract more entrepreneurs. . . . Chicago needs to create a more connected, vibrant entrepreneurial community to supplement its physical infrastructure—transportation, and digital access. . . . The successes of other cities provide a compelling argument for the benefits Chicagoland could gain by developing these linkages" (NEGSC 2001, 1). The Pritzker Pavilion and Cloud Gate are gestures working to make these hopes become reality. Another feature of the park that does this is the McCormick Tribune Ice Rink.

The McCormick Tribune Plaza and Ice Rink (2001)

CREATION—The outdoor McCormick Tribune Ice Rink was the first attraction in the park to open (see Figure 36). At the ceremony on December 20, 2001, Mayor Daley announced: "Today we proudly unveil the first piece of what will become one of the finest recreational and cultural spaces of any city in the world—Chicago's Millennium Park" (Office of the Mayor, 2001d). Funded by the McCormick Tribune Foundation, the rink is free to the public. Skate rentals and blade sharpening are available in the warming area, which also has lockers and an entrance to the adjacent restaurant. In season, the rink is open seven days a week from 9 a.m. to 9:45 p.m. During non-winter months, it is used as an activity center and an outdoor venue for the Park Grill Restaurant with seating for three hundred (see Plate 16). Original plans called for the rink to be sited at the northeast section of the park on upper Randolph Street. The decision was made to move it to the northwest section of the park, to street level on Michigan Avenue between Washington and Madison streets, in order to provide easier access to public transportation and to make it a more centralized facility.

RE-CREATION—The ice rink is designed as a multipurpose space. While it is spatially fixed, it achieves flexibility through its changing seasonal and temporal uses. The user base shifts according to the day of the week and the time of day. During the week, for example, locals use the space to skate, eat, or seek diversion during their lunch hour or after work. They are joined by students, vacation

36—McCormick Tribune Ice
Rink, January 2003

camps, and other groups. On the weekends, families make use of the facilities. Visitors are found there at almost any time.

From my observations, beginning in January 2002 shortly after the rink's opening, it appears that users were fairly evenly divided between locals and tourists. And from my conversations with officials and locals, it appears that the rink and its adjacent venues are welcome additions to the downtown area. During a visit in early January 2002, Ed Uhlir noted: "It is already a popular gathering place. In the evenings and on weekends, the rink is packed. They already need more lockers in the warming area. People who work in the area are bringing their skates or renting them as well during their lunch hour" (Uhlir 2002). During that same visit to Chicago, a fellow bus passenger—unaware of the rink until exiting nearby it—commented to me: "This is great! It's wonderful to see something like this right here on Michigan Avenue. I have about 45 minutes to kill. I think I will investigate it. I hope they have a wading pool, or fountain, a space where kids and adults can find relief from the heat in the summer, like they have at Navy Pier. There are so few spaces downtown to escape the heat. We could really use that here when it gets warm" (Satler journal entry, January 7, 2002).

From my subsequent visits, it seems that many of this bus passenger's concerns have been realized. With the opening of the Park Grill in December 2003, locals and visitors are provided with a real restaurant that offers a contemporary feel, good food, and a great view of the rink and Michigan Avenue. The indoor and outdoor dining spaces offer respite from the weather, without being removed from the activity or the possibility of people-watching. The feel is similar to that of dining along the riverfront. Trees and grass along with the Crown Interactive Fountain in the adjacent plaza on the south side and the Peristyle and fountain on the north side provide that welcome relief from heat in the summer. The Kapoor sculpture and Gehry pavilion above the rink fill the vista with visual treats for skaters, for those watching the skaters, and for those dining or simply taking in the environment around them as they pass by the site.

The decision to move the rink onto Michigan Avenue enhances its use and enlivens the surrounding area, which already benefits from the Art Institute, from the colleges and universities that have expanded along South and lower North Michigan avenues, and from residences that are being renovated or built here. The park has enlivened real estate development along Michigan Avenue and east on Wabash. The placement of the rink actually on Michigan Avenue increases this potential. The only feature that detracts from spontaneous interaction with the rink is the pathways leading up to the park from Michigan Avenue. Unfortunately, the pathways run parallel to the rink. If they ran diagonally, they would allow people to approach entrances more quickly and easily, thus fostering a more natural flow. The design here seems more focused on the symmetric aesthetic (the grid), perhaps as a result of the rink's siting on Michigan Avenue.

The Crown Fountain

Designer, Jaume Plensa
(2004–2005)

CREATION—The Crown Fountain (see Plate 18) is located just south of the McCormick Tribune Plaza and Ice Rink, on Michigan Avenue, between Madison and Monroe streets. Designed by Jaume Plensa of Barcelona, the interactive fountains feature a continuously changing exhibition of electronic images, light, and water. The fountains are intended to function for nine months out of the year. During the other three months, the electronic images continue without the water.

RE-CREATION—The inclusion of water (when weather permits) not only embraces flow in its most elemental way, it also incorporates the natural feature so essential to Chicago's identity. Whereas the Crown Fountain and display recall the huge cup-shaped fountains that previously stood on this site, the new creation symbolizes flow appropriate for the informational and technological age: the displaying of huge digitalized faces that change in expression and spurt water. The fountain affords a virtual reality that reflects the desire to make the Central Area a hub for the circulation of ideas. Disseminating visual information on the street in a public way restores or refines the social function of the street. The Crown Fountain is designed so that people interact with what they see, rather than merely reacting to it. This distinguishes it from more passive or cool media afforded by screens or facades simply displaying information or images. Since this portion of Michigan Avenue is quite wide and busy, the use of oversized images of ordinary (and multiethnic) people helps restore "ownership" of this space to people. On hot summer days, it is the norm to see dozens of children and adults walking through the water with great smiles on their faces. The fountain also buffers noise from Michigan Avenue and focuses on the idea of communication and reflection. In this case the communication is of a more basic nature: the sound of laughter and the vision of delighted faces. And that which is to be reflected is the ability to experience this in the heart of the city. It helps give the street back to the people.

Wrigley Square and Millennium Monument (Peristyle)   Architects, OWP&P (2003)

CREATION—Funded by the William Wrigley Foundation, the Peristyle is a nearly full-sized replica of the semicircle of Doric-style columns that originally stood in Grant Park from 1917 until 1953 (see Figure 37). The Peristyle is located at Wrigley Square, in the northwest corner of Millennium Park. The square includes trees and grass, sitting space, and a fountain that is active when weather permits. Here again, the sound of playful water mediates the sounds of traffic on the busy North Michigan Avenue–Randolph Street intersection.

RE-CREATION—The Peristyle and square create a space of place in this hyper-mobile section of the Central Area. Sited slightly west of and at a lower elevation than the Pritzker Pavilion, the Peristyle brackets the northwestern edge of the park. The Peristyle may seem a bit anachronistic amid the modern urban landscape including Gehry's pavilion, but in fact it acts as counterspace, making more of the city's many layers of architectural history accessible and fluid. At this site, Burnham and Bennett meet Gehry, the twentieth century meets the twenty-first, and the origin and future of the city's cultural standards intersect. Formally, the Peristyle and the Pritzker Pavilion help uphold the city's efforts to build a city that embraces and fosters culture. And having them coexist in this way encapsulates the scope of the city's evolution.

In a practical way, the Peristyle serves as a landmark for individuals who want to meet companions in this part of the city or who want to orient themselves to the park and to the area more generally. This area is heavily used by residents, commuters, and new users because of the diversity found here: hotels, cultural

37—Peristyle and Chicago Cultural Center, January 2003

venues, offices, shops, residences, and transportation hubs. Such landmarks, furthermore, provide a point of departure for the expansion of the Central Area, especially to the west and the south.

In addition to its relationship with the new Music Pavilion, the Peristyle stands across Michigan Avenue from the landmarked Chicago Cultural Center, built in 1897 by Shepley, Rutan & Coolidge. The exterior of the block-long structure is derived from Italian Renaissance precedents. Its massiveness is balanced by its strong horizontal axis, making it a formidable presence, but one that complements the horizontality of the park, amid the city's skyscrapers. In this way, the Peristyle and the Cultural Center reinforce one another temporally.

According to architectural historian Dolores Hayden: "Storytelling with the shapes of time uses the forms of the city, from the curve of an abandoned canal to the sweep of a field of carnations, to connect residents with urban landscape history and foster a stronger sense of belonging. The places of everyday urban life are, by their nature, mundane, ordinary, and constantly reused, and their social and political meanings are often not obvious" (Hayden 1995, 227). All three forms—the Peristyle, the Cultural Center, and the Music Pavilion—are defining gestures; each is simultaneously a space of flows as well as an identifiable node. Together, they help to thicken as well as to redefine the ever-changing meaning of this pivotal site.

Chase Promenade (2003)

CREATION—A creation of nature rather than of construct, the Chase Promenade covers eight acres of parkland east of Michigan Avenue and just north of Monroe Street, adjacent to the McCormick Tribune Plaza and Ice Rink. The promenade is composed of two hundred trees of various types—there to ensure a diversity of color and texture with the changing seasons and to make the promenade a temporal as well as a spatial marker. Like the Great Lawn, the Chase Promenade celebrates the unbuilt rather than the built; it provides transition space between constructs and from the hard edges defined by Michigan and Monroe. The promenade along with the Lurie Garden bracket the southern edge of the park (on Monroe Street) with greenspace.

RE-CREATION—The Chase Promenade is a popular place for visitors and locals from the new residences on Michigan Avenue, nearby colleges, and the Art Institute to eat lunch, read, or just seek respite from daily routines, a scarce and very welcome commodity in the downtown area. As Jensen notes of such pockets of green: "Here you might come and go as you pleased, throw yourself on the grass or sit down under overarching trees" (Jensen 1990, 35). Tossing a Frisbee is also a common activity here. Chances are Jensen would have approved of this relief for urban stress. The promenade's location just off Michigan Avenue serves as counterpoint to the circulation and connectivity provided by the street. Millennium Park, however, does contribute to circulation by way of its auto and bicycle garages, pedways, and busways.

Parking Garages

CREATION—The Millennium Park Garage is accessible from the lower levels of Randolph Street and mid-level Columbus Drive; bus and rail systems run adjacent to the garage and provide a link to multiple transportation systems (Millennium Park Project 2002). Encouraging multimodal transportation, levels 5 and 6 of the garage offer parking spaces for three hundred bicycles in Chicago's first full-service bike station (see next chapter).

RE-CREATION—The garage contributes to the expansion of the Central Area as a transportation hub, in this case for automobiles coming into the Loop area. While garages are not typically structures that architects pay much attention to aesthetically, the Millennium Park Garage does possess a sense of the extraordinary. It offers, as Santiago Calatrava notes, "a beautiful entrance to the city, so that your first experience in the building, the first experience of quality happens in the garage" (Calatrava 2002, 7). Commenting on a garage he built for a museum in Milwaukee, Calatrava further explains: "A garage can be a wonderful place because you can imagine it to be like a beautiful lobby. Many people in Milwaukee, a city where many people move with cars, arrive into a museum, which is a piece of art through a garage. And I thought this is a good place, to express quality [and] to bring some light down" (Calatrava 2002, 7).

The Millennium Park Garage reflects this concern for aesthetics as well as functionality. The windows, some of which are made of block glass, afford a great deal of light and create a quality of lightness and well-being. Cleanliness, clear eye-catching signage, and the choice of mostly white for coloring further enhance the feeling of well-being, so the users enjoy what is a special, noteworthy place as Calatrava describes. The addition of a Chicago Police Lakefront Bicycle Unit in the facility adds to the sense of security in and around the garage and park area.

Busway

CREATION—With funding from the Metropolitan Pier and Exposition Authority (which received a ninety-nine-year lease in exchange), the City of Chicago will create a two-and-a-half-mile dedicated bus lane in order to improve access from downtown hotels to McCormick Place for Chicago's thousands of conventioneers. The busway will run under Millennium Park between Randolph Street and the convention center. CDOT commissioner Thomas Walker explains:

By routing convention buses to the Lakefront Busway traffic on Lake Shore Drive, Columbus Drive and Michigan Avenue will be significantly reduced and will help make Grant Park a more family-friendly place. The busway will encourage remote parking and public transit usage, and remove hundreds of buses from busy downtown roads. We're reducing traffic, cutting pollution from idling buses, minimizing noise in Grant Park and strengthening Chicago's position as the world's leading convention center all at once. (Millennium Park Project 1999–2000)

RE-CREATION—As Park and Burgess observed decades ago, all attempts to expand and link an area (the park, in this case) to other parts of the city extend the center and foster a more reflective relationship between center and peripheral areas. Busways serve to enhance the park area as a node to an ever-expanding district as well, by moving people in and out of the Central Area to and from more peripheral ones. The park, by way of the busways under it, becomes extrovert—connected to surrounding elements that were previously disparate. Busways expand and diversify the transportation LANs and WANs the city is working to create, in several ways. They make visible the level below the street and orient people (mostly nonlocals) to a mode of transport they might typically ignore. Rethinking mass transit for all user types equalizes and perhaps elevates this mode of transport. It realigns center and periphery, and local and out-of-town users, and has us literally look beneath the surface of the street for connecting arteries giving life to the city. The invisible is made visible and (if well designed) can elevate an ordinary space to one more impressive. In discussing train stations Calatrava notes: "If you think for example, that maybe in a museum, half a million people attend in a year and in a station you get half a million in one week, you understand. It means they are important places. And they are places that you can treat with a lot of dignity. It makes me very much aware of the fact that stations can regenerate also the city or give a lot of character to the city in this place" (Calatrava 2002, 6). The ordinary user (resident or commuter) going about his or her everyday activities becomes the source of inspiration and redefinition. And the new city user (tourist or businessperson) is given a very positive first impression of the city.

Focusing on people's everyday activities is an important premise of the Chicago School of Sociology. In the face-to-face interactions and daily experiences people engage in, the larger social order is reified. This micro-order is the glue that defines and sustains a community. Similarly, in architectural gestures that attend to such routines, the community is reified. Again, to quote Calatrava: "[I]t's . . . the opportunity to give a whole new character to the area around. So [stations or terminals] are also very efficient instruments in terms of changing the lives and influencing the neighborhood. . . . There is no better homage to the past and to the circumstances of it than to make connection with a lot of life, with everyday life, of those people coming there. You know that life is going ahead" (Calatrava 2002, 6). Millennium Park's garages, busways, and pedestrian and bicycle pathways also address concerns of the Los Angeles School of Sociology. Specifically, as new attention is given to the interdependency of center and peripheries, and to nondominant spaces and users, the urban landscape gives way to greater environmental integration.

The Lurie Garden

Architects, Gustafson Guthrie Nichols, with Piet Oudolf and Robert Israel (2004, 2005)

CREATION—Most of the creations of Millennium Park explored so far emphasize built forms and cutting-edge technology. The Lurie Garden, which opened in July 2004, is also testament to the creativity and technological efficacy of engineers and landscape architects. But the garden, unlike the park's other features, emphasizes the unbuilt, offering an introverted space where people can disconnect from the rest of the park and city. In doing so, the garden seeks to achieve the second goal of the *Plan of Chicago* (1909): "providing sufficient park area to insure good health and good order" (Burnham and Bennett 1970, 47). In contemporary terms, it can be considered a space of silence. On its rather small and unlikely site in the park, the Lurie Garden manages to make its presence felt with all the power and diversity of spaces much larger. Most important, it proves that a garden can grow in the middle of the city, even on top of a garage roof.

The garden is the winning submission of landscape architects Gustafson Guthrie Nichols, LLP (GGN), plant specialist Piet Oudolf, and theatrical lighting designer Robert Israel for the international competition held to elicit the garden's design. Rather than submit separate entries, Gustafson decided to collaborate with Oudolf and also enlist Israel, thus creating a dream team of sorts. This interdisciplinary collaboration itself bridged boundaries and produced a design with a complex organic relationship with the landscape. Lurie Garden is sited on a 2.5-acre parcel at the southeast corner of Millennium Park, with Columbus Drive and Monroe Street forming its more gridded edges. Here, nature merges quietly with the built forms and with the site so that an ambiguity remains as to whether it is man-made or a naturally occurring phenomenon. The garden exemplifies a provocative handling of the interplay between distinct and seemingly disparate orders or perspectives on an equally contested site (see Plate 19).

The primary elements of the garden are the Lurie Hedge, the Meeting Grove, the Extrusion Plaza, the Dark and Light Plates, and the Seam. Much of the concept and construction of the garden is described by members of the design team, whose verbal sketches and visual narratives offer useful insights into how such a team of architects, landscaper, and lighting expert might work together. Having these as a guiding map offered a way for me to orient myself to the "whole" of their idea for the park. This composition can also be used as an analytic tool for considering broader issues of interdisciplinary teamwork in planning for and solidifying communities in urban terrains defined by new and divergent parameters.

The garden's primary organizing device and spatial divider is the Lurie Hedge, a fourteen-foot sculpted hedge, and a living wall. It appears to support the "gleaming headdress" of Frank Gehry's Music Pavilion, which Gehry refers to as "a tiara for Cindy [Pritzker]," who was one of its benefactors (Gehry 2002a). According to Oudolf: "It was Gustafson's idea to have the hedges as an overarching feature of the Garden. The big 'shoulder' hedge gave a main element and offered a sense of shelter in a dramatic and dynamic sense. [It is] essential as background and to create privacy, either to enclose the whole garden or, by way of windows cut out of the hedge, to make 'rooms' within it" (Oudolf 2002a). The use of the term *shoulder hedge* comes from the garden's original name, the Shoulder Garden, an allusion to the Carl Sandburg poem referring to Chicago as "the city of broad shoulders." Its name was later changed to Monroe Garden to denote its location and finally to Lurie Garden in honor of its benefactor. The term *room* is symbolic rather than literal; it is used by landscape architects to denote plates or forms set off from other parts, but not totally enclosed.

The Meeting Grove is a "welcoming room," formed by a canopy of arching flowering trees, that offers visitors the first view from the top of the stairs as well as a place to sit and gather. The broad canopies create open, shaded resting areas and contrast with other textures and features of the Garden (GGN 2002, 12). The Grove has a cloud-like ceiling created by a broad tree canopy that floats over to the Dark Plate.

The Extrusion Plaza is a broad space defined by the curved green wall of the Lurie Hedge on the east and a curtain hedge on the west. The space is organized by linear hedges in machine shapes and rectilinear wood seating platforms that appear to be solid objects extruded from the ground, "where people can sit and watch each other move in organized patterns, as packets of information through the landscape and also catch glimpses of the colorful garden interior through whimsical windows sculpted in the Shoulder Hedge" (Waldheim 2001, 22; Loveridge 2002–2005, e-mail August 19, 2003). The plaza both allows for the human social impulse to people-watch and socialize and simultaneously addresses the urban need to accommodate socially active, quick-paced circulation venues, where visitors are both audience and show.

The Dark and Light Plates create two contoured planting "rooms," covered in perennial compositions of bold contrast to reflect the city's and site's complex history and future, respectively. The Dark Plate with its mysterious, wild, textured plant palette offers opportunities to sit in small groups and watch the flow of people moving through the Meeting Grove. The Light Plate, with a bright, controlled, and freely textured plant palette, is an open-ended space built on a subtle ridge. Its tilted plantings and paths allow an abundance of light to enter. Climbing the path to the high point of the plate, the visitor is offered reflective views of the whole garden, the Art Institute across Monroe Street, and the city's skyline (GGN 2002, 22, 24; Loveridge 2002–2005, e-mail August 19, 2003).

The Seam, composed of a curved and battered stone wall, a stepped wooden platform, and a series of gently rippling pools of water, is the edge where the two plates touch and diverge (see Figure 38). Symbolically, it is also where past and future meet. The choice of elements—from the most formative to the most fluid—is a provocative way to express the dual nature of Chicago. As Manuel Castells notes, as the city undergoes the morphological changes brought about by shifting from an industrial to an informational economy, it also undergoes a shift from spaces of place (actual) to spaces of flows (virtual). In large part these spatial types define a dual or global city (Castells 1989). The seam is composed of a wood platform over water because Chicago's strategy for controlling the natural landscape was to lift the city up, building wood walkways over the marsh, covering the wet land and leaving it beneath. So the way to walk from the past (the Dark Plate) to the present or future (the Light Plate) is to discover the wooden plant form and to glimpse the underlying water looming in the crack or gap between the plates.

The Plates and the Seam honor this duality. Taken separately, they have been said to symbolize the city's past and future. In juxtaposition, these elements make it possible to rethink relationships and connections temporally and spatially by allowing or encouraging a shift of frame. Using the frame of a space of place, they act as barriers: walls, which enclose; platforms (edges), which divide

or separate; over water, which excludes and isolates. Seen in the frame of a space of flows, these features are transformed into screens, paths, and conduits, all intended to connect and move people to dispersed points in place and time. The Seam literally and analytically makes the shift transparent, not by imposing a line that separates the two plates, but rather by offering a sense of vital connection between seemingly disparate spaces. In a textural way, the Seam also acts as character lines on a face. It evokes the sense that there is a life story unfolding. In this way, it keeps history alive and relevant.

RE-CREATION—What can we learn from the language of landscape architecture that can then be applied to building design and building communities? The garden articulates the notion that landscaping can make its own sense of place without using an architectural language. The narrative born of the vocabulary of landscape architecture is at once quieting and confounding: a strong calm. Oudolf refers to this as "controlled spontaneity." Its contemplative stance offers those who enter a world where creativity supersedes formula. The challenges posed for and responded to by the garden's design can provide broader insights about the role that landscape architecture can play for the complexities of urban landscapes and urban living in postindustrial times.

Our view of the landscape and our relationship to it has been changed significantly by our ability to view the planet from new vantage points. What is landscape art at the beginning of the twenty-first century? What is our relationship to nature? (Lin 2000, 6:04)

What is the spirit of our time? You see your cities growing, occupying landscapes. We are in a moment of rethinking our relation to nature. On the other side, nature is probably the most wonderful, the most natural school to learn forms, shapes. We are also part of nature. Our vision of nature is crucial. (Calatrava 2002, 3)

Spaces referred to as "rooms" and "windows" act as devices that suggest inner and outer worlds. So there is an opposing energy or tension created with which one can move fluidly without denying the integrity of either. This is an enlightened way to compose the garden and to frame the visitor. Visitors move into and through the planting, experiencing the garden via a network of paths and seating elements. Along the walkways, the visitors are invited into the garden interior where its forms and materials are encountered in a more intimate manner (GGN 2002, 6).

Each of the garden's gestures takes the individual well beyond both the garden and the city, into a world of his or her own making. "The garden creates a beautiful picture and captures your attention" (Oudolf 2002a). In Calatrava's view: "Something that is a creation of your mind; beauty approaching nature because we observe, translate and create—makes it an artificial event. Its organicity [involves]. . . how the parts belong to each other, which you recognize like in nature, that a small part of the building is enough to recognize the whole building" (Calatrava 2002, 10–11). That is to say, the garden acts as a master plan. It sets the stage for the performance but it does not end it.

The imagery of the theatrical stage is particularly appropriate for a garden in an urban setting. Users in fact form the fourth wall on city streets or in public spaces, fluidly and necessarily shifting back and forth between their dual roles of observer and performer (Goffman 1963). To paraphrase writer Vivan Gornick: "On the city street, nobody watches, everyone performs" (Gornick 1996, 3). As visitors occupy the garden's spaces in a series of sequential staged theatrical relationships, they become a vital element defining the space; they are "players in a drama of their own devising" (Waldheim 2001, 14).

More specifically, the notion of built versus unbuilt is turned on its head. As Oudolf explains: "By turning the conventional view of gardening upside down, it is possible to create a vision of the garden, which sees nature as supreme. . . . Rather than controlling and taming nature, the gardener merely orchestrates living things that have their own rhythms and processes over which one has little control" (Oudolf 1999, 117). The gardener superimposes the two layers one upon the other. Literally, the static formal layer includes hedges, paths, and the outlines of borders while the perennials and grasses comprise the informal (Oudolf 1999, 82). The resulting garden is double-coded; it allows the user to move fluidly between the two contrasting impulses of control and spontaneity. Oudolf prefers the term *sublime*. The "sublime is meant to describe scenery that is majestic and awe-inspiring. Historically such scenery was regarded with disquiet, even horror. But for those who appreciate raw nature, or have a real feeling for plants, they will love the feeling that what they have created has actually taken over. The planting no longer feels part of them; it has a life of its own" (Oudolf 1999, 115; 2002a). Thus, the frame and the framed enliven one another through their contested yet interdependent relationship.

In Sassen's representation of an urbane terrain, the garden is a space of silence, the space in between spaces of place and spaces of flows. Silence not only has a presence, it is necessary to a successful intersection of the disparate spatial types. This concept can be understood also in terms of rhythmic structure. Two-dimensional sound, for example, is the result of a succession of beats or groups of beats. Sound can be heard three-dimensionally, however, as "the projections of a two-dimensional process into gestural space" (Asgedom 1996, 247). That is, there is a transformation that occurs by way of interaction and interpretation, which is the invisible but essential part of what we hear. Gestural space is created by the garden's frame and elements; it is the virtual thread running throughout the garden and the park. In this space there reside tremendous energy, power, and potential. And elements within the space foster and take on the same energy and potential. In essence, the Lurie Garden makes the "what" and "how" of building a community within the urban terrain transparent as process, image, and system. It can therefore be used as a literal and analytic device to understand an urban community within its dynamic and three-dimensional context.

COMPOSITION ELEMENTS

Curves and Movement

All gestures of the garden exist in order to frame the user, yet the garden can frame without confining because it articulates a new relationship between vertical and horizontal, figure and ground, inside and out, which creates affective space. Curves are among the most basic and most important elements for achieving both goals—to frame without confining and to create space that moves people emotionally. Curves, as they are used here, counter the grid features of the city and emphasize natural shapes (including human shapes) rather than built or mechanical ones. The garden's curves direct users' vistas and movement, without the constrictions or restrictions of straight lines or paths. As Jensen recognized: "It might be a great stunt to have our parks developed along straight and rigid lines, but how can the human form with its many curves fit into such a scheme? . . . Straight lines are copied from the architect and do not belong to the landscaper. They have nothing to do with nature, of which landscaping is a part and out of which the art has grown" (Jensen 1990, 38). It might be added that straight lines have nothing to do with social interaction. In many respects they inhibit people's ability to discover the environment and others for themselves, as Goldberg's architectural designs for River City acknowledge.

The Lurie Garden echoes the predilection for curves used by Jensen and Goldberg, among others, in several ways. There are subtle structural curves in the garden's architectural features: paths, walls, and seating. But the more pronounced use of curves—and with it, a huge nod to organicity and to its users—is achieved through the choice of plantings, the textures and patterns and how they play to the seasons and lights. Curves also reemphasize the original line of the urban landscape rather than force the landscaping to give way to the cityscape. In Oudolf's view: "Landscape architecture nowadays is more urban development than saying something about the landscape" (Oudolf 2002b). Space of curvature reminds the user that a landscape, even one in the urban terrain, is still primarily about the land.

Curves also vary perspective within the enclosed space of the garden. Moving through the garden and then to other parts of the park connected by the garden, "the paths elevate the sight lines and change the relationship between the plant material and the pedestrian. The effect is the feeling that the pedestrian is ascending above the landscape; floating over the earth" (GGN 2002, 31). If components work together and if one is in touch with the big picture, the moment can become "timeless, peaceful and euphoric" (Asgedom 1996, 257).

The rhythm of the curves continues in other features of the park, for example in the Cloud Gate and the music pavilion. In many ways, the garden frames the pavilion. Looking at the pavilion from the various elevations of the garden, it seems as if the top of the pavilion is crowning the garden. Structures and nature merge. Together, they create something quite unique in an otherwise rigidly ordered urban terrain—an ecstatic response where "future, past and present belong together with co-equal [value and] originality" (Asgedom 1996, 253). This composition stands in sharp contrast to the merging of built and unbuilt forms found in the highly formalized Grant Park, adjacent to Millennium Park. The juxtaposition of the two parks creates another space of silence within which to reflect and to attend to transition and duality.

In Oudolf's view, a garden should not be viewed as static, "where there is no natural spontaneity, and nothing of a sufficiently fine texture to move in a breeze." In gardens full of perennials and grasses, it does not take long to find something that is moving. "Movement is one of the characteristics of life, so we associate it with energy and dynamism; a garden of movement responds to nature and feels alive, whereas one that still seems dead. This is why these grasses are so valuable if you want to imitate the movement of reed beds in the wind," and if you want to catch the light in exciting and disparate ways (Oudolf 1999, 104, 105, 98). Movement also creates sounds, which draw attention to the absence of noise. Light and sound comprise the other compositional elements of the garden.

Light

Light is crucial in a garden, and yet, as Oudolf notes, most garden designers devote little attention to how it falls on plants. Most use light that is flat and frontal, but varying how and where the light falls "can transform the way plants look, so it makes sense to position those plants to receive the maximum benefit. The same plant can look different depending on whether it is lit from behind or in front" (Oudolf 1999, 97). Jensen too recognized the importance of lighting: "Light and shadow and their distribution during the entire circle of day and night are important fundamentals in the art of landscaping" (Jensen 1990, 61). Light has a similar significance for architecture, as Maya Lin writes: "The play of light through a building . . . is the most intangible element in architecture, yet one of the most powerful, affecting how we feel in a space and shaping how we will walk through the space. So much of what we think of as architecture has mass and weight and physical form, yet as important to me is this completely intangible material" (Lin 2000, 10:04).

Efforts by the design team to maximize the use of lighting for its functional and theatrical, emotional effects in the garden are dramatic and innovative. Israel's contribution especially "is evident in its lighting day to night transformation, voyeuristic views, metaphorical naming devices, and narrative structure. As in theater, lighting forms a part of the narrative structure of the drama, with colored lights illuminating plants and creating a way to distinguish the project by night and day, season to season" (Waldheim 2001, 15). In the Lurie Garden, light is used in a theatrical way, to punctuate voids, allow light to spill into areas and dramatize features:

At night, the garden transforms into a subtly glowing "container" of light. The Dark plate transforms into the heart of the Garden, the destination space for meeting and strolling; fog like mists are created. Visitors are enveloped in the room created by the softly lit branches. Cool, blue-toned light, resembling natural moonlight is cast from informally placed pole mounted fixtures and filters down through the branches to cast dappled shadows on the brick paving of the Cloud Plaza—the effect of the "moonlight." The Light plate in contrast is lit in a crisp, neutral-colored, and consistent wash. (GGN 2002, 43)

Features such as the Lurie Hedge, the Extrusion Plaza, and other entry areas serve as neutral perimeters that clarify way-finding to the park's other spaces. They act as transition zones to the garden's "container of light" (GGN 2002, 41). In essence they are spaces of silence, and their silence is profound. The Lurie Hedge serves as the solid form that contains the glow of the interior garden. This back lighting also allows the user to focus on shapes and textures, if substance is strong enough to stand up to the light.

Oudolf makes an interesting observation: "A good planting should have enough variety of shape to look interesting in a black-and-white photograph—looking at it again in color should add another dimension, but a secondary one. Color has much more to do with the overall mood of the planting. Different aspects of a plant may play a key role in a combination at different times of the year. This responds to . . . the dimension of time. . . . Combining different shapes and textures generates a creative tension that keeps both the eye and the imagination interested" (Oudolf 1999, 42). Residents of Chicago have grown accustomed to the interplay of shadow and light in their built environment. But regenerating the roots of light and shadow with natural landscape forms creates another link between the city's past and present.

Oudolf's remarks point also to spatial relationships. Specifically, absence can have a presence. A noticeable absence is a powerful device. In Japanese design, the "ma" or the space between objects has value and integrity in its own right. This use of light (and shadow) focuses attention on other aspects of the garden. On spaces-in-between, on the emptiness, lighting becomes back lighting rather than highlighting. This technique draws attention away from itself, serving as a counterpoint of sorts, which achieves strong impact. Like silence, this lighting can speak eloquently and powerfully. In its starkness, shifting the focus away from color can be a powerful social device as well. The duality created by the sounded and the unsounded holds similar potential.

The Sounded and the Unsounded

The counterpart of visual, geometric, haptic space, that is, the order of auditory space, is equally vital to the user's experience (Asgedom 1996, 259). It has a duality and reflexive quality, very much like the "ma" created by light and shadow.

In making music, musicians concern themselves as much with the pauses in between as with the notes played. This relationship creates the soundscape. Silence is as much a part of the music as the sounds. Natural and man-made sounds are present throughout Millennium Park. While the park has musical venues in Pritzker Pavilion and the Dance and Music Theater, the Lurie Garden is perhaps the site of music in its purest form. Mime Marcel Marceau once remarked that music is so very close to nature, it is cosmic. At the same time, one might add, the movement of nature creates music. As the park's most natural space, the garden is the most musical; it combines space for silence and reflection with space for the sounds of nature.

In many ways, the park and the garden within it are spaces in conflict with the commercial processes that drive cities. Rem Koolhaas has refined the commercial role of cities to note that over the past two decades, "shopping has become our most reliable and if not our only kind of emblem of what is urban, or only symbol of what is urban" (Koolhaas 2002, 9). The park offers a soft boundary to this city characteristic by disengaging from its surroundings in shapes and rhythms. The garden, however, stands in complete disregard of and direct opposition to what surrounds it. It is a counterspace within a counterspace, the purest place of all in terms of what it hopes to achieve: escape from the shapes, sounds, rhythms, and intentions that structure the city as marketplace. In the garden, recreation returns to the value of time, in the absence of clock or marketplace. Moving into or out of the garden, one is spatially and temporally transported as in no other space in the park. Here, users are invited to realign themselves with who they are—natural creations, not mechanical robots. Sounds and silences of the natural world, the daily or routine sounds in particular, offer the greatest rhythmic expression (Asgedom 1996, 246).

The garden offers the strongest counter to what Koolhaas feels has permeated not only all of urban life but all of a city's identity: the commodification of time. The garden gives to time, and to all that lies within it, intrinsic value. The garden serves as a reminder of what leisure means, in its purest sense: doing nothing, taking a breath, holding the breath between activities. Making space for doing nothing allows a person to be, and perhaps to become. The profound absence of constructed form and activity is perhaps the most radical statement made in the park. The garden reifies the networked structure of new global cities that allows them to look beyond traditional boundaries and ideologies for their identity and to bring global grids down to local scale. The garden deepens and expands the city's vista; making city and center more resilient, more deeply diverse, and more interdependent than traditional cities or smaller communities could ever be. The garden may offer the city a new emblem of what urban can and should be.

RE-CREATION REVIEWED

Millennium Park is a concise and complete artistic gesture and social event. It is also a significant indicator of how Chicago has chosen to approach its transformation. The inclusion of landscape architecture as a vital component of this process enables the city and its planners to return to their origins, to reflect on their original abilities and intuitions as they create new bridges for the century just begun. Millennium Park promises to reshape Chicago and more specifically the Central Area into a place where some spaces flow easily into one another, where some require a bridge, and where some spaces exist in sharp contrast with neighboring sites.

The Millennium Park plan offers a synergistic, pliable vista and shape for the park and surrounding area. Into what had been, until now, a formal, symmetrical, and classic recreational facility, the plan introduces new forms and relationships—asymmetry, informality, flow, both built and natural—and the recognition of a new and increasingly significant type of city user. This approach is ingenious and logical, for it makes no sense to imitate parks or gardens designed for places hundreds or thousands of years ago. Sculptor Isamu Nouguchi believes we need to tear patterns apart and look at the possibilities in the context of modern architecture (and modern society). Whether the park can fulfill all its ambitions waits to be seen. Certainly no one structure alone can accomplish this. In his discussion of Gehry's newly completed work in Los Angeles, the Walt Disney Concert Hall (2004), Jencks observes: "It is vain to ask art or architecture to make up for political, economic or social inadequacy. Yet it still makes sense to ask a public building to symbolize a credible public realm, to set a relevant direction and act as if its meaning could be universalized for society at this time and place" (Jencks 1993, 102–4). Here we are also reminded that public spaces are the primary site for public culture. In Millennium Park, this idea might be slightly rephrased and updated to denote the park's status as a site for public cultures.

The more magnificent the tradition, the greater the challenge to create for today's world. Millennium Park both moves the city forward and draws it back to its roots, offering the space to experience an ecstatic moment of vision: "the moment where former possibilities and models are extended, interpreted and reinterpreted in the present to be projected as understanding in the future" (Heidegger 1962, 437). The future and continuity of the legacy of architecture and sociology *and* landscaping already established in Chicago seems ensured in this vital part of the city. In a city of bridges perhaps this is the most enduring bridge Chicago needs to provide.

The Lurie Garden on Monroe Street and the Pritzker Pavilion on Randolph bracket the park. As both frame and framed, they open and envelop this space in the city's Central Area. More important, they provide point and counterpoint both to one another and to the other features of the park. And they are also markers and catalysts for what lies beyond them. At these northern and southern boundaries of Millennium Park, we find evidence of the expansion of the Central Area. New neighborhoods are emerging west, north, and south of the Loop. Center is branching out and periphery is reaching in with an eye to greenspace. The city is once again raising the bar for architecture and design in order to restore its world prominence in architecture by creating the architectural landmarks and masterpieces of tomorrow. It is also moving beyond existing boundaries, real and virtual, in order to forge that future.

39—EL on Wabash Avenue,
November 2000

PART

IV

Realigning Center and Peripheries

We are now in a process of constantly redefining ourselves. Things that were separate now intersect and become part of a programmatic continuum. (Koolhaas 2002, 7)

One of the consequences of globalization is that cities and, more particularly, city centers are increasingly dependent on surrounding areas for their definition and viability. This interdependency is noted by both the Chicago and the Los Angeles schools of sociology. Proponents of the Chicago School posit that the "typical process of expansion is from the core outward," whereas those representing Los Angeles School argue that "it is the peripheries that determine what remains of the center" (Wirth, in Park 1967, 206; Dear 2002b, 16). The different relational dynamics between center and periphery as depicted by the two schools may not be as oppositional as they seem. If center and periphery are placed in a context where they can be viewed simultaneously, and where their relationship is understood to be a reflexive one, what emerges is a frame and place that allows for both viewpoints. That is, the consequence of this realignment is a "centrality" defined less by any one place or placement and more by an expanding network of multiple sites and users.

The synergistic realignment between center and peripheries that is unfolding and reshaping Chicago's Central Area today is explored in the following section. In the chapter "Branching Out," emerging neighborhoods south, north, and west of the Loop are identified in order to illustrate the shape and direction the city (center) is taking by "sending out its tentacles to include sources of supply not available in its immediate vicinity" (Wirth in Park 1967, 183). In the chapter "Reaching In," some of the city's efforts to realize the socioeconomic growth and development envisioned in the *Central Area Plan* and *A New Economy Growth Strategy for Chicagoland,* among others, are examined through the center's efforts to "gather materials essential to sustain itself, but also transform these and send them out again" (183). While some of the projects and plans explored here lie outside the geographic or political boundaries of the Central Area, they can be understood as analytically and functionally linked to the visions for the Central Area and as provided for in these plans, that is, they are central to and part of the city's vision for the New Central Area. In some cases, these projects point to the achievement of goals; in others they are reminders of what remains open and unresolved. Together they reveal that the realignment requires a new analytic infrastructure as much as a physical reshaping.

The Central Area Plan (CAP) envisions a Central Area "characterized by its rich interplay of uses. . . . Residential development can be found adjacent to offices and around the corner from regional retail" (CAP, 33). Residences can now also be found adjacent to waterways and parks, for example, in the area formed by the new alliance between Millennium Park and the Michigan Avenue Streetwall, comprised of nearly fifty uniquely designed historic buildings. While the streetwall and Millennium Park are each a separate and complete statement, they complement and enliven one another. The streetwall harks back to the city's original boundary while Millennium Park moves the city beyond it. The streetwall reifies the commercial and residential; the park reifies culture and recreation. Michigan Avenue, Columbus Drive, Randolph Street, and Monroe Street capture the networks of connectivity both local and beyond. Millennium Park draws its power from the ephemeral spaces and dynamic activities it houses and creates. The streetwall derives its power from the monuments, which testify to the city's architectural and historic past. Together, they create a rare nexus of past and present, built and unbuilt. Millennium Park and the Michigan Avenue Streetwall not only frame a new residential area, they also set the standard for what will be built in the future, and together, they are helping to reshape this part of Chicago's Central Area. More specifically they are realigning the areas immediately surrounding them, as well as parts of the city that would previously have been considered peripheral.

HISTORIC MICHIGAN BOULEVARD DISTRICT—
MICHIGAN AVENUE STREETWALL

On February 27, 2002, twelve blocks of Michigan Avenue between 11th Street and Randolph Street were designated a Chicago Landmark District. This district represents the city's development during the late nineteenth and early twentieth centuries. It is home to some of Chicago's finest individual buildings, and many significant cultural institutions such as clubs, hotels, and prestigious office buildings. The streetwall has been said to look as if some of the best of Chicago just gathered along the lakefront and posed for a group photo. Among the architects whose works stand here are Adler & Sullivan, Louis Sullivan, Daniel H. Burnham, Holabird and Roche, Marshall and Fox, Henry Ives Cobb, S. S. Beman, and Graham, Anderson, Probst & White (City of Chicago, DPD 2003). In Mayor Daley's

40—*above*—BP Bridge over Columbus Drive looking toward the Michigan Avenue Streetwall, August 2004

41—*right*—Historic Michigan Avenue Streetwall, August 2004

view: "This collection of buildings can be seen as symbolic of the cultural, commercial and architectural heritage of Chicago"; and according to James Mann, former Midwest director of the National Trust for Historic Preservation, the street presents "the signature of Chicago architecture" (Office of the Mayor, 2001a).

The origin of Michigan Avenue as a streetwall facing Grant Park dates back to 1836, when the city's first subdivision map labeled all land east of what was then called Michigan Boulevard as public ground to remain forever open, clear, and free. The strip began to be set in stone and brick in the late nineteenth century when advances in skyscraper technology spurred construction of taller buildings. By the 1860s the west side of the street was developing as a fashionable residential strip. By 1900 the street had become the home of the city's most prestigious cultural institutions devoted to art, music, literature, and theater. The aging of the streetwall and threats of demolition of some of the structures motivated the city and interested parties to preserve this architectural treasure by giving it landmark status.

As with landmarking along Greater State Street, the intention is to preserve the avenue's character and to work with its surroundings. In contrast to State Street, where retail and commerce dominate, the Historic Michigan Avenue District is and has traditionally been defined by its residential and cultural venues. And unlike the contrast with constructs on State Street, which draw from the power of the grid and the skyscraper, Michigan Avenue is influenced by the neighboring unbuilt, natural features it faces: Grant Park, Millennium Park, and the Lake. Conceptualizing this area as a residential and cultural district makes social and economic sense. It also makes design sense.

The draft guidelines for the district suggest that renovation and adaptive reuse preserve original or historically significant materials and architectural features, repair rather than replace, replace with compatible features or materials, allow for unusual new ideas in new construction, but always preserve the integrity of the district's character. A number of the vintage structures along South Michigan are functionally obsolete and not conducive to business, but, with similar floor plates and lots of windows, they are ideal for residences or hotels. Architect Donald Hackl, president of Loebl, Schlossman, and Hackl, also believes more residential development along the streetwall "would energize a part of the city that now lacks a 24-hour life cycle. Not enough people are living there. It has no sense of neighborhood. More residential would mean more people on the street and make it a livelier part of town" (Hackl, in Handley 2001a).

Some property owners object to landmarking because of its potential of "encumbering property without any economic benefits." Those in support of preservation of the streetwall, however, point to the contribution these existing structures can make to the current needs of the city (Handley 2001a). In a letter to the *Chicago Sun-Times,* Bob O'Neill, president of Grant Park Advisory Council, wrote: "Landmarking makes buildings economic engines, collectively creating character and generating tourism revenue" (O'Neill 2002).

This emerging neighborhood benefits from the confluence of the renovation of Greater State Street, the landmarking of this portion of Michigan Avenue, riverfront development, and both Grant Park and Millennium Park. Other cultural venues also play a role. The Auditorium Building (1899; designed by Adler

& Sullivan), which is now Roosevelt University, and Orchestra Hall (1905; designed by Burnham & Company, renovated in 1966 by Harry Weese and Associates), which is now home to the Chicago Symphony Orchestra, are but two examples of the well-renowned venues located here. Residences are clearly geared to the middle class, that is, the new middle class. According to real estate agent Tracy Cross: "25 percent of all residential sales in the greater downtown area are in the Loop and Near South Side and 30 percent of those are coming from the suburbs" (Handley 2001a). Here, buyers predominantly consist of empty-nesters, people interested in taking advantage of cultural venues of the city, and professionals tired of long commutes. They are affluent and tend to be a bit older than residents in other portions of the downtown area. Conversions and new construction are responding to both the natural and the economic exigencies of this area.

The McCormick Building (1908), designed by Holabird and Roche, has been converted to condominiums and marketed as the Residences at 330 S. Michigan. The facade of limestone, red brick, and terra-cotta has been restored in compliance with the city's historic guidelines. Another vintage structure designed by Holabird and Roche and converted into condominiums is the former Crane Company Building (1913), at 836 S. Michigan Avenue. It was gutted to make way for thirty-six residential units base-priced from the lower $200,000s to more than $2 million. The Blackstone Hotel (1909), designed by Marshall and Fox, has also been converted into condominiums. Overlooking the green of Grant Park and the blue of Lake Michigan at 636 S. Michigan Avenue, the twenty-one-story building has units ranging from four thousand to eleven thousand square feet at prices ranging from $2.2 million to $6 million for a full floor. Sales are brisk. These projects take advantage of their proximity to Grant Park and the Art Institute to enhance the condos' value as urban property and to make them more desirable places to live.

Two projects specifically built to capitalize on the older landmarks and now the new one, Millennium Park, are worthy of closer examination. Six North Michigan, sited near the southern edge of Millennium Park at Madison Street, is a residential conversion; the Heritage at Millennium Park, located at the park's northern edge at Randolph Street, is a newly built mixed-use complex. Both work with their immediate surroundings but also push the existing boundaries further than ever before. They are noteworthy for their ability to focus attention on Millennium Park and points eastward, while simultaneously moving people from the Lakefront back to the Loop. Concise expressions of the new synergy, they not only complete the Loop but also expand it.

Architect, Richard E. Schmidt (1899; converted and renovated 2000–2004)

Six North Michigan Avenue Condominiums, in the Montgomery Ward and Company Building

An $80 million renovation, which began in early 2000, has converted the former administrative headquarters and catalog warehouse for Montgomery Ward and Company into Six North Michigan Avenue Condominiums (see Figure 42). The Montgomery Ward and Company Building was originally designed in 1899 by Richard E. Schmidt, and it was renovated in 2000–2004. The building now houses 123 one-, two-, and three-bedroom luxury condominiums and duplex penthouses. When units went on sale in 2001, prices ranged from $225,000 to $1.6 million (Handley 2001a). Its first occupants moved in two years later. The residences are designed to appeal primarily to couples without children and to those looking for an in-town or second residence. There is retail space available on the street level and parking on floors 2 through 4.

This project has chosen to use its location, North Michigan Avenue, in the new name as a way to reestablish its new place. But the architecture and the physical siting within the larger urban landscape are what give it presence and make it a space of place. Nicknamed the "Busy Bee Hive" at the turn of the century, to emphasize the work ethos of Montgomery Ward and Chicago, this twenty-story skyscraper was the city's tallest building when it opened in 1900, and for years afterward it was a popular tourist destination.

42—Six North Michigan Avenue, January 2002

Architect Richard E. Schmidt combined functional Chicago School–style accents with decorative Italian Renaissance accents in his design. The landmark's most popular architectural characteristic was a three-story pyramidal roof tiled in gold terra-cotta panels, and an eighteen-foot-tall gilded weather vane in the shape of a female figure, designed by J. Massey Rhink. This symbol of progress, sited at the peak of the roof, was lighted with four electric beacons. It was removed in 1947 (Lowe 1985, 145). Even without the iconic feature, the structure continues to contribute to the visual history of the Historic Michigan Boulevard District (Busk 2002). It is a reminder that not all of the city's skyscrapers followed the aesthetic precepts of the Chicago School, or perhaps it is a reminder that the Chicago School and city were and are more interested in a sense of style than in any one, particular, style.

The building is easily noticeable from the lakefront or Columbus Drive, not only because of its corner location and height but also because of the incline that exists as one moves west from Columbus Circle to Michigan Avenue, which elevates the viewer's line of vision. At the same time, the building offers a spectacular view of Millennium Park's McCormick Skating Rink as well as the rest of the park and the lake. The development's sales manager, Cindy Mattioli, notes that residents are able "to step outside their front door and see a beautiful outdoor development with fountains, gardens and ice-skating." And, "because of the park, no one will ever be able to build a high-rise across the street and block the view" (Busk 2002).

The development is in the heart of the city's cultural center and nightlife, with theaters, great restaurants, shops, and access to the Chicago Cultural Center and Art Institute of Chicago as well as the museum campus (Busk 2002). Prior to renovation along South Michigan Avenue, Randolph Street, Greater State Street, and the riverfront, this site was considered peripheral. Using the park and the streetwall as new framing points, however, Six North Michigan now achieves a more central place in the city's new Central Area. Thanks to its form and function, it provides a missing piece of the CBD envisioned by the Central Area Plan.

The Heritage at Millennium Park—130 North Garland Court

Architect, Solomon Cordwell Buenz and Associates (2004–2005)

The Heritage at Millennium Park, designed by Solomon Cordwell Buenz and Associates (2004–2005), is the first new construction in the Millennium Park–Streetwall area. The Heritage takes the CAP vision for "a Central Business District where people live as well as work" another step forward. With no sites available along Michigan Avenue for a new project, developers decided on a site one block west, at the intersection of Wabash Avenue and Randolph Street (see Figure 43). Seven East Loop retail buildings were razed to make way for the million-square-foot development valued in excess of $250 million (Spielman 2001d). The entrance to the Heritage is at 130 North Garland Court, an alley behind the Chicago Cultural Center, which was widened, repaved, and landscaped for this purpose.

The Heritage at Millennium Park contains two distinct elements: a fifty-seven-story north tower with an outward curving wall of windows facing the lake, and a twenty-eight-story south section with an inward curving facade. The 356 condos are built in a forty-nine-story tower atop a broader eight-story base, which includes twenty retail storefronts on the first two levels along Wabash and Randolph Street, a six-level parking garage for residents and the public, and a venue the developers have offered to lease to the city for one dollar a year for cultural events (Ruda 2001). The tower capitalizes on unobstructed views of Millennium Park and Lake Michigan, because residences start on floors overlooking the nine-story Chicago Cultural Center immediately to the east. Many west-facing units have views of the Loop and River North. A landscaped park and sun deck is located on the roof of the garage at the ninth-floor level on the Wabash side. There is also a deck facing the lake on the twenty-eighth floor, a dog walk on the eighth floor, and an indoor lap pool and exercise room.

Like Six North Michigan Avenue and projects built along the river, the Heritage at Millennium Park incorporates a prestigious location into its name, which frames the relationship between the building and its site. But unlike Marina City, RiverBend, or even Six North Michigan Avenue, for example, the Heritage at Millennium Park must balance its temporal as well as its spatial origins. The term *Heritage* evokes the past—a cultural and architectural tradition. It emphasizes history in terms of people as well as place. Identification with Millennium Park, itself a new space, places the structure in the present and connects it to greenspace. The name is an accurate portrayal of the many dualities and connections this structure intends and achieves.

The Chicago-based architectural firm of Solomon Cord-well Buenz and Associates was selected to design Heritage at Millennium Park. Here, as they have done with projects along the riverfront and elsewhere, they have used their understanding of the site and its architectural history as inspiration for the design. Their perspective and actual design is also guided, however, by the larger urban landscape that defines Chicago. At this unique and pivotal location, they have drawn from water, park, and street. Using curved green glass and other building materials helps to bring the water inland, or to incorporate the imagery of what will be an expanded waterfront, thanks to Gehry's pedestrian bridge in Millennium Park. Looking at their work, one can see the influence of Sullivan, Mies, Burnham, Goldberg, and the river's signature building at number 333 West Wacker, designed by Kohn, Pederson, and Fox.

The design and materials of the Heritage at Millennium Park also respond to features of the site and to the long-term goals for this area. Expanding what was an alley to the forty-five-foot-wide Garland Court resolves the constraints at street level by using the grid without forcing the building to remain on a traditional axis. Widening what essentially was an alley opens up the site at street level. There is a sense of lightness and airiness that invites people to come into the street. A modern chrome sculpture at the corner of Garland Court and Randolph Street also helps attract the attention of those walking along Randolph. The now more substantive and supportive base helps to balance the Heritage's height so that the building better fits its surroundings. Chicago's DPD helped to shape the final design. At the time of its planning, assistant commissioner of the city's DPD Ty Tabing suggested "We wanted the building to fit the context of the South Michigan Avenue Streetwall, which is one of the treasures of the city and is now being landmarked. We wanted less height than the developers proposed. We wanted less of a monolithic building and more of a slender tower" (Tabing, in Handley 2001b). Originally, the developers wanted a 650-foot building; they received approval for 620 feet.

43—The Heritage at Millennium Park, Chicago Cultural Center, and Peristyle, August 2004

The Heritage is envisioned as a "cultural set-aside" linking with the Randolph Street theater district. In response to the city's request for a complement to the Chicago Theater District along Randolph, the structure includes a twenty-five-thousand-square-foot space on the third floor, which may become a museum or an entertainment facility and which, Tabing believes, "will have a public benefit" (Tabing, in Handley 2001b). It will be up to the city's Department of Cultural Affairs to decide how to use this space. Possibilities include a small gallery, an exhibit room, or a lecture auditorium. Other possibilities for its use include a space for very small theatrical productions or additional space for programs such as

Gallery 37 or the Cultural Center (Handley 2001b; Spielman 2001d). The hundred thousand square feet at the base of the building are important. Tabing stressed: "The city's long-term vision is to get shoppers to cross the river from North Michigan Avenue and spend time in the Loop" (Handley 2001b).

The Heritage at Millennium Park is also reshaping Wabash Avenue. By expanding the residential area, the Heritage connects this portion of Wabash to the Loop and park areas via Randolph Street. This will help breathe new life into an undeveloped corner and an area in need of diversity and revitalization. The north–south street is covered by the Chicago Transit Authority elevated tracks used by three commuter lines. One key element of the plan will be the preservation of the facades of four existing buildings on Wabash. Though not landmarks, the five- and six-story structures will maintain the historic look of the street with its EL tracks running down the center.

Because the Heritage at Millennium Park will be linked with the city's underground pedway system, it will be possible to walk to many locations without going outside—a tremendously attractive option in Chicago. Even without the pedway, the Heritage is close to many of the city's most desirable and, for locals, most necessary amenities. Residents are a block or two from the theater district and Harold Washington College, three blocks from the Art Institute, across the street from the Cultural Center and the Marshall Field's flagship store, half a block from Millennium Park, and a block from the lake (Spielman 2001d). Trains and buses as well as main roadways are immediately available. Yet Alderman Burton Natarus, whose Forty-second Ward includes the Heritage at Millennium Park site, notes: "We don't have a system of moving people around the Downtown area without cars. Will this have an impact on the area? You bet it will." He views the intersection of Michigan Avenue and Randolph, one block east of the site, as "one of the worst intersections in the United States" (Ruda 2001).

The South Loop and Near South Side

There is also concern about the future of other buildings along Michigan Avenue. Will more South Michigan Avenue buildings become condos? Landmark designation and the new park will bring a huge boost in property values to a section of the city now considered one of the most beautiful and desirable. Most agree that there is a residential market and the most valuable spaces are those with unobstructed views of the lake. Solomon Cordwell Buenz architect John Lahey believes that "Condos with a view to Millennium Park will be like Central Park in draw. Prices and rents will reflect this. [Prices range from $246,500 to $2.7 million for spaces ranging from 809 to 3,866 square feet.] But it's still cheaper to live in a condo than rent" (Lahey 2001). The marketability of the interior units without the view, however, remains in question.

The buildings that comprise the South Michigan Avenue Streetwall and Historic District collectively create "the beautiful house that allows Grant Park to be the city's front yard" (O'Neill 2002). But what will happen further south? The South Streetwall on Roosevelt Road, the last row of buildings framing Grant Park, is completely undeveloped and not yet designed. Consequently, the Grant

Park Conservancy has initiated the Parkitecture movement. Parkitecture is a regular ongoing series of panel discussions and public input forums about architecture and design in and around Grant Park with the goal of encouraging "high quality innovative design of the new Grant Park buildings facing the park as well as the structures and landscaping within it" (Grant Park Conservancy 2004). This area is but one part of the burgeoning South Loop.

The South Loop was created through the reclamation of rail yards and printing houses for residential development at Dearborn Park and Printers Row, beginning in the late 1970s. Since then, the South Loop has emerged as a successful, affordable, mixed-use residential community that features adaptive-use rental units as well as for-sale spaces. *The Economic Base and Sector Analysis, Central Area, Chicago, IL, 2000–2020 Report* (City of Chicago DPD 2001) indicates that, in the 1990s, loft development spread to neighborhoods from Printers Row to the whole Central Area, including the Near South Side. Modestly priced lofts add an important housing option, especially to the younger segment of the population, those between twenty-five and thirty-four years old, drawn to the city for the job expansion, especially in companies that rely on younger, well-educated workers. Yet fewer buildings are available for residential conversions.

The Near South Side includes the Central Area's greatest concentration of large parcels of land for redevelopment and the best opportunities for available river-edge improvements. Here, a barrage of new residential developments, geared primarily for middle- and upper-income residents, is in various stages of construction. Many structures sell over 50 percent of their units before they are anywhere near completed. Sites include the Columbian, at the corner of Columbus Drive and Roosevelt Road; State Place (see Figure 44), at the corner of State Street and Roosevelt Road; and the Museum Campus area, where complexes called Museum Park, Lakeside, and Prairie Place (phases 1 and 2) are completed or near completion. These new complexes are primarily south of Roosevelt Road, but some hover around the Printer's Row District.

44—State Place (New condominiums on State and Roosevelt), South Loop, July 2003

45—The Central Area and
vicinity. Chicago Conven-
tion and Tourism Bureau

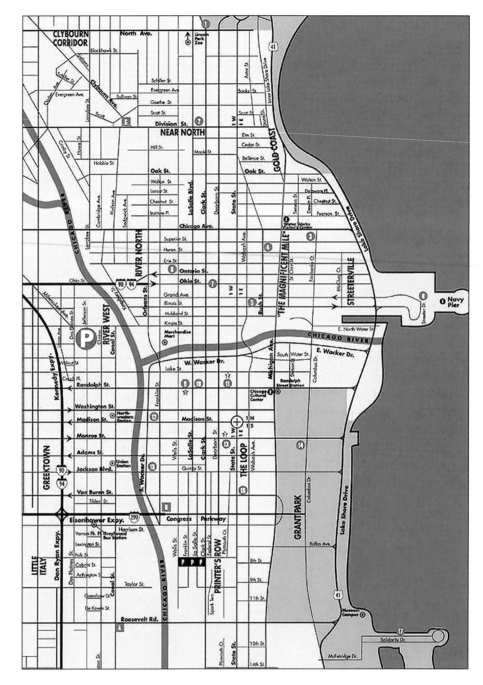

In addition to housing, amenities such as shopping, parks, cultural venues,
and educational facilities as well as improved transportation are making this an
attractive area for those priced out of the market in the core of the Central Area.
Currently, however, there are no bridges over the river between Roosevelt Road
and Eighteenth Street, so recommendations for this area highlight building new
bridges over the river in addition to residential and retail development (CAP, 59).
There is a call for continued retail development and for the creation of a parkway along both sides of the river with an extended riverwalk to facilitate connectivity between this area and the rest of the Central Area (CAP, 56).

NEWFOUND NEIGHBORHOODS—NORTH AND WEST

Currently, the preferred residential neighborhoods are found North and West of the Loop. Unlike the Near South Side, and even the Loop, where development inches forward building by building, if not block by block, whole neighborhoods are being reconfigured at a rapid pace. These include River North, Lincoln Park, Lakeview, Bucktown, Wicker Park, and the West Loop.

46—River East, January 2005

River North—roughly bounded by the river (south and west), Clark Street (east), and Oak Street (north), for example—has become an area of fine art galleries, high-end antique shops, home furnishing stores, and upscale restaurants and boutiques. It is also a popular entertainment district. At the turn of the century, Old Town was a modest neighborhood for working-class families directly west of the Gold Coast. Lincoln Park was both a large public park that bordered Lake Michigan and an upscale neighborhood filled with gracious high- and low-rise buildings and homes bordering the park. As the city grew, Lincoln Park expanded to encompass another working-class area to the west called Sheffield, which accounts for the bulk of the neighborhood. Old Town and Lincoln Park are similar in feel. They are diverse communities with eclectic blends of architectural style, and the expected gentrified amenities for shopping and eating.

Hovering on the border of Lincoln Park is Lakeview, also known as Wrigleyville because of its ties to Wrigley Field. Lakeview was originally an enclave of German and Northern European blue-collar workers living with their families in neat family dwellings and brick-and-greystone two-flats. Today these are increasingly inhabited by college students and young professionals who are drawn to the amenities offered in the neighborhood and to easy access to the downtown area.

Bucktown and Wicker Park, located in the near northwest, have become highly desirable gentrified areas within the past five years. Artists in search of larger spaces and cheaper rents than can be found downtown have gravitated toward such areas, which offer abandoned factories and industrial spaces. In Bucktown today, bars, nightclubs, restaurants, and shops along with renovated lofts and living spaces have replaced former factories and vacant storefront spaces. South of Bucktown is Wicker Park, currently the hippest neighborhood in the city. It is situated where Damen, Milwaukee, and North streets conjoin. Division Street to the south is Wicker Park's other main artery. As in the other neighborhoods described above, art galleries, boutiques, and trendy restaurants have begun to fill the area.

The area formerly known as West Town—now designated variously as the New West Side, the West Loop, and the Near West Side—is still so new that people cannot yet decide what to call it. Once the site of dilapidated industrial buildings and walk-ups, the area caused developers and planners, beginning in the late 1980s and 1990s, to search downtown for abandoned or ignored warehouses and factories suitable for adaptive use (see Plate 20).

On and west of Canal Street, near the Merc and other corporate structures, newly constructed residential, mixed-use complexes are also beginning to dot the landscape. RiverBend and Metra Mart on Canal Street, just east of the Merchandise Mart, are noteworthy examples. These are being joined by the newly converted Traffic Court Building (now the Reid-Murdoch Center) and the Montgomery Ward Warehouse (now e-port). These complexes are significant in that they add new construction and mixed-use spaces to the once industrial and then corporate landscape in the Loop and either on or close to the Riverfront. In addition to residences, the area now houses the city's most important contemporary art galleries and serves as a hub for acclaimed restaurants and sources for high-end home furnishings. The area caters to the new gentry—affluent consumers who demand boutique-type shops and gourmet restaurants. This includes people working in the nearby area and those visiting the Central Area in addition to neighborhood residents.

FRACTAL FORMS—DUAL VISIONS

New transportation and communication networks are transforming what were once peripheral or fringe areas into parts of the central core. But proximity to the center still counts. As the "fringe" areas described here reveal, an area is provided with cache by aligning with the center, not by distancing itself from it, which acts as a rebuttal to those skeptics who question the significance of the center or those who question the need for the center at all. More than ever (or perhaps, once again), centrality, albeit one now derived from fractal forms and asymmetrical connections, is defining Chicago.

During the 1980s, housing values displayed little tendency to appreciate in locations closer to the city center. According to a report by the Chicago Federal Reserve, by the end of the 1990s, however, proximity to the central city had become very important in housing prices, which declined by 7.5 percent per mile as they moved away from the CBD. This trend continues, no doubt reflecting the ongoing process of gentrification in formerly low-income Chicago neighborhoods (Krontoft, McMIllen, and Testa 2001). The report hypothesizes that traffic congestion may be a factor in the decision of professionals who work in central cities to live there as well. Commuting from surrounding suburban areas into downtown Chicago has become costly in terms of both time and irritation, which induces many households to opt for a center-city residential location. There is, as Tabing has alluded to, the recognition that "people want a little more out of the quality of their lives than shopping in Schaumburg or other malls" (Tabing 2000). Seeking to ride this wave of discontent with suburban living, and to take advantage of the more favorable image of downtown or city living, developers have sought to capture the market of affluent buyers by offering residences and amenities that cater to their needs.

Statistics bear this out. The landscape of the city center is one of growth; but growth has been uneven in a number of ways. While the number of households grew from 36,800 in 1990 to 52,000 in 2000, the balance between rental and for-sale (condominiums and lofts) housing shifted toward the latter (City of Chicago DPD, 2001, 63). In March 2001 there were signs that "Chicago area's hottest residential market—downtown— . . . started to cool. . . . In the downtown area, the inventory of unsold units increased to 3,900 at the end of the first quarter from 3,200 at year-end 2000" (Roeder 2001d). Figures provided by Appraisal Research Counselors, Ltd., indicated that more than 10,500 downtown units would be marketed in 2001, the largest figure in the building boom that dates from about 1996 (Roeder 2001d). This number was downgraded to 9,700 the following year. Another 9,200 units went on the market between 2002 and 2003.

In early 2002, "despite a growing number of unsold condominium units and numerous new projects on the way, analysts who follow the downtown housing market said that long-term trends favor developers. That would mean a return to a robust market that, since the mid-1990s, has seen construction cranes encircle the Loop and allowed the developers to test buyers' tolerance for price hikes" (Roeder 2002a). For the first half of 2002, there were about 1,000 condo sales per quarter in the inner city, which is considered a decent pace. Some projects were pushed back to 2003 or 2004. Because of nervousness about the market, lenders placed restrictions on sales to speculators, requiring that 50 percent of units be sold before construction can start, compared with the requirement for 20–30 percent preconstruction sales a couple of years ago (Roeder 2002a). By either standard, sales continue strong. Newer developments such as 20 North State (Street), in the heart of the Loop, and State Place, in the South Loop, are easily meeting the more stringent requirements. Upon its opening in 2004, 20 North State was completely sold out, and over 50 percent of State Place had been sold by July 2003, when construction had only just begun. Those tracking the local market continue to believe the appeal of the city is not going away. Phil Nyden, director of the Center for Urban Research and Learning at Loyola University, goes further: "This phenomenal growth right now in the Loop with upscale high-rises, new buildings, condos and apartment buildings is stunning. It is a major development in the City of Chicago" (Nyden, in Skertic and Hermann 2002).

The story is very different in the rental market. While, in the 1980s, rental housing accounted for 86 percent of the new units added, in the 1990s, 42 percent of new housing units were rental. And of those units under construction after 2000, only 25 percent were rentals. *The Economic Base . . . Report* indicates: "Demand for an annual average of 1,800–2,000 units over the next 20 years is reasonable and represents about 8 percent of the annual household growth forecast for the metro area and 1 out of every 10 new office-using jobs in the study area" (City of Chicago DPD 2001, 85).

Although Central Area workers and current renters continue to want and need rental units, project economics favor condominium development. This is because many rental properties built in the 1980s received government financing, requiring commitments to affordable housing. As the financing expires, more conversions can be expected (City of Chicago DPD 2001, 69–71). Loft conversions have been an important housing type in the Central Area, as they tend to be more moderately priced than new construction (68–69). This is one of the reasons that adaptive use or loft conversions gained popularity in the 1980s and their appeal continued into the 1990s, when most of the available spaces for conversion were exhausted.

Aside from loft conversions, the question of affordability for this population segment has resulted in explorations for options previously either reserved for areas outside the city limits or not considered at all. This is the reason behind Dearborn Park and the other developments south of the Loop, behind loft conversions and new housing west of the Loop, and behind the rehabbing of whole neighborhoods, especially on the Northwest Side (Longworth 2002). Most affected is the population sector comprised mostly of young professionals between the ages of twenty-five and thirty-four.

Households with children continue to be a minor segment in the growth of the Central Area, in part because they are also being priced out of the market, and also because few appropriate housing types have been built to accommodate this family type. The mayor has strongly advocated developments that will appeal to families with children. In response, developers are including two- and three-bedroom units as well as a day-care-center space for the Central Area. But families also insist on good education, so schools will also have to become part of the plan to bring families with children back to the Central Area of the city.

ENTERING "THE GLOBAL ERA"—NEW DISPARITIES, NEW ALIGNMENTS

As Chicago enters what journalist Richard C. Longworth describes as "the Global Era," the city must find its place amid still other asymmetries, in particular, those etched by outcomes of gentrification, globalization, uneven growth, and the polarization between wealthy and poor. Demographic and economic growth for the city and city center reflects these trends. Census data for the year 2000 indicated that the Central Area's population increased from 63,200 in 1990 to 90,500 in 2000. Growth was most evident in the ethnic neighborhoods, which absorbed many new immigrants, and in urban core neighborhoods populated by high-income and mostly childless households (Krontoft, McMillen, and Testa 2001). Chicago's median household income for 1999 was $38,625, up 12.6 percent from the 1990 census figure when it is adjusted for inflation. The average Hispanic neighborhood's median household income for 1999 was $43,214, and the average African American neighborhood's was $36,298. In comparison, the median household income for whites and Asians was $61,952 and $49,808, respectively (Mumford Center for Comparative Urban and Regional Research results, in Skertic 2002).

In many ways, two Chicagos are emerging: the newly gentrified and predominantly white neighborhoods and the low-income black and Hispanic communities. Census data for the year 2000 supports this as well. In 1999, Lincoln Park had the highest median household income ($68,613) of all of Chicago's community areas. Oakland, a predominately black community was ranked the lowest, with the median household income at $10,739. Even within Lincoln Park, which is 87 percent white and 5 percent black, the median household income was $73,956 and $16,418 for whites and blacks, respectively. In only eighteen areas of the city is the black median income higher than the citywide median, compared with thirty-four areas for Hispanics and forty-five for whites (Skertic, Guerrero, and Herguth 2002). In 2002, nine of the ten poorest community areas in Chicago were more than 94 percent African American and located predominantly on the West and South Sides, while the ten community areas with the highest median income were roughly the same as in 1989—north of the Loop and predominantly white—although their ranking changed slightly (Skertic and Fornek 2002). Asians, in Chicago, are typically found in neighborhoods with a median income of $56,935.

Robert E. Park reminds us that "Land values, since they reflect movement, afford one of the most sensitive indexes of mobility" (Park 1967, 61). When Park applied social distance as an overlay to the physical shape of a city, he had these very considerations in mind. While the overlay of social distance has taken on global as well as local parameters, poverty fundamentally is and always has been about distance from power in exactly the prismatic ways it was constructed by the first generation of Chicago sociologists. As the city becomes workplace and home to the wealthy, it also becomes workplace and home to those at the lower end of the spectrum, including new immigrants. They also need places to live that are affordable and accessible to the downtown area. New gentrification may exacerbate the isolation of minorities, economically as well as residentially, if mixed-use and mixed-income projects are not expanded to include this population segment of the city.

When race and ethnicity are factored in, location and social distance take on more complex but very tangible meanings and consequences. With respect to residence, changes in Chicago's population and ethnic composition have done little to desegregate blacks or Hispanics within the city. Between 1970 and 1990, residential areas where the population was comprised primarily of blacks grew and became more clearly defined. The same trend occurred for Hispanic communities. Further, blacks and Hispanics are more segregated from one another (Abu-Lughod 1999, 336–37). Residential segregation impacts access to education and employment. The findings of a study conducted by the Chicago Urban League on Chicago and suburban Cook County employment support this, showing that "the major sectoral zones within the city in which minorities are heavily concentrated [areas that average 70 percent black in population]—namely West and South of the Loop—are exactly the zones that have suffered the greatest losses of employment and are likely to continue to do so" (Abu-Lughod 1999, 338–40). Economic opportunity declines or disappears in many poor areas with certain minority bases.

Although globalization may have been an exacerbating factor, it has not caused this gap. Rather, the existing disparity between African Americans and whites is a local problem. In Abu-Lughod's view, the prognosis for Chicago's future depends upon "whether the trend toward the marginalization of poorer African Americans within the city can be reversed, whether a more stable coalition between African Americans and Latinos can be constructed . . . [and] whether the social fabric of the Chicago region can be mended sufficiently to yield synergism rather than continued counterproductive fission" (Abu-Lughod 1999, 357–58). Phil Nyden concurs with this view: "we are only as successful and secure as our poorest neighborhood" (Nyden, in Skertic and Hermann 2002). Isolation makes increasingly less sense when applied to conceptions of connection and community for cities in the "global era." So does fusion, in its traditional uses in cities, that is, having the dominant overtake and silence the nondominant. In the case of Chicago, we can ask, how can Chicago safeguard against encroaching gentrification and the omission of the poor in the city's reshaping?

Benet Haller offers one consideration as to how neighborhoods might be recognized and how they might relate to one another. As noted, he predicts that, in all likelihood, some neighborhoods in the Central Area will remain distinct and in the hands of the locals, rather than give way to the "new city users" as has been the case in much of the Central Area. These neighborhoods might be said to represent counterspaces with respect to the predominant look and feel of the Central Area. Haller believes this is not necessarily a bad thing, because such areas serve a vital role in keeping localism a priority in an ever-growing global terrain where new city users are of primary interest. So the presence of distinct neighborhoods in the downtown area, as well as beyond it, may well be an asset for and a necessary component of the city center.

Interaction, therefore, need not undercut identity, if neighborhoods are able to complement instead of compete with one another. This form of interaction can increase connectivity and reduce social distance. In E. W. Burgess's terms, peripheries can "centralize decentralization" through an agglomeration of smaller entities, which "coalesce into sub-business areas visibly or invisibly dominated by the central business district" (Burgess, in Park 1967, 47). But peripheries also decentralize the center by expanding its scope and by increasing its impact and power. It is in this dynamic landscape that Chicago must be placed. One way in which these disparate but essential components of the city can find common ground is to employ the new version of multi- or mixed-use structures but to do so in poor as well as in middle- and upper-income areas. For Chicago's Central Area, "mixed" will have to include both race and social class as well as use.

According to the *Central Area Plan,* "Chicago enjoys a long-standing reputation for weathering change and surmounting obstacles. It has a history of doing visionary things for practical reasons" (CAP, 1). It also has a history of taking risks that, while not always perceived as practical, have contributed to the city's growth and achievement. "There is," architect Santiago Calatrava acknowledges, "as much constancy in greatness as there is in change" (Calatrava 2002, 10). The first generation of builders used change and risk as momentum for their efforts to frame the city's morphology. Chicago continues to nurture this aesthetic and rhythm, and architects and sociologists continue to build and explore the city, Chicago style. With another phase of the city's growth and change well underway, we might ask, where is Chicago looking now? Where will the next projects come from? And where will they lead Chicago?

The CAP envisions a Central Area that "is many centers in one, operating within many geographic spheres, ranging from global to local" (CAP, 1). In order to address these "multilayered" relationships, the plan targets four key areas of interest, which will be considered on the following pages through projects and plans exemplifying efforts to resolve them. These four issues are how to house the poor, how to support shopping and retail business, how to provide a multimodal transportation hub, and how to promote tourism. Several projects lie outside the physical boundaries of the Central Area, yet they embody the vision of the Chicago that is yet to be. These projects are, in essence, nodes generating energy back toward the center. And together with the center, this network of nodes is helping to shape the New Central Area and, more generally, Chicago.

HOUSING THE POORS

As the Heart of a Great International City, the Central Area must continue to bolster Chicago's claim to being America's most livable city and become an international model for environmental planning. (CAP, 1)

In order to make Chicago, in the words of Mayor Daley, "America's most livable city," first and foremost the city must provide its residents with affordable and adequate housing. In his 2002 State of the City address, the mayor stated: "Chicagoans are entitled to neighborhoods that are safe, clean and affordable; neighborhoods that are great places in which to live and raise families" (Office of the Mayor, 2002a). The CAP specifies: "The Central Area should offer a broad range of housing options in the downtown market for workers, students, empty nesters, family and the elderly through the use of public and private funds" (CAP, 28). These provisions must also extend to the city's poor.

In 1999, with input from the city, the Chicago Housing Authority (CHA) developed its Plan for Transformation, which, according to the mayor, "will make Chicago a national model for the new century and replace the legacy of failure with hope and progress for the families and seniors who live in public housing" (Office of the Mayor 2002a). With this plan, the CHA seeks to "renew the physical structure of CHA properties, promote self-sufficiency for public housing residents, and reform the administration of the CHA (CHA 1999). Specifically, the ten-year plan calls for rehabbing the city's twenty-five thousand public housing units and all of its scattered site developments and senior citizen buildings as well as constructing new mixed-use housing. Generally these developments will consist of one-third public housing, one-third affordable housing (rentals to those at or slightly below the city's median household income), and one-third market rate for-sale homes.

To reduce the isolation of poor communities and to build neighborhoods, the CHA Plan has instituted new programs linking residents to employment and community resources. It has begun recruiting new businesses into these neighborhoods, implemented a mixed-income strategy of occupancy, and initiated construction or improvement of other institutions such as schools, parks, libraries, and police stations. In these ways, the City hopes to "transform housing developments into active thriving communities" (CHA 1999, annual report for 2004). In addition, the city initiated the Hope VI Program, which provides the CHA with grants to facilitate the Transformation Plan. While the program was targeted for termination by the administration in 2004, provisions were included in the FY04 Omnibus Appropriations bill to fund the program and continue it through 2006 (City of Chicago 2005). As of 2004, the halfway mark for the plan, 52.2 percent of the twenty-five thousand units slated for renewal had been rehabbed. At least thirty-five hundred families had been relocated to other CHA developments or neighborhood communities of their choice; four thousand residents had been directed to or placed in new jobs, and all of the city's scattered site developments were in process of rehabilitation (City of Chicago 2004b; CHA 1999, annual report for 2004; Office of the Mayor 2002a).

Over the next five years, city plans call for building five hundred more Single Residence Occupancy (SRO) units and rehabbing another one thousand; building ninety units of supportive housing for homeless families; and, in partnership with the CHA, developing two transitional shelters that would temporarily house as many as 150 families per year. With the intention of providing families with support "each step of the way," the plan will pay special attention to non-leaseholders moving out of CHA housing in an effort to avoid the possibility of homelessness (Office of the Mayor 2003). These measures are part of another plan (initiated by the city in 1993) to deal specifically with the most dramatic consequence of the housing affordability crisis: the appearance of an increasingly large group of people without permanent housing. The Plan to Eliminate

Homelessness has a dual agenda. First, it aims to move from a system focused on temporary shelters to a system that moves people quickly into permanent housing, provides social services, and addresses the causes of homelessness. At the same time, the plan aims to prevent homelessness by helping residents keep the homes they have and by subsidizing mortgages or rents until the wage earner can retrain or find new work (Office of the Mayor 2003).

Susan Wachter of the Wharton School has identified specific areas of federal policy that she believes have contributed to the prevention of homelessness. These proactive measures include a shift to Section 8 or vouchers to decrease the concentration of low-income households and the work of the Federal Housing Authority (FHA), the Community Reinvestment Act, and Fannie Mae and Freddie Mac to increase home ownership among low-income households. During the 1990s, the rate of home ownership surpassed 50 percent of households for the first time in U.S. history (Krontoft, McMillen, Testa 2001). While governmental policies can facilitate better outcomes, the private sector will ultimately have to be included in any plan that intends to build "the most livable community in America." As CHA's CEO Terry Peterson notes: "In the end, this plan isn't just about building housing and strengthening communities. It's about building meaningful and rewarding lives" (CHA 1999). Reconnection with the community is vital. The CHA and the End to Homelessness plans acknowledge that transformation entails physical as well as social and economic change. They pose new frames in which to identify homeless people and what they require.

Poverty and homelessness are typically viewed as predictable consequences of the widening gap between the number of low-income housing units and the number of households that require such units. According to sociologist Madeline Stoner, the lack of housing and services for vulnerable people is a logical precursor to homelessness (Stoner, in Dear 2002a, 220–21). But the problem is more complex. Rather than a consequence of a marginal position with respect to the dominant social, economic, and political forces of urban life, homelessness should be seen as a consequence of being caught up in and situated exactly at the point of convergence of these forces. That is, perceptions, actions, and reactions of the dominant culture create the frame that marginalizes and excludes people's access to shelter. Stoner believes that strategies for new global economies must recognize the correlation between homelessness and extreme poverty. In addition, "the housing supply and built environment must reverse the social isolation of contemporary single and small households. The human environment also needs to develop formal social supports to augment . . . the informal systems . . . and to rebalance the human and built environment to challenge the fortress mentality of privatopias" (Stoner, in Dear 2002a, 231).

As Chicago finds new form, it must continue to search for parameters that can realign its most disparate and difficult parts. Mixed-income strategies and multiuse, adaptive, and flexible housing forms are some of the policies and designs that reflect the city's efforts to achieve this connection. Ways to provide inhabitants with a sense of security still require consideration. Security is as necessary for the tourist or businessperson seeking temporary lodging as for residents seeking more permanent housing. Indeed, security is a concern of people of all classes, but it is clearly most important for those without any sense of permanence in their lives. As one homeless person explained: "Everyone should have some decent roof overhead. We're all entitled to that. A home is the idea of who you are. Once you have shelter, then you are able to develop the idea of how you can get yourself out of the trouble you are in" (Satler journal entry, September 5, 2000).

In addition to increasing the number of units available and reducing their isolation from the rest of the city, planners should factor the design and aesthetics of the housing into the plans. Here the intersection of architecture and sociology can play a vital role. Architects and sociologists can help create spaces that facilitate a sense of well-being and reduce or remove some of the boundaries between communities and their inhabitants. What has seemed an insurmountable gap between the city and its most disconnected can be bridged. "The challenge," according to Sassen, "is how to bridge the inner city, or the squatters at the urban perimeter, with the center. In multiracial cities, multiculturalism has emerged as one form of this bridging. A 'regional' discourse is perhaps beginning to emerge, but it has until now been totally submerged under the suburbanization banner, a concept that suggests both escape from and dependence on the city" (Sassen 2000, 141). Some architects seem aware of and ready to meet this challenge. Frank Gehry reflects: "Architecture is a small piece of this human equation, but for those of us who practice it, we believe in its potential to make a difference, to enlighten and to enrich the human experience, to penetrate the barriers of misunderstanding and provide a beautiful context for life's drama" (Gehry 1989).

Historically, Chicago has offered architects and planners a great deal of freedom and support to go outside existing boundaries of building and designing. At the same time, Chicago has also been the site where confinement and depersonalization have been paramount in designs for public housing, most notoriously in the Cabrini Green and the Robert Taylor projects (Venkatesh 2000). The CHA is well aware of this legacy. The Transformation Plan, in their words, "represents a new beginning for public housing in Chicago. It's an opportunity to change the stigmas of the past, and create a new culture of success and hope" (CHA 1999). There is evidence of this new image in projects such as Archer Courts.

Architects, Landon Bone Baker (2002–2003)

Archer Courts—Phases 1 and 2, 2220–2242 South Princeton

The Archer Courts development is located just south of the Loop, in the heart of the city's Chinatown. Built in 1951, it was one of the eight city-state housing developments built to house the people displaced by the construction of the Eisenhower Expressway. Unlike many other buildings in the CHA Courts Program, Archer Courts remained a stable, clean, and community-oriented development. Its population consisted of working-class, lower-income, and elderly residents. However, in 1999, Archer Courts deteriorated to the point that its viability was questioned by some community leaders (Landon Bone Baker 2004–2005). Rather than see the fifty-year-old, seven-story, 147-unit housing complex torn down, the Chicago Community Development Corporation bought it from the CHA and renovated it, taking advantage of the federal financing provided by 1997 legislation for rehabilitating eligible subsidized housing. The corporation, founded by

Anthony Fusco and Daniel Burke, hired Chicago-based architect Peter Landon. At a cost of $6.5 million (half of the cost to tear it down and build a new structure), they transformed a crime-ridden and dilapidated structure into an award-winning, mixed-income housing complex (Phase 1), without displacing any of the 670 residents. The resident population in 2003 was diverse: 70 percent Chinese mostly of retirement age, 25 percent African American families with children, 3 percent Caucasian, and 2 percent Native American (Blair 2003).

For Landon, the primary goal of the renovation was to humanize the complex, to "break down the scale" (Landon, in Blair 2003). He walked through every unit and talked to many of the residents in order to get a sense of the people and their needs and preferences. This gesture, in turn, gave residents a sense of ownership and empowerment. For the developers, the primary goal was to make Archer Courts "a good neighbor to the surrounding area" (Blair 2003), and so they spent time reaching out to the predominantly Chinese community. Success for both architect and developers in many ways depended upon the look of the building. As Fusco realized: "as long as it had that prison like external, we couldn't break down the [social or psychological] barriers" (Fusco, in Blair 2003).

On the outside of the complex, the transformation was achieved through innovative and creative use of color. The strategy is most eloquently manifest in the glass curtain wall and trim treatment behind it (see Plate 21). To break down the scale of the curtain wall, Landon divided it into panels with plain glass for some and frosted for others. Together, the panels create a complex layered effect, adding depth and architectural impact (Blair 2003). Other primary elements included extensive landscaping and outdoor pavilions ("leong-tengs") to provide areas for meditation and the practice of Tai Chi (Landon Bone Baker 2004–2005; Landon and Baker 2005). In addition, the prisonlike fence on the periphery of the site was transformed by the addition of metal plaques bearing Chinese cultural symbols. The fence provides one form of security for residents; other security features include an intercom system for entry, better lighting throughout the complex, and on-site management offices and staff.

Inside the buildings, the dark, dingy enclosed corridors that residents had formerly avoided were painted in bright primary colors and were brightly lit, so that they became safe connecting pathways. The corporation added laundry rooms; a computer learning center, which provides computer classes and e-mail facilities; communal spaces with attached kitchens; a hall that serves as a party or meeting area; and a wellness center for elderly residents, where medical staff from nearby medical centers come several times a week. All units were upgraded with new appliances, new thermal-pane windows, mini-blinds, vinyl floors, and fresh paint. To add a touch of personality, units were equipped with features requested by the individual residents. For example, families (mostly African American) were given larger units, more counter space, and more electrical outlets. To accommodate the older, shorter Chinese residents, kitchen cabinetry configurations were changed and layouts were slightly altered.

Construction of Archer Courts Phase 2 began in 2002 and opened in 2003 (see Plate 22). It was fully occupied in 2005. The development is part of the City of Chicago's Homestart Program, an initiative by Mayor Daley to encourage the development of slightly-below-market-rate properties. As such, it is a mixed-income development, offering market-rate and below-market-rate home-ownership opportunity along with CHA rental units. Specifically, the complex consists of forty-three, three-story townhouses with garage and roof deck, for rent or purchase. Thirty-four of the townhouses went for market rate; five went to those earning 80 percent of the city's median income, with the city providing tax increment subsidies; and four went to those eligible for public housing. Phase 2 was built on vacant land west of the original Archer Courts Phase 1 buildings. Phases 1 and 2 are connected, using "continuing walkways, landscaping themes and similar building systems." Phase 1 "explores reuse rather than destruction," whereas Phase 2 "tests a relatively under-explored affordable building-system and furthers the discussion of prefabrication in building and housing. The Archer Courts project as a whole presents an interesting case study of successful economically, racially, historically and architecturally mixed development" (Landon Bone Baker 2004–2005).

In recognition of this extraordinary success, Archer Courts has won design awards from the Richard H. Driehaus Foundation and the American Institute of Architects as well as the approval of residents and the surrounding community. According to a child in the complex: "I feel good about coming home. We're not in the slums anymore." And one elderly resident, who has lived there since 1987, stated: "Everyday I thank the people who made my apartment better" (Blair 2003). We all should.

Archer Courts is an example of "doing a visionary thing for practical reasons." It proves that public and private efforts can work together to produce housing that improves both the lives of residents and the viability of the larger community. Archer Courts is changing the face of housing for the poor and the faces of those who are poor. It also reminds us that, while design does not cause behavior, it certainly affects it. The architects understand this project to potentially be "a prototype for similar developments throughout Chicago" (Landon Bone Baker 2004–2005).

There is evidence of this taking place in other CHA projects. Replacing Chicago's once infamous housing projects are developments intended to form the base for new neighborhoods. Massive high-rises are being replaced by mid-rise and low-rise, mixed-income housing units at scattered sites so that the sense of isolation is removed. Cabrini-Green has been decentralized into various projects on and off site. Francis Cabrini Extension North, for example, will consist of four mixed-income communities: Old Town Village East and West, Village North, and River Village South, sited within the Old Town neighborhood. Homes are near a number of restaurants, retail establishments, schools, parks, and public transportation (CHA 1999, annual report for 2005). The Hope VI Revitalization Plan for the Robert Taylor Homes, designed by the architectural firms of Landon Bone Baker and Johnson and Lee, incorporates new streets that reconnect the site to the existing city street grid. The size of the blocks is scaled for walking and easy cross interaction between the blocks. While each block is "designed as an individual element," it is also designed to relate to the larger whole (Landon Bone Baker 2004–2005; Baker, e-mail May 13, 2005). In many ways, the plan captures the essence of the hybrid space that Chicago aspires to be. A similar outlook is reflected at the other housing developments owned by the CHA.

Raymond Hilliard Center   Architect, Bertrand Goldberg
(1966)

As old symbols of housing are giving way to new ones, preservation has also found its way into the mix. The Raymond Hilliard Center was designed by Bertrand Goldberg in 1966. Even at that time it was recognized as a cut above the rest of the housing projects designed for the poor. Architecturally it utilized innovative forms and features, reminiscent of Goldberg's other landmark building, Marina City. Outsiders and residents recognized Goldberg's efforts. It was the only project that did not require police for security. More than thirty years later, the Hilliard Center was recognized for its architectural and social efforts when it was entered into the National Register of Historic Places in 1999. It is currently undergoing extensive renovation, but the facade will stay true to Goldberg's design, and the center's aim will stay true to his intention of providing appropriate (and different) housing for young families and for the elderly.

But Hilliard's import today is supplemented by the activity occurring around it. Located south of the Loop, it now finds itself just west of the McCormick Convention Center in an area experiencing much revitalization because of its proximity to the CBD. New signs of life, including a new supermarket, coffee shops, and other retail establishments make the possibility of integration more feasible. There are public investments such as a new police station, the National Teachers Academy, and transportation improvements. The Hilliard Center was and remains a beacon in its cutting-edge design and in its goal of providing residences for the diverse types of people who comprise the poor or, more accurately, "the poors." It is socio-architecture at its best.

From Houses to Homes to Community— *Joining Architecture and Sociology*

It is significant that innovative, award-winning architects are now designing homes for "ordinary" residents. This gesture not only reflects the commitment of architects to enhance the cityscape and the lives of those who inhabit their spaces, but also the willingness of the city to support these efforts, on behalf of these city users.

Housing is, perhaps, where the most basic and essential point of intersection between architecture and sociology lies. Architecture is concerned with creating shelter, with making space for people to inhabit and use. Urban sociology—and sociology in general—developed around the key concept of community; and community is essentially about activities and the spaces in which they occur. In other words, architecture builds and sociology studies. Both frame and are framed by human interaction. Therefore, housing and community should stem from this stronger but more pliable intersection of interests. As Goldberg observed: "Our American search for causes of social maladjustments has mistakenly shifted the emphasis of this search to housing. Housing follows our changes—it does not create them. . . . Ethnic groups have emerged with clearer identity. New housing will be aimed toward forming communities from these disparate elements. We should think how we want a humanistic urban environment to perform. The architect can do whatever we think" (Goldberg 1993).

New connections must be created among architects, sociologists, and other professionals from many disciplines. All are now investigating these issues as distinct "communities" of inquiry, coexisting but not really interacting with one another. An analytic shift—one that would provide reflexive intersections and greater interaction among disciplines—would afford a new understanding of the relationship of the various parts that create the difficult whole that is urban community. This shift would make it possible to reframe marginal groups as necessary, albeit unequal, in relation to more central groups.

In addition, housing and community can benefit from an aesthetic that engages all the senses, the aesthetic provided by landscaping. As Jensen suggested nearly a century ago: "Art grows out of native soil and enriches life as a people attempts to express and develop this growth. It is contemporary to life itself and is fastened in the chain of human endeavor. It comes from within, stimulated by environments and influenced by the customs and habits of people" (Jensen 1990, 2). In March 2002, Mayor Daley noted the importance of greening the city in micro and macro efforts: "Parks are essential building blocks of strong neighborhoods. Trees, flowers, a small park, even a sidewalk bench can soften the rough edges of a city, add some color, calm your nerves and make you feel a little more at peace with your environment. What do all these amenities have in common? They improve our quality of life" (Office of the Mayor 2002b).

Architects and sociologists would do well to consider adding landscape architects to their community of inquiry. Millennium Park and the Riverfront Development Plan as well as sites along the northern and main branches of the river exemplify the possibilities of such interdisciplinary collaboration. We can hope and encourage this fertile combination to flow south, along with more housing and economic opportunities, so that this branch of the river and its local communities can be more tightly knit into the fabric of the city. In these ways, the goal of making Chicago "America's most livable city *and* . . . an international model for environmental planning" may come closer to being realized (CAP, 1).

The city seems to be making earnest inroads toward this goal. The Westhaven Park Project, scheduled to break ground in the fall of 2005 and also part of the Hope VI Revitalization Plan, could be considered a "green" development. The units will all be Energy Star rated, which means 30 percent more efficient than the Chicago Energy Code. Landon Bone Baker are the architects for this project, sited in the West Loop, and according to one of the design architects, Catherine Baker: "we are very happy about this." The mayor has facilitated a "green" permit program in which the city will waive permit review fees and will expedite the permit process for such projects (Landon and Baker 2004–2005, Baker 2005). The architects were also able to incorporate work spaces and living spaces into the project, adding another mix to the infrastructure of the neighborhood. This further enhances the mixed-use notion, in communities most in need of the notion of "mix" that includes income and use. These gestures envision the city within the global as well as the local context. A community of the twenty-first century must possess this duality of purpose.

SHOPPING, RETAIL, AND THE SERVICE SECTOR

The Downtown of the Midwest, the Central Area must continue to grow as the center of regional business and the Midwest's "Main Street" of great retail. (CAP, 1)

47—Westhaven Park Project, August 2005. *Bruce Bondy*

Retail has been discussed in each section of this book because it is a common thread that runs throughout the renovation of the Central Area. As Rem Koolhaas and Guido Martinotti (among others) maintain, retail has become very significant in urban identity and in our lives, albeit in ways that differ from the retail of the past. For the newly emerging, nineteenth-century Chicago, with access to both urban and rural markets, retail possibilities for the city's budding entrepreneurs seemed limitless. Montgomery Ward was among the first to capitalize on rural markets in his mail-order business. Using the expanding rail system and postal service, the Ward catalog created a greater demand for manufactured goods and changed the way midwesterners shopped. Richard Warren Sears with his partner Alvah Roebuck formed a successful mail-order business based on a similar strategy. Meanwhile, Marshall Field developed his own style of merchandising—elegant retail stores with an emphasis on service, creating a "shopping experience" (Wendt and Kogan 1952). Today, his company continues to update and transform itself in order to provide patrons with "a shopping experience."

In the twenty-first century, shopping permeates almost every aspect of our lives in ways and places that make it routine and almost invisible. At times, shopping has overwhelmed a space. But there are spaces that overwhelm shopping. That is, in many contexts shopping is a necessary activity—purchasing goods to satisfy needs. In the examples discussed here, however, the design and aesthetics of the space create an experience that elevates shopping above its basic function. More important, perhaps, is that in these venues, the public is given the opportunity to return to and use spaces that were previously becoming ever more privatized, oppressive, or mundane.

Crate & Barrel—646 North Michigan Avenue

Architects, Solomon Cordwell Buenz and Associates (1990)

Crate & Barrel at 646 North Michigan Avenue stands out for a number of reasons (see Figure 48). As the flagship store of a locally based company that now extends nationwide, it is testament to the continuing strength and uniqueness of retail in Chicago, or more correctly Chicagoland, because its headquarters are centered outside the city proper in Naperville. Visually, the building obliterates boundaries of inside and outside. Glass and aluminum afford transparency so that customers and passersby can simultaneously see and be seen. Natural light, pine, and oak give the interior a relaxed, midwestern feel and look. This feel flows onto the street from the diamond-patterned oak flooring inside the door to

48—Crate & Barrel on North Michigan Avenue, January 2002

the smooth concrete of the same pattern that extends from the storefront to the curb (Sirefman 1996, 124). The design gives a nod to Sullivan's Carson Pirie Scott with its curved facade and horizontal as well as vertical strength. Socially, the public and private realms are turned inside out and outside in, in the poshest of locations—North Michigan Avenue. The structure democratizes space without sacrificing elegance for a store that sells housewares at fairly modest prices.

If shopping has become, as Koolhaas believes, "our most reliable, if not our only emblem of what is urban," eating out is not far behind. While perhaps not

usually considered a retail venue in the traditional sense, a restaurant can function as a place that serves and sells local character, injects a new culture into an
existing frame, or fuses a variety of cultures within its site and changes the character of the whole. A restaurant not only offers opportunities to users, it is an
economic engine and a social incubator. In many ways, a restaurant reflects the
city's diversity, complexity, and dynamism in microcosm. Therefore, descriptions
of several restaurants are offered here, in addition to more traditional retail venues, especially for their ability to overwhelm the basic, biological function of eating and create a multilayered, multisensory experience. These restaurants also
serve to illustrate how retail and service sectors have expanded and are expanding cities by connecting centers and peripheries.

Rhapsody, at 65 East Adams Street (between Michigan and Wabash)

Architects, Aria Architects
(1997)

Rhapsody (see Plate 23) is part of the Symphony Center space. The restaurant
consists of three eating spaces: the main dining room, the Conductor's Room,
and the enclosed garden. Use of varying color palettes, natural and artificial
lighting, and expansive windows helps distinguish the eating spaces from one
another and to connect them to one another and to the outside. Moving from
Rhapsody's bar—amber and brown with dim golden light—to the Conductor's
Room—yellow and pale green with natural light streaming in from the wall of
glass, which can be opened onto the urban garden—is a transition that is fluid
and fresh. What is most striking about the outdoor room of the restaurant is its
design and the lush garden. Rhapsody is a flower that blooms in the shadow of
the EL, amid the concrete-and-steel structures on Wabash Avenue. Sited low to
the ground, with a roof that resembles petals of a flower, the restaurant appears
to be a part of the garden. Jim Horan, Rhapsody's architect, was inspired by the
Paris Metro, so, while organic in one sense, the design has urban roots as well,
made more relevant by its association with the "train" systems in the two cities.
Benches have been placed in the garden for year-round use, affording people an
opportunity to take in the garden, to watch and listen to the EL and the city as
they move in working mode. Rhapsody is a nice example of how a multisensory
design can take people out of one realm and transport them into another. The
unlikely siting of the garden offers an element of surprise and delight for restaurant patrons as well as for those who come upon it from Wabash Avenue. Constraints imposed by various landmark preservation issues required the development of an "acceptable interface with the main building" (Horan 2003).
Rhapsody's architect has accomplished this fusion in a way that honors the fluidity of the music venue it adjoins.

Rhapsody readily caters to local patrons. But thanks to its connection with
the Symphony Center, its proximity to the EL on Wabash, and its well-earned
reputation, its customer base includes many new city users. Rhapsody thus expands its economic and aesthetic viability to the city. Rhapsody also connects
Wabash to newly renovated areas, Millennium Park and the streetwall on the
east and Greater State Street on the west. Seamlessly interwoven with the Symphony Hall, Rhapsody is nonetheless a destination point in its own right. More

than simply adding to the existing space, Rhapsody and the Symphony Center create a different kind of relationship. Physical and social boundaries are blurred, and this blurring in effect solidifies the identity of each component while creating a new whole that is truly a hybrid space. This new whole does not house or frame its components; rather, it is formed by their asymmetrical juxtaposition and by their diverse uses and users. Such hybrid spaces are a growing trend found in museums, music halls, theaters, and most interestingly, train and air terminals.

Rock 'N Roll McDonald's—600 North Clark Street

Architect, Frank Camacho,
with International Design
Architects (1983, 2005)

Rock 'N Roll McDonald's opened in 1983 and quickly became a landmark for this part of the city. The restaurant is one of the oldest in the chain and the third busiest in the country. In conjunction with the company's fiftieth-year celebration, McDonald's decided to rebuild this flagship store so that it would reflect the new direction of the company—"forever young"—and the neighborhood's changing users and their needs, while still respecting the history of the city (Camacho 2005). Its transformation embodies the diversity and complexity found in neighborhoods experiencing new gentrification, as in River North, where this McDonald's is located. The new McDonald's at 600 North Clark juxtaposes, and in some cases blurs, a number of dualities: the sense of the old with a sense of the new, a space of place with a space of flows, and inside with outside. It too is a hybrid space.

Framing the structure are the traditional name and golden arches, which provide recognition. But the building's exterior and interior expand the possibilities for dining within a familiar fast-food venue. The building's exterior pays reverence to the architects that have shaped Chicago. The southern facade evokes Louis Sullivan's Carson Pirie Scott, while its northern facade recalls the modern glass-and-steel profile of the works of Mies van der Rohe. The new McDonald's actually consists of three distinct spaces. For customers on the go, a widened drive-through area now accommodates two lanes of cars. For customers who prefer to stay and eat, the restaurant offers seating for three hundred (double its original capacity) in a two-story building that includes a roof garden (Herman 2004). The two levels are connected by an escalator and elevators.

The first level continues the high-energy feel of a fast-food restaurant, where people can meet, get their food, and move in and out quickly. Traffic flow for three hundred is achieved by the size of the building, by the side entrances, and by having enough space between the order area and the seating area on this level (Herman 2004; Camacho 2005). Communal tables replace small individual ones found at most McDonald's, giving the space the feel of an oversized kitchen where people comfortably gather to share a meal with others.

The second floor is more low-keyed, offering a place to have quiet conversation among friends, to make use of wireless access and virtually connect, or to unwind and take in the view of the garden or the streetlife by way of the floor-to-ceiling glass windows. Amber-toned lighting, the spatial arrangement of seating, and the comfortable furniture help achieve the relaxed feel of a living room, or more accurately, living rooms. The architect divided the huge space into

smaller "rooms," which are positioned along the perimeter. Each "room" is furnished with black-leather-like Barcelona chairs and couches and glass coffee tables, made famous by their designer Mies van der Rohe. The main eating space offers booths as well as stand-alone tables seating from two to four people. Seating for singles or small groups continues along the perimeter behind another service area, which offers lighter fare such as coffee, tea, bottled water, and pastries. This region overlooks the roof garden and a view of downtown Chicago. The walls of the back area display some of the rock and roll memorabilia that was the hallmark of the original restaurant. The larger portion (which includes a 1967 Corvette, a life-size Marilyn Monroe poster, a Gibson guitar, and many photos and records) is now housed in a stand-alone enclosed space between the main building and the parking lot. The old-and-new restaurant was intended to be more than a place to eat, and this is why the decision was made to keep the memorabilia.

Sociologist George Ritzer has written a great deal about the McDonaldization of society, referring to structures and processes whose outcomes favor hyperrationality and dedifferentiation (Ritzer 1992). While this is accurate in many cases, this McDonald's and the McCafé on North Wabash exemplify designs that strive to have the opposite effect. There is a blurring of fast-food dining and what is referred to as casual dining in more traditional restaurants. One venue is taking a cue from the other, making it more difficult to pigeonhole either format. These overlaps may raise the standards of and expectations for all venues in terms of food, service, and design. Most important, who we might expect to patronize or even own the restaurant is blurred and expanded. The 600 North Clark McDonald's is owned by Marilyn Wright, a Croatian immigrant. She owns

49—Rock 'N Roll McDonald's at 600 N. Clark, August 2004

nine other stores. Immigrants and women can move up the ladder, by way of fast-food or more traditional restaurants. This McDonald's is meant to serve as an icon for the future of the corporation and the city. In this capacity it could well be revealing itself to be an archetype for building within the asymmetrical realignment of high and popular cultures, of spaces of place and spaces of flows, of dominant and nondominant cultures.

Serving Up the City to the World—The Highs and Lows of the Service Sector

Beyond merely exemplifying another form of retail, restaurants constitute a subset of the largest-growing sector for jobs in global cities: service. Chicago's CBD has prospered from the continued growth of business service industries that began in the 1980s. An intense concentration of specialized legal, management consulting, accounting, communication, business education, meeting, travel, and other services has bolstered Chicago's position as the commercial capital of the midcontinent, at a time when other midwestern cities face a disadvantage in their industry mix, which remains concentrated in production manufacturing.

Professionals in this labor pool often command high earnings and constitute the city's new gentry. Yet, while the numbers of jobs increase, opportunities for upward mobility within the service sector are decreasing. Hospitality and retail intersect with Chicago's second-largest source of income, tourism, as well as with businesses that cater to the city's new gentry, so we might expect to see workers climbing the ladder. Marilyn Wright is a case in point. Yet these jobs typically do not offer much upward mobility, and many workers find themselves trapped at the lower end of an income spectrum that is exhibiting an ever wider gap between high and low. If we look at who comprises this segment of the labor force, we find a high proportion of women, immigrants, and younger workers. So, while opportunities for these groups need to be nurtured and expanded, and achievements noted, workers at the lower rungs need to be valorized for the essential work they perform *at that level*. Their labor is vital in both the informal and formal sectors of the economy. They are part of the global economy, and their cultures are essential components of global cities.

Yet despite their significant contributions, these workers are granted only marginal status. The economic boom for some often comes at the expense of the disadvantaged many. This is not a new development in the history of Chicago. A workforce comprised largely of new immigrants built the canals, laid the rails, and labored in factories. Many of the craftsmen arriving in the late 1880s found their skills made obsolete by mass production and mechanization. Low wages, oppressive factory conditions, and economic downturns put thousands out of work and gave rise to two watershed events in labor history—the Haymarket Riot in 1886 and the Pullman Strike in 1894. These two events remain pivotal moments around which the labor movement still rallies (Schnell 2002). The demand for service workers had been declining since the 1950s, but when the service sector began to boom in the 1980s, minorities and immigrants again filled the workers' ranks (Sassen 2001b, 9).

In comparison to other midwestern cities, Chicago continues to receive a large influx of immigrants (Krontoft, McMillen, and Testa 2001). Census data for the year 2000 show that 21.7 percent of Chicago residents were foreign-born, up from 16.9 percent in 1990. Inside the command centers, or traditional CBDs as we envision them, there are in fact multiple areas and cultures, which offer the city many resources. Retail and other businesses in the center, as Sears on State Street is doing, could make nondominant populations more visible and viable, both as workers and as consumers. Restaurants too are responding to the heterogeneity of the population by reflecting these differences in their menus and in the design of their architectural space. The "center" or "dominant" culture can encompass only part of the city. Peripheral areas, particularly many of the immigrant communities, house the rest.

The peripheries hold opportunities for nurturing business and retail in ways that complement the Central Area. Marginal areas can be as vital as the center, yet they are not in competition with it. By catering to locals, the businesses are able to focus on what and whom they know best. Success in business is about numbers and location. Today, inside and around the corporate command centers of Chicago, immigrants and other marginal groups are still being undervalued, despite their work that makes possible the city's participation in the global economy. It is important to remember that, as Sassen explains: "Globalization is a process that involves multiple economies and work cultures. . . . It is interesting to note again how the dominant economic narrative argues that place no longer matters, that firms can be located anywhere thanks to telematics, that major industries are information-based and hence not place-bound. This line of argument devalues cities [and much of the invisible workforce] at a time when they are major sites for the new cultural politics" (Sassen 2000, 143–44).

But success in business is also about service, both the service providers and their products. Developing the local, marginal areas would give residents venues to work and shop. Proximity to the center encourages members of the dominant culture to come and experience something unparalleled thus spreading business and retail beyond one area and facilitating fluid movement into and out of the traditional center. Rather than envisioning the Central Area as a hub in the traditional sense, Chicago can become a network of hubs for its diverse residents and visitors.

Therefore, Chicago can become a regional Main Street by drawing from and supporting its nondominant cultures in local businesses and by offering greater opportunities to people and places that previously would not have been considered. The renovation of State Street serves as prototype for this vision. Rather than becoming a generic version of "Main Street," State Street features its own local identity. Diversity and distinctiveness are a large part of what constitutes the city's assets and its potential. As a global Main Street, Chicago should reflect all the communities that shape it. At the same time, Main Street needs to intersect with as many streets—both real and virtual—as possible. By acting as a nexus for all the other paths and groups that come and go to and from it, "Main Street" achieves dynamism and inclusion. This is the Main Street that accommodates the landscape of the twenty-first century.

Chicago has also extended the idea of Main Street through "exportation" of local businesses. *One-off* is a term that refers to venues that are offshoots or spin-offs of the original but not clones or replications. These shops and restaurants adapt the design, service, or menu to their individual sites, yet they still offer the flavor of the original. One-offs are especially worthy of note for the role they play in accommodating local and global users in the city's two airports.

Pegasus on the Fly and the Berghoff Cafe O'Hare are but two of the many eating spinoffs found at Midway and O'Hare airports, respectively. Airports are in many ways becoming cities within cities, so that efforts to reproduce features that give them the feel of a "local" neighborhood make sense. Integrating such venues in airports, train stations, and the like is a growing and successful trend. Venues that must reflect increased hypermobility and hyperconnectivity also need to find ways to accommodate human speed and scale. In this case, restaurants help slow the pace, create comfortable spaces, and provide relief from many of the mundane, albeit necessary, activities of modern life. Because airports themselves are both mundane and vital to the city, planning their future as "thoroughfares" has become a major focus in envisioning Chicago as a transportation hub.

MULTIMODAL TRANSPORTATION HUB

The Central Area must strengthen its position as a transportation hub. The Center of the Chicago Metropolis, the Central Area currently houses 40 percent of the region's office market. To remain an economically competitive business location, it must be accessible and connected. (CAP, 1)

According to historian David Brodherson: "the claim was made in 1927 that 'all airplanes lead to Chicago.' From the early 1920s the airport, much like the skyscraper became important to Chicago as an expression of progressive government and commerce, urban pride and competition. In 1924 Charles H. Wacker declared that airfields were 'one of the first necessities toward the development of this city as a center of the aircraft industry'" (Brodherson 1993, 73). These "declarations" take on greater urgency today. As the city moves to reposition itself in the global marketplace, it also finds itself needing to redefine itself nationally and regionally. Both of Chicago's airports (O'Hare and Midway) are in the process of massive reconfiguration. Because their plans and designs respond to users and those affected by changes on the ground, the emphasis they put on local and global issues differ. Whereas Midway's renovation plans emphasize localism, ongoing plans and developments for O'Hare reflect its necessary global thrust. Together these airports are meeting the dual needs of the city and, in the process, are reshaping it.

Midway Airport Renovation (2001–2004)

Physically occupying just one square mile, Midway has a history that stretches back to the beginnings of commercial aviation. Dedicated in 1927 as Chicago Municipal Airport, it was in its early years the world's busiest airport. Renamed

Midway in 1949 after the World War II naval battle in which planes played a decisive role, it was the leading airport between the coasts until the early 1960s, when air travel exploded and O'Hare, twenty miles to the north, and other new airports were built. The importance of Midway declined over the course of the next two decades. By the early 1980s, it was almost abandoned. But then, suddenly, it started to come back to life as a hub for value-priced airlines like Southwest Airlines and American Trans Air (ATA). The terminal, dating back to 1947, was originally designed to accommodate 3 million passengers a year. Midway's recovery has been astounding: in 2004 alone, the airport served 18.5 million passengers.

The Midway Airport Terminal Development Program was officially completed in June 2004. The $927 million project, funded by federal transportation grants, airport-generated revenue, and passenger facility charges, includes a new terminal, more service area for ticketing and baggage claim, larger gates, and new concourses, as well as new shops and restaurants, and a new parking garage. The improvements aim both to increase capacity and to ease the congestion that has been a growing problem in recent years.

The most noticeable change at Midway, however, is the new 678,000-square-foot terminal building, which opened on March 7, 2001. With the airline ticket counters and baggage claims on two different levels, travelers can more comfortably arrive and depart. According to aviation commissioner Thomas Walker: "[It] offers greater efficiency for the airlines and provides the conveniences and services travelers expect from the nation's premier point-to-point airport" (Midway Airport 2002b, 1). My own observations at the new facility in July 2001 serve as an example of one traveler's reaction based on use "before" and "after" the renovation:

Arrived in the new Midway terminal. The building is airy, light, and clean. The entire place was spotless and the workers were fervent about keeping it that way. The building for the most part is white with lots of skylights which on a sunny day like this was great. It really reinforced the sense that a terminal could house planes but also make the passenger feel important. The light and spaciousness made the terminal feel more like a bridge than an enclosed or fixed place. The new baggage claim area was also bright and efficient. Signage and new conveyors are excellent. When the luggage came out of a long shiny stainless steel overarching conveyor, it *gently* slid down the rotating portion. It was set up so that the baggage, even large, irregular types would not fall or stop the flow. From anywhere around, there was easy and ample pick up space. The height of the baggage claim also cut down on excessive lifting in order to get the baggage off. Exiting the airport from this area to mass transit, cab stands, or parking was easy. More renovation is going on, but the improvement from my previous visit was astounding. It was like coming out of the darkness and into the light. (Satler journal entry, July 6, 2001)

As more people use air travel to commute and as more of their time is spent waiting in terminals, airports achieve (or can achieve) new meaning. To put it another way, airports can become venues that open more than airways to the people who pass through them; they can offer a bit of the city in which they are located. The new and improved Midway terminal makes inroads toward this redefinition. It has merged aesthetic grace with thoughtful, efficient design, and both are geared toward the needs of the users. This is the Chicago way.

The city is also hoping that a revived Midway will act as a catalyst for new development on Chicago's southwest side, a depressed residential and industrial area that has largely missed out on the economic boom of the last decade. Aviation commissioner Thomas Walker believes: "in tripling the size of the airport and adding a lot of new services and amenities, the new facility will have a significant effect on the surrounding community" (Midway Airport 2002b, 1).

Before the expansion, the facility contributed $2.5 billion annually to the local economy and provided fifty thousand jobs, both on- and off-site. After the expansion, those figures are to rise to $7 billion annually and ninety thousand jobs (City of Chicago 2004a). Midway offers potential for the creation of ancillary services such as hotels, restaurants, and meeting spaces for businesses. To encourage new development in the surrounding area, the city established six districts along Cicero Avenue and other TIF-eligible streets. The first beneficiary of the program was ATA, which announced that it would build a training center for pilots and other personnel and participate in the construction of a one-hundred-room hotel on ten acres of land just north of Midway on Archer Avenue. ATA's recent declaration of Chapter 11 has altered some plans and put others on hold. But, as of early 2005, the airline has stated that Chicago is one of the hubs it intends to keep.

On Cicero Avenue, the area's main commercial artery, the city recently completed an extensive streetscape renovation on the blocks that stretch from the Stevenson Expressway to Midway. The project installed islands and planters down the middle of the thoroughfare in an effort to make it more attractive to retailers. The first new business to move to the formerly blighted strip is a seventeen-hundred-square-foot drive-through Starbucks Coffee at the southeast corner of Cicero and Forty-Seventh Street. The restaurant is one of two Starbucks in the Chicago area co-owned by the Johnson Development Corporation, a division of Magic Johnson Enterprises (Sharoff 2001). Starbucks's and ATA's participation in the project may serve as the green light for other businesses to follow, in much the way Toys R Us did on State Street. As part of Mayor Daley's vision for a transformed southwest sector of the city, retailers are being lured into the airport and neighboring area. There is, of course, the possibility that chain stores, as opposed to small local enterprises, might take over. Cicero Avenue, like State Street, struggles for the delicate, precarious balance between recruiting retail and maintaining community identity.

Gestures of balancing can also be found in the design of the new terminal. Because the facility straddles Cicero Avenue, it was designed as two buildings, which total just under a million square feet. They are connected by a covered pedestrian bridge. The new check-in and ticketing areas are on the east side of the street; a food court and two new gate concourses are on the west side. The renovation allowed Midway to expand from twenty-eight gates to forty-one. The location of the airport influenced its internal and external design elements. Steven Reiss, one of the principals of HNTB Architects and Engineers and the chief architect of the Midway terminal facility, noted: "Because . . . you can see downtown even on a foggy day, we thought it was important for Midway to be an architectural extension of the city. The main materials are brick, painted steel and glass and the colors are a little warmer than typical for an airport terminal" (Sharoff 2001).

Additional efforts to integrate the terminal with the city and the community in which it resides can be found within the terminal itself (see Plate 24). One is the choice of concessionaires. Of the ten restaurants in the food court, nine are branches of local establishments, including Harry Caray's, Gold Coast Dogs, Manny's, and Potbelly Sandwich Works. According to the Department of Aviation (DOA) deputy commissioner for concessions, Eric Griggs, the idea was to "show off the best of Chicago." In return, Midway offers its concessionaires a large market. Sales in 2000 reached nearly $17 million; Griggs expects that figure to more than double in the future (Griggs, in Sharoff 2001). Another local gesture finds form in the airport's artwork, which features creations of Chicago artists. One is *Rara Avis,* created by Ralph Helmick. From a distance, viewers see an image of Illinois's state bird, the cardinal. But as they walk closer to it, they realize the sculpture is actually composed of twenty-five hundred small metal planes, linking natural and manmade flight.

These retailers and artists add the local layer to the worldwide, the LAN superimposed upon the WAN. Every airport must be a WAN. But an airport can choose also to become a LAN, in order to distinguish itself and create a distinct identity. This is no different an aspect from any other component of a community, which must—like each human being—also balance individual and social components in forming its persona.

O'Hare Airport's Modernization Plans (1981–1995, 2001)

As Mayor Daley declared in his 2002 State of the City Address: "Over the next twelve years, world trade is expected to grow two to three times faster than the world's gross domestic product. As a result, transportation—an area in which Chicago excels—will be one of the fastest-growing segments of the world economy. . . . O'Hare Airport is absolutely vital to Chicago's continued growth as an international center and as the economic engine of our region's economy" (Office of the Mayor 2002a). The O'Hare Modernization Program (OMP) is the second comprehensive expansion and reconfiguration plan that O'Hare will have undergone since it opened in 1963. Both plans faced years of debate, false starts, and opposition. Both plans not only reflect the need to accommodate new types of air travel and increasing numbers of air travelers but also challenge engineers, planners, and architects to accommodate residents in the nearby areas, with sensitivity toward the environment as well. Primarily, both plans are designed to reconfigure O'Hare so that it will maintain its own and Chicago's position as the nation's premier international gateway.

O'Hare is currently the country's busiest airport, in terms of numbers of planes arriving and departing daily. The airport already generates 450,000 jobs and $38 billion in economic activity for the Chicago region and the state of Illinois. The city estimates that modernization of the airport will create 195,000 more jobs and another $18 billion in economic activity (O'Hare 2004).

In 1981, Chicago's DOA initiated the first plan, which was completed in 1995 at a cost of $2 billion. The master plan for rejuvenation and expansion was drawn up by a team composed of the architectural firm Murphy/Jahn, along with Schal Associates and the engineering company Environdyne Engineers. This plan added two new terminals, new roadways, a new rapid-transit station, and a 240-acre cargo area. Murphy/Jahn, Inc. (formerly Naess and Murphy, then C. F. Murphy & Associates) designed the United Terminal and the peripheral rapid transit station connecting to it. Perkins and Will designed the International Terminal and the internal transit system, the so-called "people mover" linking the airport city together.

The second reconfiguration plan, the OMP, signed into law by Governor Blagojevich on August 6, 2003, will reconfigure O'Hare's current intersecting-airfield layout into a more modern, parallel configuration at an estimated cost of $7.25 billion. This will allow the airport to reduce weather-related delays by 95 percent and overall delays by 79 percent. The OMP will also bring a new western terminal facility, with more airline gates and parking, connected to O'Hare's main terminal core by an automated people-mover system (O'Hare 2004; Newbart and Sweet 2005).

O'Hare's existing airfield has seven runways, all but one of which intersect. The first step will be to build and open the far north runway, allowing the airport to accommodate three arrival streams instead of the two it now handles. The second phase will involve the creation of a western terminal facility. The first step here will be to extend an existing runway, and to open a new runway (and close an existing runway) on the western side in order to provide additional runway length, airfield capacity, and operational flexibility. The final step will extend another existing runway, build and open two new parallel runways, and close two existing ones on the western side. It may also involve construction of additional gate facilities in the west terminal area and the airport's existing core. It will also enable the development of new roadways at the west side of the terminal (City of Chicago 2004e). The OMP must acquire 433 acres from the districts in Chicago, Des Plaines, Elk Grove Village, and the Village of Bensenville through the O'Hare Land Acquisition Program. The plan, along with a separate environmental impact statement, was reviewed and on September 29, 2005, approved by the Federal Aviation Administration (FAA). Within hours, opponents sought and were granted a temporary stay by a federal court (Newbart and Sweet 2005; Konkol and Spielman 2005).

Critics of the plan point to the demolition of industrial parks, the noise and environmental damage in neighboring communities, and the difficulty of securing true fair market value for homes and businesses. Some also claim that the "hub" system more generally is monopolistic (Evans 2002, 5; Tita 2002, 4, 27; Associated Press 2002, A9). In response to this last criticism, a report was issued and a congressional hearing held on June 14, 2002, to look into accusations that the [then] seven major airlines were conspiring to divide up the market into geographic areas controlled by hubs. O'Hare (where 80 percent of all flights are controlled by United and American airlines) was used as an example of the "monopoly" control the airlines can hold over their hub cities. Representatives Henry Hyde and Jesse Jackson Jr. asked the Justice Department to investigate. The primary supporters of the anti-expansion movement are the Suburban O'Hare Commission (SOC)—a triumvirate of mayors from Elk Grove Village, Bensenville, and Park Ridge who favor building a third Chicago-area airport in Peotone. Airlines contend that Peotone is too far from the city to attract a viable number of passengers. According to airline logic, hubs at major metropolitan airports serve as a gathering point for passengers from several cities and generate full flights. Mayor Daley asks, "If you can't expand O'Hare Field, how can you expand economic opportunities?" (Konkol and Spielman 2005). Perhaps the real question is "The expansion of opportunities for whom?" The debate, like the plan, continues to unfold.

Considering the role of airports in recent decades, Brodherson pointedly noted: "City planners and politicians have proudly replaced housing projects and highways with airports as the latest form of urban renewal" (Brodherson 1993, 95). The current plan for O'Hare seems to have countered this trend, thanks in part to new users and in part to the changing conception of airports. Contrary to Brodherson's belief that airports are places through which people go rather than to which people go, it seems that airports in some ways are indeed becoming spaces of place. This is the case especially for the transnational businesspeople but also for more of the population flying on a regular basis.

It is significant that the plans for O'Hare and Midway (one an international airport and the other a point-to-point) both use the term *premier airport*. It seems clear that, in its attempt to secure a prominent role in the global market, the city recognizes that while information can be transported virtually, the need to move people and goods must continue to factor into plans and design for facilities and infrastructure. Today's airports, while acting as hubs, do not conform to traditional notions of the term in either role or appearance. Aside from increased volume and speed, they are being designed as social gathering places for the growing cadre of new city users.

Both airports are also characterized as extensions of the local community. As Brodherson noted: "O'Hare and Midway grew to be cities within cities instead of static movements of architecture" (Brodherson 1993, 73). As such, in addition to affording transportation, they can extend the notion of circulation to include the diversity of cultures found in Chicago, within their facilities. True mobility would foster such a definition for airports. But airports also bear the responsibility of accommodating the needs and concerns of those living close by and of the environment more generally. A city cannot be entirely virtual. Neither can any of its components. As airports take on their new roles as a city's front door and living room in addition to being a circulation hub, they face the same identity crisis the city does, in trying to achieve a dual persona. Concentrating command centers while dispersing production sites, while seemingly paradoxical, seems an essential trait of dual cities and their components. This duality is found on the ground as well as in the air.

The ability to connect and circulate goods and people remains among the city of Chicago's highest priorities. Because decisions dealing with transportation must include both local and global parameters, efforts are increasingly geared toward making Chicago a multimodal city. Among the many projects underway to rework the city's thoroughfares for automobiles and mass transit, there are two that reflect the city's efforts to rework the automobile into the old and new visions of Chicago. One project is a local gesture in form and function; the other project adapts an "import" to fit local needs and aesthetics.

Revive Wacker, Phases B and C (2002+)

A street running in all directions (north, south, east, and west), Wacker Drive was designed as "a distributive artery for seven major north/south streets and nine east/west streets" (City of Chicago 2002). Its renovation was physically and temporally divided into three sections: Section A, from Franklin Street to State

Street; Section B, from Randolph Street to Franklin Street; and Section C, from State Street to Michigan Avenue. Renovation of Section A was completed in November 2002.

Watching the renovation process during my visits to the city, I marveled at the engineering and design of Wacker Drive and the massive amount of work required for its restoration and upgrading. The project went forward through Chicago winters and summers. Local office workers and people passing the riverfront on their way to other places would pause to watch. At times, passing from the north end to the south end required major detours. Rather than become annoyed, however, people seemed to notice what they had taken for granted for so long: how vital and yet how unassuming this pathway is for the interconnectivity of the city. As of August 2004, much of the main work has been completed on the remaining sections, while finishing touches continue, including a memorial to Chicago's Vietnam veterans.

London-Style Taxis

On Wacker Drive, State Street, and Michigan Avenue, one will notice black, retro-looking cabs. In an effort to revive its lagging business, Yellow Cab, the city's largest cab company, proposed to introduce these London-style taxis and sought the mayor's permission to place "wrap advertising" on the fenders and doors to finance the forty-thousand-dollar vehicles. Yellow Cab also proposed to install in every one of its cabs a twelve-inch interactive screen, which would be subsidized by advertising on Web sites. The screen, embedded in the safety shield that separates driver from passenger, would feature information about hotels, restaurants, theaters, and museums as well as updates on the stock market and news (Spielman 2002c, 2003b).

The city has responded favorably to this proposal, although it raised issues regarding cab licensing and advertising. According to Jerry Roper, president of Chicago's Chamber of Commerce: "It positions Chicago as a futuristic place that introduces new services and innovations. This is exactly what a city that attracts as many international and domestic tourists as we do needs" (Spielman 2002c). The London-style taxis made their debut in the city in 2003, making Chicago one of a growing number of U.S. cities—including Boston, Las Vegas, and several cities in California—offering such transportation (Spielman 2003b).

The idea of blending old and new technology and style seems consistent with other projects Chicago has initiated in order to redefine itself as a dual city. The taxi is a nice vehicle for melding past with present, space of place with space of flows, on multiple levels. It forges communication with transportation, thus interweaving both meanings of circulation. Furthermore, it serves local users while it also serves and perhaps even draws in tourists. The London-style cab imbues this most mid-American city with a layer of international flavor. Even as this new cab reaches beyond the Loop for inspiration and energy, however, it remains a decidedly local gesture. Chicago has already positioned itself as a city ready, willing, and always more able to accommodate transnational users. London-style taxis are a gesture toward that end.

Millennium Park Bike Station—239 East Randolph Street

If the city has its way, more bicycles will be sharing the roadways with cabs, cars, and buses as a viable commuting option. As unlikely as it might sound, there are indications that this goal may be met. In 2000, the DOT prepared *The Bike 2010 Plan.* This plan expands on *The Bike 2000 Plan,* prepared by the Bicycle Advisory Council in 1992, which offered twenty-nine recommendations to encourage bicycling. Both bike plans complement the CAP's efforts to expand bicycle lanes and to improve bicycle transit access and use, parking, and safety for the city's ninety miles of bikeways.

One sign that these efforts are coming to fruition is the Millennium Park Bike Station located in the fifth and sixth floors of the northeast section of the Millennium Park Garage (see Figure 51). The location connects the bicycle station and its users to the pathways of the new Central Area. And with its proximity to the Randolph Street Metra Station and the McCormick Place Busway, the bicycle station advances the goal of making Chicago multimodal. The bike station was initially intended to be underground. However, the architects decided it should have "a more attractive and official presence so the people would know about it" (Steele, in Livingston 2005). The above-ground portion of the station features a

51—Bike station at
Millennium Park on Randolph Street, August 2005

glass curtain wall and an interior atrium that offer cyclists a welcoming entry, along the lines of Calatrava's view that garages need not be dark and unattractive; rather, they can make important first impressions. Muller and Muller designed the atrium's skin to maximize energy efficiency and natural ventilation. The vertical surface features "a series of stainless steel cables on which plantings will eventually grow and climb to create more shielding" (Steele, in Livingston 2005).

The feeling of light and airiness is continued inside. The station offers three hundred free parking spaces on two levels. Cyclists pay one dollar a day for use of locker rooms and showers (with discounted monthly or yearly passes available). Other amenities in the station include on-site bicycle repair, bicycle rentals, a shop where riders can purchase bicycle-related items, and a café offering healthy food and beverages. The Chicago Police patrol unit stationed in the building provides all users with a sense of security for the entire garage. Though the facility caters to bicyclists, runners and in-line skaters are also welcome.

In keeping with the city's commitment to becoming more environmentally responsive, the station features 120 solar panels that generate a portion of the facility's needed electricity. Funding for the project came from the Federal Congestion Mitigation Air Quality program. This program, which is jointly administered by the U.S. DOT's Federal Highway Administration and the Federal Transit Administration, under the TEA-21 Act, is designated for projects to ease traffic and congestion and improve air quality in Chicago (biketraffic.org 2004; Uhlir 2002; City of Chicago 2004c).

At the station's opening, Mayor Daley noted that "[this] is yet another step toward our goal of making Chicago one of the most bike-friendly cities in the country" (City of Chicago 2004d). According to David Steele, senior designer for the station: "It actually has become somewhat of a landmark for bikers in Chicago" (Steele, in Livingston 2005). Since its opening, use of the station has been at or near capacity and there is a wait list for lockers. This station is the first to be built in Chicago, the first of its kind in the Midwest, and one of only a handful in the nation's larger cities. But judging from its success, indications are that it will soon be joined by other stations in the city. The lakefront trail runs through the park and almost the entire length of the city, making what some may have viewed as an unlikely transportation option more and more of a viable option for Chicago residents and commuters . . . and tourists.

TOURISM

As Chicago's Downtown, the Central Area must continue to set the vibrant standard for the rest of the city, offering innovation and excitement in its diverse districts and great neighborhoods. It must create even more reasons to visit. (CAP, 1)

Tourism (and tourists), while vital and welcome in many respects, can overshadow other needs and users of the city. This balancing act must continue if the city—a living organism—aims to become a heteropolis. It is not an either/or choice, but an all/and programmatic continuum that the city must continuously reexamine and readjust. Navy Pier, Millennium Park, the new Theater District, newly built hotels, and planned renovations for O'Hare Airport and the Mc-Cormick Convention Center can be viewed as evidence of the city's increasing emphasis on tourists. But efforts have been made to provide for a more inclusive range of users. One site that reflects interest in local identity and that is, in many ways, a representation of community is the newly renovated Soldier Field Stadium.

Architects, Holabird and Root (1925) and Wood + Zapata (renovation, 2003)

Soldier Field

Sports are a pervasive feature of everyday urban life. Most metropolitan newspapers devote upward of 20 percent of each day's edition to sports. In many cities, there are stations devoted to sports talk shows, which attract thousands of listeners, and workers devote a great deal of "water cooler" conversation to local teams and events. Team loyalty gives the large, often anonymous, urban environment a small-town feel. Sports afford a sense of identity for a city's inhabitants and, for newcomers, offer entry into the community of their adopted home. Sports are also big business for a city, and Chicago is a big sports city. The renovation of Soldier Field—or more correctly the adaptive reuse of this landmarked structure—says much about the city and its residents.

Dedicated as a memorial to those killed in World War I, the original stadium was designed by Holabird and Root as part of the Chicago Beautiful program and was intended primarily for track and field events. It now hosts the city's football team. The concrete structure's Doric style reflects other venues along the Lakefront, including the Field Museum of Natural History (1919), the John G. Shedd Aquarium (1929), and the Max Adler Planetarium (1930). The stadium underwent a number of renovations to correct sight lines and to accommodate larger numbers of people. The latest renovation took place in 2002–2003 (see Figure 52). The stadium's new form is respectful and reflective of the city and its residents. But it does not recede into the rest of the cityscape. It is straightforward, dynamic, and innovative.

Instead of relegating sports venues to suburban areas accessible only by car as so many other cities are doing, Chicago made the choice to keep sports within the city. At the same time, instead of tearing down the old stadium, Chicago also decided to preserve the perimeter of the old stadium and literally to place the new stadium inside it. The approach is very similar to what was done with buildings on State Street, which were retrofitted with technology and amenities befitting needs and desires of modern workplaces. In a way, Soldier Field is the new workplace for its players, and the new play space for spectators.

Essentially, Wood + Zapata inserted "a high-rimmed soup bowl (the new arena) atop a dinner plate (the existing stadium)—creating a nesting composite, leaving the two components separate and distinct, but enriched by association" (Giovannini 2004, 116). The juxtaposition of symmetrical space with asymmetrical space, emphasized to meet functional needs, creates a sense of new energy and dynamism. "For the gap between the new and existing footprints, the architects carefully calibrated distances and details so that the outside of their modern shell and the inside of the old one face each other and define the piazzas in between, with mobile food and drink concessions" (Giovannini 2004, 120). People

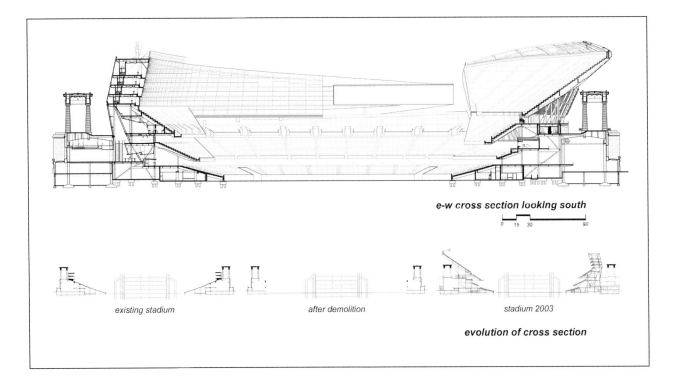

e-w cross section looking south

0   15   30   90

existing stadium   after demolition   stadium 2003

evolution of cross section

enter the stadium through the original, restored facade, then pass through the transitional space formed by the confluence of the two forms before entering the wide, open bowl.

The use of extreme cantilevering exemplified by the trusses that serve as armatures for the two LED scoreboards and by sharply angled steel columns beneath the bleachers makes the composition possible and dynamic. Aesthetically, these gestures create a strong sense of verticality, which balances the large horizontal span created by the field. Functionally, cantilevering offers maximum seating for a stadium that is shorter than the original.

This seating configuration is made possible by deep cuts in the structure at the end zones, affording spectators stunning views of the city's downtown skyline. Architectural critic Herbert Muschamp notes: "As a result there is extreme intimacy: with the field, the city and Chicago's heroic tradition of leadership in the building arts" (Muschamp 2003). Perhaps Wood + Zapata drew inspiration from Frank Lloyd Wright, who wrote: "Instead of post and beam construction . . . you have a new sense of building construction by way of the cantilever and continuity. In this simple change of thought lies the essential of the architectural change from box to free plan and the new reality that is *space* instead of matter" (Wright 1960, 285).

During my visits to Chicago, I passed Soldier Field every day while traveling by bus to the Loop. Admittedly, I was sad to see it gutted during the winter of 2002. Subsequent visits brought curiosity and anticipation about how the construction would take form, whether it would be completed in time for the 2003 season, and how it would fit into this site and the larger cityscape. Chicagoans too seemed anxious. The *Chicago Sun-Times* offered regular photo updates and progress reports online. Chicago architect Stanley Tigerman noted that, "during construction, when the supporting structure was exposed, it had a familiar

52—Soldier Field, 2004.

Wood + Zapata, Inc.

expressionism commensurate with Chicago's true architectural tradition, and reflected in both the first and second Chicago Schools of Architecture" (Tigerman 2004, 118). My fellow bus passengers were less philosophical but, for the most part, as passionate about the stadium as they were about the game itself. As the bus passed the site, their facial expressions and remarks ranged from dejection to inquisitiveness to downright anger; rarely was there ambivalence. Most of the time, the stadium became a topic of conversation, bringing strangers together for a little while. Such is the nature of urban life.

The renovation became the object of all the speculation, emotion, and expectation that normally center on the games themselves, until the stadium opened in September 2003. But even then debate did not really stop. The "new" addition to the stadium evoked controversy over cost ($385 million, now the second-largest expenditure on a project after Millennium Park), the disruption of the landmark building, and the look of the final design. But these debates took a secondary place to the games played on the field, which is exactly what should have happened. A venue for activity should enhance and energize but not overshadow. The new stadium represents asymmetry at its best—in what takes front stage and in how parts align. It also represents innovation at its best. Muschamp states: "[Soldier Field] should be a model for cities that are looking toward architecture to strengthen their identities as contemporary cultural centers" (Muschamp 2003). He echoes Park, who believed: "Cities, and particularly the great metropolitan cities of modern times, so far as they can be regarded as the product of art and design . . . are with all their complexities and artificialities, man's most imposing creation, the most prodigious of human artifacts" (Park 1974, 2:133). Soldier Field is a catalyst for architectural change. It is also a reflection of the changing life of the postmodern city. Hopefully it will continue to inspire debate, inside and out.

RECENTERED—BLOCK 37 (108 NORTH STATE STREET)

The *Economic Base . . . Report* states: "The Central Area can position itself to be more competitive and attractive with improved transportation and enhanced cultural, recreational, retail, and educational facilities" (City of Chicago DPD 2001, 81). The place where this potential may be playing itself out most conspicuously is Block 37, renamed 108 North State Street, in the heart of the Loop and very close to where the city originated (see Figures 53 and 54). Block 37 stands at a juncture in terms of the direction it will take. The latest plans call upon all four of the CAP's directives.

The devolution of Block 37 dates back to Mayor Richard J. Daley's tenure. The current chapter in the story begins in 1983, when Block 37 was first proposed for development under Mayor Harold Washington. The mayor selected a team of three high-profile companies, including JMB and Metropolitan Structures, which joined to become FJV Venture to serve as the project developer. In 1989, under Mayor Richard M. Daley's direction, the city cleared the block of its former structures—office buildings, a grocery store, and two movie theaters—to make way for a 2.2-million-square-foot office and retail project. Then plan after

53—*above*—Block 37,
January 2005

54—*left*—Block 37, July 2001

plan was discussed forever, while the site remained vacant. In 2001, the city re-purchased Block 37 from FJV and moved to secure a "master developer" in order to put together a mixed-use plan for Block 37. In early 2002, the city issued a re-quest for proposals (RFP), as it was called. The Virginia-based Mills Corporation, which teamed up with Chicago-based condominium builder MCL in presenting a plan, was picked to oversee development.

The city chose Mills because officials thought retail would be a driving force be-hind the development, and Mills has extensive experience building malls both across the country and locally, in Lake County. Mills had first contacted City Hall about Block 37 in 1999, but at the time, the cost of the proposed plan seemed po-tentially to present too steep a cost for taxpayers. In the 2002 proposal, Mills touted its ability to make the block a tourist destination "indispensable by day and indescribable by night." Retail experts believed the company had left behind its "outlet mall" image by working with full-price stores and would add other attrac-tions. Most significant, Mills offered contacts with all retailers, "from expensive shops to discounters" (Washburn and Kirk 2003; Spielman and Roeder, 2003).

Following a two-day workshop in early 2002, Mayor Daley was urged to make the vacant North Loop parcel a year-round draw by incorporating everything from a jazz center, a movie theater complex, gambling venues, and a continuous Cirque du Soleil, to a transportation center with express trains to O'Hare Airport. British-based department store Harrod's expressed interest but later backed out.

In 2004 WBBM–Channel 2 (or CBS2) agreed to move their headquarters to the site and build a showcase media center for their TV station and radio outlets. Mills negotiated plans with a developer to build a residential tower, and again with the Chicago Transit Authority (CTA) to build a high-speed rapid rail transit station providing high-speed service to and from Chicago's O'Hare and Midway airports at the lower, pedway level. The latter, according to Tabing, "poses engi-neering challenges out the whazoo" (Tabing 2000–2005, e-mails August 29, 2002, and June 4, 2004 [quote]). And in an effort to disconnect Block 37 from its old negative image, the site was "officially" renamed 108 North State Street.

Plans for 108 North State continue to solidify. In April 2005, Ralph Johnson of Perkins and Will Architects unveiled plans for the site featuring approximately 400,000 sf of office space, a 200–300-room hotel, and a 200–300-unit residential tower (with greenspace on the roof), in addition to CBS2 Chicago headquarters and broadcast facilities and the CTA transit station (GSSC materials). In May 2005, the Mills Corporation announced the acquisition of six new retail, enter-tainment, and restaurant tenants, most of which are "firsts" for Chicago (GSSC 2001–2005, e-mail May 2, 2005).

Also in May 2005, the Chicago City Council approved the redevelopment plan. Under the provisions of a city ordinance, the developer (Mills) will be re-quired to set aside 10 percent of the residential units for moderate-income resi-dents or contribute one hundred thousand dollars per unit to an affordable housing fund (Washburn 2005). Some feel the percentage should have been dou-ble that. Block 37 at 108 North State Street continues to generate debate. This is fitting for a space that seems destined to remain contested space amid plans to provide it with new life. The promotion statement for the 108 North State Street

Web site aims to foster a new image: "A world-class multi-use urban destination . . . offer[ing] a twenty-first-century shopping experience, entertainment venues, restaurants, a state-of-the-art transit station, metro style lofts and condos, a hotel and spa and commercial spaces" (www.108NorthStateStreet.com).

108 North State Street represents the confluence of all that Chicago is and is yet to become, the confluence where past and present meet. It is fitting, perhaps, that plans for this site include transportation and communications networks in addition to retail venues that accommodate both residents and tourists. Reenlisting this site as a nexus of connectivity and circulation brings the idea of what the center should be full circle. That the proposed venues utilize the rich architectural and historical legacies of the site while also taking advantage of advances in technology to stimulate, inform, and transport individuals in environmentally friendly ways confirms what Park and his cohorts, early in Chicago's development, understood as the ecology of cities and their centers. As Park explained: "Transportation and communication, tramways and telephones, newspapers and advertising, steel construction and elevators—all things . . . which tend to bring about at once a greater mobility and greater concentration of the urban populations—are factors in the ecological organization of the city" (Park 1967, 2). Today, 108 North State has added to the mix some new users and some new formulations, including virtual and environmental ones. Boundaries may have blurred, but not the awareness of the impact and opportunities resulting from the various relationships that are possible between center and peripheries.

The difficulties encountered in creating and realizing plans that address increased diversity and interdependency—beyond the center, city, or even the country—make issues involving the morphology of Block 37 more typical than atypical as the twenty-first century progresses. In these ways, Block 37 has served as contested space—a reminder that Chicago is about growth and development, but that growth, which must involve human activity and reflection, will not occur in a uniform or predictable way. Chicago would do well to adopt the cautious optimism expressed by architect Renzo Piano: "The dilemma or paradox of building is that only when you finish the structure or building do you know how close you've come to the vision" (Piano 2002).

It is perhaps fitting that, very near the site where it first sprouted, the city should now be facing the difficult enduring decisions regarding its future. It is risky to ask that the space accommodate all components of the Central Area's Plans, but risk goes with greatness and risk is part of Chicago's makeup. John Zukowsky characterizes Chicago by way of its duality and contradictory persona in the following way:

Chicago . . . has a greater responsibility to architectural history than most other American cities. . . . If anything, Chicago's traditions encourage rather than discourage land development, thereby continually challenging architects to respond or react to the city's past. Thus, a dualistic, contradictory nature has existed throughout the history of Chicago and its architecture. . . . [T]his dualism of the contradictions between the forces of history and the avant-garde is an almost schizophrenic characteristic that runs throughout Chicago's cultural condition. (Zukowsky 1993, 30)

With this duality in mind, perhaps there is another way to interpret risk and greatness here. Block 37 reminds us of another vitally important component that the city must cultivate: spaces of silence. Writer Ross Miller, in his comprehensive account of Block 37, *Here's the Deal,* notes that it "is currently a gold-plated hole in the ground, a dead and bleak vacancy at the heart of a great American city" (Miller 1996, note to the reader). He expresses the views of many. But perhaps the city can put Block 37 to a better use by encouraging human activity and engagement rather than by demanding more in the built sense; that is, by asking more of it socially. Until the McCormick Rink opened in 2001, Block 37 was the site of "Skate on State" in the late fall and winter. During the spring and summers through 2004, venues such as Gallery 37 set up residence here, offering respite and opportunities for learning about and exhibiting crafts and artwork. During one weekend in August 2004, Block 37 hosted a summer festival entitled *From the Middle East to the Midwest,* produced by Genesis at the Crossroads, a Chicago-based nonprofit ethnic arts organization. Their intention is to "utilize the arts as a vehicle for civic dialogue, and promote awareness, appreciation and celebration of cultural diversity" (letters and materials from Genesis group, 7/6/04).

The importance of public space and venues that bring more of the inside out, and bring the energy and vitality of all areas of the city back to public spaces, has been discussed but cannot be overemphasized. To do so in the middle of the Loop adds another layer of meaning and significance to the notions of centrality and city street/block. Perhaps middle can be interpreted as heartland, so that Block 37 (108 North State Street) is in this sense the city's heart(beat), in much the same way as Chicago is America's heart(beat). Maybe that is why this block has remained and perhaps should remain, symbolically if not literally, open-ended and unfinished, but far from empty.

CHECAGOU, CHICAGO, CHICAGOLAND

Another shift in frame is already in the works for the CBD and areas that surround it. In February 2005, two mainstays of the Central Area's old guard—the Greater State Street Council and the Central Michigan Avenue Association—announced a merger, creating "a new, expanded organization, with significantly more clout for promoting Chicago's central business district" (GSSC 2005). The new association, called the Chicago Loop Alliance, represents an area now referred to as the East Loop, a forty-block service area bordered by Dearborn on the west, Lake Michigan on the east, and Wacker Drive on the north. The district extends south to Congress along Wabash, State, and Dearborn, and to Roosevelt along Michigan Avenue. The intention of the merger is to draw from Greater State Street and Central Michigan Avenue in order to compete with the expanding West Loop. This realignment confirms and reinforces the analytic shift many have already taken regarding their perception of where and what the center is. Jeffrey Inaba, one of the architects retained by the CLA to promote the new area, views the East Loop as "the most dynamic area in the city . . . garner[ing] its complexity and richness from the unique blend of old and new that repeatedly reflects itself in each of its microcosms, from theaters and museums to retail and educational institutions" (GSSC 2005). One of the design concepts in a proposed plan for the East Loop involves using the EL-covered Wabash corridor in ways that make it an asset as opposed to a liability. The plan calls for upgrading lighting, offering under-the-EL events, and also landscaping *under* the EL using a hydroponic nutrient-film technique (Loop the Loop, GSSC 2005). Once again the city is poised for change, once again the city draws from its roots as it looks forward, and once again it manages to turn a problem into an asset. That is the Chicago way; that is Chicago—old and new.

Checagou

Checagou was the name given to the river (and later the city) by Native Americans, to denote a flowering wild onion that grew there. The river seemed more a marsh than a river, and the city was yet to be. While some avoided the wild onion because of its strong odor and the difficulty of digesting it, some found beauty and purpose in it. Jensen for example, noted: "Native water plants grace the margin of this river, both for a completion of the water picture and for practical reasons. They prevent erosion by wave action and keep children from

55—*right*—Wild onion—
Allium sp. Alliaceae.
© *G. D. Carr*

falling into deep water" (Jensen 1990, 84). As far as Chicago has come (or gone) from being Checagou, nothing could provide a more appropriate image for this city than this multilayered, multisensory plant.

The three sections of the city described here reference natural elements of the environment, including the flowering wild onion plant. On State Street, preserved buildings and new street fixtures honor the onion and the other vegetation endemic to the site. Overlaying these natural forms onto built features reifies and helps identify the space of place that State Street was and has become once again. Development along the riverfront is utilizing the water and its plant life as inspiration and as elements in new designs. Built forms, greenery, and flowing water have been combined and give new uses and meaning to the riverfront and to the structures alongside it. And the image Jensen depicts is returning to the site, enhanced and made more fluid by way of the riverwalk. In Millennium Park, the duality of spaces of flows and spaces of place meet, and interpretations of the flowering wild onion are apparent in each spatial type. Gehry's work offers, perhaps, a high-tech representation of this flowering plant, complete with substance above and below the surface. The Lurie Garden features many indigenous plants as well as symbolic representations of the city's transformation from marsh to urban terrain. Here, nature and construct are turned on their heads. Gardens grow over and from constructed terrain. Beneath ground-level one finds life as well, in the form of a parking garage, bicycle station, and busway, a nexus of circulation fueling the streetlife above it. The park is a composition of new and unexpected forms that reinforce and make more apparent the original line of the urban landscape.

All three sites provide a multilayered, distinctive way of connecting disparate forms and perspectives. It is the layering of different temporal and formal constructs, each with its own set of values and frames, that gives the city its richness and meaning. But Checagou as city (Chicago) is more than its original line and natural environment. It is also a composition of communities—people and their relationships with each other and with their environment.

Chicago

Beyond visual references to the city's namesake, one can find and use the organic sense of the wild onion to understand the social character of the city. "Wild" implies a lack of social ordering, the absence of the imposition of civilization upon an area or people. Not yet constrained or conforming, people and forms retain a sense of spontaneity. Park believed that "Civilization . . . [was] the result of man's effort to use the resources of his environment in order to change nature and, where possible, make it less raw, more comfortable and less difficult to endure" (Park 1974, 2:132). Architect Renzo Piano upholds this view, noting: "Architecture is about [the human side of] telling stories; it is illusion, a tale of a city" (Piano 2002). What transforms illusion into reality, or spaces into places, is to be found in the experiences people have in them. It is perhaps when civilization can engage nature, rather than silence or deny it, that the city and its people can be vitalized. Chicago is such a place.

This may, in part, explain why Chicago, now as then, finds itself as a gathering place for architects and sociologists, among others who want to push the existing limits and tell stories. Arguably, Chicago far and away has more great buildings than does any other American city. With all else that has been discussed, it may well be that this in part comes from its horizontal as well as its vertical scale. Chicago seems to always have been inextricably tied to the street and the life enacted on it. Comparing the prairie with the mountains (or the sea), Jensen notes: "Man cannot comprehend the solitude and the spiritual message of the mighty mountains, but he can understand the message that he can measure in relation to himself, something not beyond his limited mentality" (Jensen 1990, 21). For him the prairies are inhabited and therefore human. It is this inclusion of people that provides a sense of security. So the introduction of people and the recognition of human scale can enhance spaces by creating a sense of place. The same can be said for the inclusion of people and human scale in the design and planning of cities. Human scale does not limit; rather, it grounds people so they may be free to imagine and create. The feel and foundation of Chicago is the prairie, that vast but graspable horizontal vista—multisensory and open-ended. It permeates buildings, people, and their relation to one another on the grid of the streets that form communities and cities.

The dynamic between nature and construct, real and illusory, is very much apparent in the wild onion, and in cities like Chicago that sustain this sense of organicity. At first glance, an onion seems solid and concrete. Yet closer examination reveals that it is formed of many layers building upon one another. Peeling back the layers one at a time brings the realization of several paradoxes. It is the transparency of each layer that creates the quality of mass. Each layer, seemingly fragile, is pliable and resilient, made so by slender, almost invisible fibers that give it the ability to withstand changes in form when it is cut, peeled, or cooked.

In its construction, the onion builds from the inside out. But the core can only be seen if one removes its layers, which destroys the whole or at least changes its form. Unfolding the layers offers another reality. So what appear to be the whole and what appear to be the source of its strength are not. Some Chicago architects understood this and profoundly altered the way architecture developed. As Frank Lloyd Wright explained, when he moved away from post-and-beam construction, "the reality of a building no longer consisted in the walls and roof . . . but in the space within the building" (Kaufmann and Rae-burn 1960, 284). Or as Bertrand Goldberg cautioned: "Don't confuse the functional location . . . with the structural efficiency. Think of the core as being the stem of the building, but that has a certain illusory quality to it because what we are really looking at is the comparative efficiency of material used at the center or used at the exterior perimeter. An eggshell is more efficient than a tree—in the use of material and the weight of its material" (Goldberg 1992, 193). The reality is more intuitive than learned, but it can appear counterintuitive if a nonorganic stance is utilized.

The sociological parallel to this stance in architecture is exemplified in the awareness that face-to-face encounters as well as larger institutions that frame these interactions give us needed windows into understanding social order. Sociologist Edward Soja, for example, believes the most sensible stance for an urbanist discourse is one defined by "the two sides of its own contradiction." He writes, "Understanding the city must involve the micro and the macro, with neither inherently privileged, but only with the accompanying recognition that no city—indeed no lived space—is ever completely knowable no matter what perspective we take" (Soja, in Dear 2002a, 416).

Thinking in this way about the city as community, one can argue that center and periphery in and of themselves have little to do with where the strength of the community lies. It is more the case that the human institutions and relationships hold the city together much like the fibers in the layers of the onion hold the onion together. People in their actions and reactions to others and their environment are the fibers that hold the city together and give it strength, diversity, and flexibility. Order is made apparent through people's actions and interactions rather than through physical constructs. That is, the presence of this powerful unifying force that creates a sense of city or community is for the most part felt rather than seen. To use a more high-tech analogy, this is how fiber optics work in communication systems. The fibers are responsible for facilitating the most fundamental component of human interaction, the ability to communicate, in this case at very large distance, but the fibers for the most part are invisible except in outcome.

While Chicago has a center that is, in many respects, geographically defined, the city has always understood the importance of circulation and connection, now virtual in addition to real. It might be more accurate to say that Chicago is a hierarchy of these interactive layers bound by one theme: that of being a community. This means the city must shape spaces around its inhabitants in order to allow them to live and work, to connect, communicate, and circulate. Moving in and out of the center has always been a part of the theory and practice of the city's morphology. But today, this movement includes, indeed transcends, spatial and temporal boundaries with growing speed and complexity.

Chicagoland—An Unfolding Hybrid Space

Today, it might be useful and appropriate to consider Chicago as exhibiting a sense of the controlled spontaneity Oudolf describes; or as Jencks puts it, "en-formality: a calculated informality . . . is more than a style and approach to design; it is a basic attitude towards the world of living with uncertainty celebrating flux and capturing the possibilities latent with the banal" and intuitive with the the reasoned (Jencks 1993, 59).

En-formality may also be read as the undoing of traditional symmetries that opens up perspectives and options that would otherwise not be apparent or possible. "The asymmetry of power . . . means that everybody for the most part lives their lives on the outside, on the periphery. At the same time, as the sheer number of differentiating relationships suggests, there are moments when one always has some power" (Jencks 1993, 123). More and more, the frame of asymmetry is being utilized in building and planning as in the realignment of the Central Area and peripheral areas, extending well beyond city limits. Or maybe it is that we are just now able to understand and view cities in this way.

What may best work as a frame for viewing and for facilitating the city's movement in this direction is the notion of a hybrid space, an unfolding space. Instead of closing off from or blending into the dominant spaces, nondominant components contest traditional relationships and existing boundaries by using features that shift the temporal as well as the spatial flows. The cityscape is at once a product of disparate and asymmetrical parts, but also sui generis. Such a frame for the city is prompted by the name used locally: *Chicagoland*. *Chicagoland* in many ways denotes this notion of broadening the temporal and spatial sense of the city's scope. It serves as an indexical or shorthand expression for the place the city is becoming and for the analytic frame required to envision it. The term *Chicagoland* evokes the synthetic and dynamic relationship between construct and nature, between "the city" (Chicago) and "the hinterland" (outerland) depicted and anticipated by Wirth, Burgess, Park, and other sociologists early in the city's history. Chicagoland captures the literal process of movement into and out of the center but also implies the social mobility that the Chicago School associated with movement. Both connotations are integral to the understanding of the city offered by the Los Angeles School. Finally, Chicagoland reflects the hybrid of dominant and nondominant cultures and spaces, where one is named and the other is not. Their naming implies an asymmetry in terms of power and recognition, but their union invokes interdependency. This is exactly what the city's center and peripheries, the city and its ever-expanding surroundings must become and come to mean in the global landscape. As cities extend their influence further and further beyond their physical limits, they are also essentially transformed by the places and users they extend (in)to in essential

56—Pritzker Pavilion,
August 2004

ways. It is in this dynamic universe that Chicagoland is finding its place; branching out and reaching in. As seen in projects described here, there is evidence that efforts have been made and that more efforts are in the works to provide for this type of connection and realignment.

In 1985, Studs Terkel wrote, "Chicago now? It's still in the throes of being born. We haven't learned how to create cities. A city should be a place to live" (Terkel 1985, 95). In what has been a rather short span of time since he wrote this, and since new plans for Chicago have been implemented, much has been accomplished. Yet there is much more to do. As with people, cities face many challenges. But it is the challenges that provide the potential for them to grow. It is urbanist Alex Krieger's view that "The most difficult challenge facing American urbanism may not be coming up with a better way to subdivide land, but to rescue, reinvigorate, reform, resettle, learn once again to love places already made" (Krieger 1998, 75). Chicago has proven that it intends to meet this challenge as well as the many others it faces. Chicago is also showing a commitment to reconnect with nature, with *its* own nature, and to find its place and be at home in a meaningful but unfolding universe. This too is what a community is at its core. For all these reasons Chicago will keep changing and telling new stories that deepen our understanding of it as well as other cities. We can at least hope this is the case.

SELECTED BIBLIOGRAPHY

Abbott, Andrew. 1999. *Department and discipline: Chicago sociology at one hundred.* Chicago: University of Chicago Press.

Abu-Lughod, Janet L. 1999. *New York, Chicago, Los Angeles: America's global cities.* Minneapolis: University of Minnesota Press.

Algren, Nelson. 1979. *Chicago: City on the make.* 1951. Chicago: University of Chicago Press.

Anderson, Nels. 1923. *The hobo.* Chicago: University of Chicago Press.

Asgedom, Maya. 1996. The unsounded space. In *White papers, black papers,* ed. Lesley Naa Norle Lokko, 237–76. Minneapolis: University of Minnesota Press.

Associated Press. 2002. Airlines use hubs to drive up prices, reduce competition: Group's report says coalition of Chicago-area mayors is opposed to O'Hare expansion; Congressional hearing is June 14. *St. Louis Post-Dispatch,* May 22.

Baker, Catherine. 2005. E-mail, May 13.

Berger, Miles L. 1992. *They built Chicago.* Chicago: Bonus Books.

Bey, Lee. 2001a. At last, hope for Block 37. *Chicago Sun-Times,* January 21. Architecture section, 1–3.

———. 2001b. City plans to redevelop skyscraper fall through. *Chicago Sun-Times,* February 20. Metro section, p. 8.

———. 2001c. The 'city' worth saving. *Chicago Sun-Times,* January 22. Architecture, pp. 1–3.

———. 2001d. Loop site may get seventeen-story buzz cut. *Chicago Sun-Times,* February 4.

———. 2001e. Monumental new use for 2 old blocks. *Chicago Sun-Times,* February 19.

———. 2001f. Waterway has a role to play. *Chicago Sun-Times,* March 12. Metro section, p. 15.

———. 2002. The Battle for S. Michigan. *Chicago Sun-Times,* February 12.

BBB. *See* Beyer Blinder Belle.

Beyer Blinder Belle. 2001. Architects and Planner, LLP. Internal fact sheets on the Merchandise Mart renovation and retail development. August 23.

Bistry, Bob (for DeStefano + Partners). 2001. Phone interviews. December.

———. 2002. Phone interview. June 4.

Blair, Gwenda. 2003. Out of the ashes, Cinderella. *New York Times,* January 2. House and Home section, p. F1.

Blau, Judith. 1992. *The visible poor: Homelessness in the United States.* New York: Oxford University Press.

Bluestone, Daniel M. 1991. *Constructing Chicago, 1991.* New Haven: Yale University Press.

Bohlen, Celestine. 2001. Built for substance, not flash. *New York Times,* January 22. Arts section, p. E1.

Booth Hansen Associates. <boothhansen.com>.

Bouman, Mark. 1993. The best lighted city in the world: The construction of a nocturnal landscape in Chicago. In Zukowsky 1993, 33–52.

Bowermaster, David. 2001. Boeing lands in Chicago airport battle. *Seattle Times,* September 4. Business and Technology section.

Bowermaster, David, and Kyung M. Song. 2001. Boeing begins a new era: First day barely noticed in Chicago, Seattle. *Seattle Times,* September 5. Business and Technology section.

Brodherson, David. 1993. All airplanes lead to Chicago: Airport planning and design in a midwest metropolis. In Zukowsky 1993, 75–97.

Bruegmann, Robert. 1993. Schaumberg, Oak Brook, Rosemont and the recentering of the Chicago metropolitan area. In Zukowsky 1993, 159–77.

Bücher, Carl. 1901. Industrial evolution. New York: H. Holt.

Buck, Genevieve. 2001. American Invesco, April 8. <american invesco.net/developer/SunTimes_4-08-.asp>.

Bulmer, Martin. 1984. *The Chicago School of Sociology.* Chicago: University of Chicago Press.

Burawoy, Michael, et al. 1991. *Ethnography unbound: Power and resistance in the modern metropolis.* Berkeley and Los Angeles: University of California Press.

Burnham, Daniel H., and Edward H. Bennett. 1970. *Plan of Chicago of 1909.* Chicago: Commercial Club of Chicago, 1909. Reprint, New York: Da Capo Press, 1970.

Busk, Celeste. 2001. Great Street comeback. *Chicago Sun-Times,* March. Shopping Districts, p. 19.

———. 2002. It'll knock you for a loop. *Chicago Sun-Times,* September 1.

Calatrava, Santiago. 2002. Interview with Charlie Rose. Transcript no. 3209, PBS: WNET, New York City. First aired May 22.

Camacho, Frank. 2005. Phone interview. August 11.

CAP. *See* City of Chicago DPD 2000a.

Cappetti, Carla. 1993. *Writing Chicago.* New York: Columbia University Press.

Castells, Manuel. 1989. *The informational city.* Oxford: Basil Blackwell.

———. 1993. European cities, the informational society and the global economy. *Journal of Economic and Social Geography* 84, no. 4, 247–57.

Centennial Fountain. 2001. <lohan.com/inst_centennial_des.html>, accessed July 31.

CHA. *See* Chicago Housing Authority.

Chall, David. 1983–1984. Neighborhood changes in New York City during the 1970s: Are the gentry returning? *Federal Reserve Bank of New York Quarterly Bulletin*, winter, 38–48.

Chandler, Susan. 2001. A multicultural state in Sears. *Chicago Tribune*, May 20. Chicagoland, p. 1.

Chicago Housing Authority. 1999. Plan for tranformation. <thecha.org/transformationplan>. This and subsequent annual reports (CHA Moving to Work: Annual Plan for Transformation) can be found at <thecha.org/transformationplan/reports>.

———. 2002. <thecha.org/News/090102_news.html>, accessed September 1.

———. 2004. Five-year progress report. CHA Web site, accessed June 14.

———. 2005. Summary of transformation plan. <thecha.org/transformplan/plan_summary.html>, accessed May 14.

Chicago Tech Today. 2001a. <chicagotechtoday.com/chicago informationtechnologycenter.shtml>, accessed August 2.

———. 2001b. <chicagotechtoday.com/chicagoinformation technologycenter.shtml>, accessed August 28.

Christopher, Thomas. 2002. The making of a woodland garden. *Martha Stewart Living* 182, no. 103 (June): 179–82.

City of Chicago. 2002. <w15.cityofchicago.org/trans/Wacker/pages/history.html>, September 12.

———. 2004a. Midway airport terminal development program now complete. <egov.cityofchicago.org>, June 8.

———. 2004b. Celebration for five-year progress toward transforming public housing. <egov.cityofchicago.org>, June 14.

———. 2004c. <cityofchicago.org/Press Release>, July 10.

———. 2004d. <cityofchicago.org Press Release>, July 19.

———. 2004e. <egov.cityofchicago.org/airfieldmodernization>, July 25.

———. 2005. Celebration for five-year progress toward transforming public housing. <egov.cityofchicago.org/city>, accessed March 3.

City of Chicago. Department of Planning and Development (DPD). 1966. *The comprehensive plan of Chicago*. December.

———. 1996. Vision for Greater State Street. <ci.chi.il.us/PlanAndDevelop/Programs/RetailChicago/51.html>.

———. 1997. Vision for Greater State Street: Next steps.

———. 2000a. Chicago's central area plan: Phase 1 progress report, draft for review. Steering committee meeting. November 30. Cited in the text as CAP.

———. 2000b. Chicago's North Loop theater district: Rebirth of a dream. Luncheon meeting, City of Chicago Department of Planning and Development and Daniel P. Coffey Associates. November.

———. 2000c. TIF program. January 10. <ci.chi.il.us/PlanAndDevelop/Programs/TIF/CentralLoop.html>, accessed December 12.

———. 2001. Economic base and sector analysis, central area,

Chicago, IL, 2000–2020 report. Compiled by Arthur Andersen. March.

City of Chicago. DPD State Street Commission. 1995. State Street renovation project. Chicago.

———. 1996a. State Street: That great street. Overview of renovation plan. January 22.

———. 1996b. State Street development project. Produced with Skidmore, Owings, and Merrill. Chicago.

———. 2003. Landmarks Division materials.

City of Chicago. Department of Transportation. 1999–2000. *Millennium Park News*. Spring 1999, Winter 1999–2000.

———. 2001. Millennium Park plan. Lakefront millennium project.

City of Chicago. Office of the Mayor. 2000. *Technology education integration plan*. Mayor's Council on Technology and Workforce Development subcommittee report.

———. 2001a. Mayor Daley hails city's top ranking as business site. Press release, February 27.

———. 2001b. Old Loop Woolworth building to be rehabilitated. Press release, February 27.

———. 2001c. Mayor Daley welcomes new Sears store to Loop. Press release, May 23.

———. 2001d. Mayor Daley, McCormick Tribune executives and private donors cut ribbon on spectacular skating rink at Millennium Park. News press release. December 20.

———. 2002a. Mayor's state of the city address. City hall, February 26.

———. 2002b. City council designates historic Michigan Boulevard Streetwall a Chicago landmark district. Press release, February 27.

———. 2002c. Chicago greening symposium. Speech delivered by Mayor Richard M. Daley. March 8. <Greeningsymposium_speech_3/22/02>.

———. 2002d. Chicago theater district welcomes Noble Fool Theater. Press release, March 25.

———. 2003. Mayor Daley releases plan to end homelessness: New strategy emphasizes permanent social services. Press release, January 21.

City of Chicago. Public Buildings Commission (PBC). 2004. Millennium Park sculpture named Cloud Gate by artist Anish Kapoor. 29 June. <pbcChicago.com/subhtml/press/pr_millennium_park_sculpture.asp>.

Coffey, Dan. 1997. Chicago redevelops State Street—again. *American City and County* 112, no. 8, 26-31.

Cohen, Stuart E. 1976. *Chicago architects*. Chicago: Swallow Press.

Collins, Randall, and Michael Makowsky. 1978. *The discovery of society*. Rev. ed. New York: Random House.

Condit, Carl. W. 1952. *The rise of the skyscraper*. Chicago: University of Chicago Press.

———. 1964. *The Chicago School of Architecture: A history of commercial and public building in the Chicago area, 1875–1925*. Chicago: University of Chicago Press.

———. 1973. *Chicago, 1910–1929: Building, planning and urban technology*. Chicago: University of Chicago Press.

———. 1974. *Chicago, 1930–1970*. Chicago: University of Chicago Press.

Cook, John W., and Heinrich Klotz, eds. 1973. *Conversations with architects*. New York: Praeger.

Corfman, Thomas A. 2000. State Street revival marches to steady beat. *Chicago Tribune*, October 20. Business section, pp. 1–2.

———. 2001a. Dearborn center to be bastion for citadel firm. *Chicago Sun-Times*, February 21. Inside Real Estate, section 3, p. 2.

———. 2001b. Rival to Block 37 project: Planned tower would vie for some retail condo buyers. *Chicago Tribune*, June 14.

———. 2001c. State Street's boom runs into economic wall. *Chicago Tribune*, October 5. Business section.

Corfman, Thomas A., and Blair Kamin. 2001. Cool economy casts shadow over new plan for Block 37. *Chicago Tribune*, January 21.

CRCD. City of Chicago. 1999. DPD. Chicago River Corridor Plan.

CRCDGS. City of Chicago. 1999. DPD. Chicago River Corridor Design Guidelines and Standards.

Cremer, Jill (for Trump International). 2005. Phone interview, March 31.

Cronon, William. 1991. *Nature's metropolis*. New York: W. W. Norton.

Daley, Richard M. 2001. A new economy for Chicagoland: Growth strategy. *Chicago Technology Today*, August 1.

Dealerspotlight. 1999. *Leicaview* (Spring): 17.

Dear, Michael J., ed. 2002a. *From Chicago to L.A.* Thousand Oaks, CA: Sage.

———. 2002b. Los Angeles and the Chicago School: Invitation to a debate. *City and Community* 1.1 (March): 5–32.

DeStefano + Partners. 2001a. RiverBend projects.

———. 2001b. RiverView projects.

———. 2001c. Waterfront projects.

Dickinson Group. 2001. The Heritage at Millennium Park. In-house materials and personal interview with Michelle Nisonboim, December 19.

Downtown is up. 1998. *Economist* 348, no. 8082 (August 22): 22–24.

Eaton, Leonard K. 1964. *Landscape artist in America: The life and work of Jens Jensen*. Chicago: University of Chicago Press.

Edgerton, Michael, and Kenan Heise. 1982. *Chicago: Center for enterprise*. Woodland Hills, CA: Windsor.

Elie, Paul. 2001. Broad shoulders, gentle shoreline. *New York Times*, May 13. Travel section, p. 1.

Ethington, Philip J., and Martin Meeker. 2002. Saber e concer: The metropolis of urban inquiry. In Dear 2002a, 403–20.

Evans, James. 2002. Bumpy runway for Bensenville owners? *Crain's Chicago Business* 25, no. 1 (January 7): 5.

Facts about Chicago, 2001. 2002. <chipublib.org/004chicago/chifacts.html>, accessed September 5.

Faris, Robert E. L. 1970. *Chicago sociology, 1920–1932*. Chicago: University of Chicago Press.

Ferkhenoff, Eric. 1995. Tradition, service, quality are central to this camera store. *Chicago Sun-Times*, May 18. Special advertising supplement, p. 2.

Fine, Gary Alan, ed. 1995. *A second Chicago school?* Chicago: University of Chicago Press.

Finley, Larry. 2002. Rising along the river. *Chicago Sun-Times*, May 31.

Fishman, Robert. 1996. Beyond suburbia: The rise of the technoburb. In LeGates and Stout 1996, 485–92.

Flesch, Donald. 2001. Personal interview. July 7.

Flicker, Russell. 2004. Phone interview, June 17.

Foerstner, Abigail. 1988. Approaching 90, Central Camera is a three-generation saga. *Chicago Tribune*, December 23. Section 7, p. 83.

Friedman Properties. 1999. Friedman Properties to restore the Traffic Court Building. Friedman Properties materials.

Friedmann, John. 1986. The world city hypothesis. *Development and Change* 17:69–84.

Friends of the Chicago River. 2001a. Mission statement. August 13. <chicagoriver.org>.

———. 2001b. CRCD Plan message points. June 25. <chicagoriver.org>.

Gallagher, Patricia, and Philip Enquist. 1997. "That Great Street" homes for a comeback. *Planning* 63, no. 1 (January): 12–15.

Gallis, Michael, and James S. Russell. 2002. World city. *Architectural Record*, March issue, 70–73.

Gateway Center IV, Chicago. 2003. <skyscrapers.com/english/worldmap/building/0.9/117140>.

Gehry, Frank. 1989. Frank Gehry: Pritzker Architecture Prize Laureate. <pritzkerprize.com/gehry.html>, accessed January 19, 2002.

———. 2002a. Phone interview, February 11.

———. 2002b. Above the curve. Transcript of interview between Frank Gehry and Scott Pelley. *CBS—Sunday Morning*. First aired July 28.

Gehry, Frank O., Associates. 2002. Millennium Park Plan. Description and sketches, internal reports, received January 18, 2002.

———. 2002–2005. E-mail correspondence.

GGN. *See* Gustafson, Guthrie Nichol.

Giampetro, Bob. 2003. What's in store. Report by Cynthia Bowers. *Sunday Morning News—CBS*. Aired November 30, 2003.

Giedion, Sigfried. 1941. *Space, time, and architecture*. Cambridge, MA: Harvard University Press.

Giovannini, Joseph. 2004. Boston architects Wood and Zapata stir up controversy at Chicago's Soldier Field. *Architectural Record*, May issue, 114–20.

Goffman, Erving. 1963. *Behavior in public places*. New York: Free Press.

———. [1974] 1986. *Frame analysis*. Boston: Northeastern University Press.

Goldberg, Bertrand. 1983. The critical mass of urbanism. Speech delivered at the Union International des Architects Working Group Habitat, in Washington, D.C. April.

———. 1991. Introduction: Involvement of water. In *Process Architecture 96: Composition of oceanic architecture*, 13, 19–24. Tokyo: Process Architecture.

———. 1992. *Oral history*, comp. Betty J. Blum. Chicago: Department of Architecture, Art Institute of Chicago.

———. 1993. What does "housing" mean in the twenty-first century? Housing conference speech, Aspen, CO, February 25.

Gopnik, Adam. 2003. Under one roof. *New Yorker*, September 22.

Gornick, Vivian. 1996. *Approaching eye level*. Boston: Beacon Press.

Gottdiener, Mark. 1997. *The theming of American dreams, visions and commercial space*. New York: HarperCollins.

Grant Park Conservancy. 2004. <grantparkconservancy.com>.

Greater State Street Council (GSSC). 1997. *Vision for the future of Greater State Street* (Vision plan).

———. 2000. Greater State Street annual summary report.

———. 2000. Greater State Street status: Summary report. October.

———. 2001. Executive committee meeting minutes, April 10, May 8, June 12.

———. 2001. Greater State Street status: Summary report. January 1.

———. 2001–2005. E-mails.

———. 2005. <greaterstatestreet.com>.

Grese, Robert E. 1992. *Jens Jensen*. Baltimore: Johns Hopkins University Press.

Grossman, Kate. 2001a. N. city making big plans for empty Loop park. *Chicago Sun-Times*, May 3. Metro section, p. 14.

———. 2001b. Unique downtown shops. *Chicago Sun-Times*, May 27. Metro section, p. 14A.

GSSC. *See* Greater State Street Council.

Gustafson, Guthrie Nichol. 2002. 100 percent design development narrative for Monroe "shoulder" garden. Project materials. April.

Guy, Sandra. 2001a. New formula for Loop Sears. *Chicago Sun-Times*, May 7. Business section, p. 47.

———. 2001b. Big names part of Sears' state opening. *Chicago Sun-Times*, May 18. Media Mix section, p. N62.

———. 2002. State Street seeks identity. *Chicago Sun-Times*, March 25, 2002.

———. 2006. Hip retailer to fashion new outfit here. *Chicago Sun-Times*, January 13. Business section, p. 62+.

Guy, Sandra, and David Roeder. 2002. McCafe concept hasn't been grounded. *Chicago Sun-Times*, May 14.

Haller, Benet (for the City of Chicago, Department of Planning and Development). 2002. Telephone interview, January 24.

Handley, John. 2001a. The next magnificent mile(s)? Historic South Michigan Avenue seems set for a major residential influx. *Chicago Tribune*, June 10.

———. 2001b. The next best thing to Michigan Avenue: How about Wabash? *Chicago Tribune*, August 12.

———. 2001c. Living down by the riverside is on the rise. *Chicago Tribune*, November 3.

Harris, Neil. 1993. The city that shops: Chicago's retail landscape. In Zukowsky 1993, 179–99.

Harris, Richard. 1991. The geography of employment and residence in New York since 1950. In Mollenkopf and Castells 1991, 129–52.

Harvey, Lee. 1983. Myths of the Chicago School. Paper no. 1, Occasional Paper Series, Research Unit, Department of Sociology, City of Birmingham Polytechnic, Birmingham, England. May.

Hasbrouck, Wilbert R. 2001. Historic avenue. *Chicago Tribune*, February 3.

Hawthorne, Mary. 1996. All alone in the city. *New York Times*, October 12. Book review section, p. 12.

Hayden, Dolores. 1995. *The power of place*. Cambridge, MA: MIT Press.

Heidegger, Martin. 1962. *Being and time*. San Francisco: Harper and Row.

Hepp, Rick. 1999. Architecture: An interview with Larry Booth. *Chicago Tribune*, December 28.

Herguth, Robert C. 2001. Wacker to be a headache till fall '02. *Chicago Sun-Times*, January 30. News section, p. 5.

Heritage at Millennium Park. 2001. <heritagecondo.com/home.html>, accessed December 12. Available.

Herrick, Robert. 1898. *The gospel of freedom*. New York: Macmillan.

Herman, Eric. 2004. McDonald's rolls out its future. *Chicago Sun-Times*, July 13.

Hermann, Andrew. 2004. One with the show, at long last. *Chicago Sun-Times*, July 17.

Hoch, Charles, and Robert Slayton. 1989. *New homeless and old: The community and the Skid Row Hotel*. Philadelphia: Temple University Press.

Holophane. 2002. Historically styled lighting helps make State Street stately again. <holophane.com/product/case/statest.html>, accessed September 1.

Horan, Jim. 2003. Phone interview, August 17; e-mail, August 19.

Hoyt, Homer. 1939. *The structure and growth of residential neighborhoods in American cities*. Washington D.C.: GPO.

Huxtable, Ada Louise. 1986. *Architecture, anyone?* Berkeley and Los Angeles: University of California Press.

———. 1988. *Kicked a building lately?* 1976. Berkeley and Los Angeles: University of California Press.

Inside Publications. 2002. <insideonline.com/site/epage/6087_162.html>, accessed July 17-23. Available.

Irace, Fulvio. 1988. *Emerging skylines*. New York: Watson-Guptil.

I-street. 2000. Tech facilities boom in Chicago. August. <i-street.com>.

Jacobs, Jane. 1961. *The death and life of great American cities*. New York: Random House.

Jahn, Helmut. 2001. Navy Pier and river projects. Murphy/Jahn, Inc., materials.

Jahn, Tony, and Andrea Schwartz. 2004. Personal interview. January 8.

Jencks, Charles. 1993. *Heteropolis*. New York: St. Martin's Press.

———. 2002. *The new paradigm in architecture*. New Haven: Yale University Press.

Jensen, Jens. [1939] 1990. *Siftings*. Baltimore: Johns Hopkins University Press.

Jukes, Peter. 1990. *A Shout in the Street*. Berkeley and Los Angeles: University of California Press.

Kamin, Blair. 1996. Stately street. *Chicago Tribune*, November 15. Section 5, p. 1.

———. 1999. Vertical triumph. *Chicago Tribune*, October 17.

———. 2001a. A clear vision: Office building boom shifts focus to a new kind of modernism. *Chicago Tribune*, January 21. Architecture section.

———. 2001b. Plan looks like a real beauty, unlike its beastly predecessor. *Chicago Tribune*, January 21. Metro section.

———. 2001c. Michigan Avenue divided on plan for landmark zone. *Chicago Tribune*, January 28.

———. 2001d. Blanket landmarketing is the best way to save Michigan Avenue. *Chicago Tribune*, February 1.

————. 2001e. Local heroes: Chicago firm creates a better Block 37. *Chicago Tribune,* February 4.

————. 2001f. Another window into the Wright world of design. *Chicago Tribune,* May 27.

————. 2001g. Building up to a lively scene. *Chicago Tribune,* September 9.

————. 2001h. Foundation for change. *Chicago Tribune,* September 9.

————. 2001i. Icons look like targets in wake of attack. *Chicago Tribune,* September 13.

————. 2001j. Trump sets sights lower: Proposes 78-story tower for Chicago riverfront. *Chicago Tribune,* December 12.

————. 2001k. Trump's skyscraper reaches for mediocrity. *Chicago Tribune,* December 19.

Kamin, Blair, and Thomas A. Corfman. 2001. Trump's vision? Architect's plan for a 2,000-foot Chicago tower may offer a peek underneath billionaire's tent. *Chicago Tribune,* September 11.

Kaufmann, Edgar, ed. 1970. *The rise of an American architecture.* New York: Praeger.

Kaufmann, Edgar, and Ben Raeburn, eds. 1960. *Frank Lloyd Wright: Writings and buildings.* New York: Horizon.

King, Anthony D., ed. 1996. *Re-presenting the city.* New York: New York University Press.

Konkol, Mark J., and Fran Spielman. 2005. Daley wins OK for O'Hare makeover. *Chicago Sun-Times,* September 29.

Koolhaas, Rem. 2002. Interview with Charlie Rose, transcript no. 3167. PBS: WNET, New York City. First aired March 25.

Krieger, Alex. 1998. Whose urbanism? *Architecture* 87 (November): 73–77.

Krier, Leon. 2001. Interview by Nikos Salingaros. The future of cities: The absurdity of modernism. <planetizen.com /oped/item.php?id=35>, accessed November 6.

Krontoft, Margrethe, Dan McMillen, and William Testa. 2001. Are central cities coming back? The case of Chicago. Chicago: Federal Reserve Bank of Chicago. December. No. 172A [special issue].

Kuroyanagi Akio. 1991. Oceanic architecture: Creating ocean space. *Process Architecture 96: Composition of oceanic architecture,* 14–18. Tokyo: Process Architecture.

Lahey, John (for Solomon Cordwell Buenz & Associates, AIA). 2001. Telephone interview, August 27.

Landers, Amanda, ed. 2001. Boeing chooses Chicago as center of new corporate architecture. *Boeing News Release,* May 10. <boeing.com>.

Landon Bone Baker, Architects. 2004–2005. Project materials for Archer Courts and Westhaven Park.

Landon, Peter, and Catherine Baker. 2004–2005. E-mails and correspondence.

————. 2005. Personal interviews, January 5.

Lefebvre, Henri. 1991. *The production of space.* Oxford: Blackwell.

LeGates, Richard T., and Frederic Stout, eds. 1996. *The city reader.* London, New York: Routledge.

Lin, Maya. 2000. *Boundaries.* New York: Simon and Schuster.

Livingston, Heather. 2005. Millennium Park Station offers viable commuting option. *AiArchitect,* March 28. <aia.org>.

Longworth, Richard C. 2002. Chicago has entered the global era. *Chicago Tribune,* August 25.

Loveridge, Gareth (for GGN, LLP). 2002–2005. E-mail correspondence.

————. 2003. Phone interviews.

————. 2003. Revised narrative for Monroe Garden. April.

————. 2004. Revised narrative for Lurie Garden, June.

Lowe, David. 1979. *The great Chicago fire.* New York: Dover.

————. 1985. *Lost Chicago.* New York: American Legacy Press.

Lynch, Kevin. 1960. *The image of the city.* Cambridge, MA: MIT Press.

Mansell, George. 1979. *Anatomy of architecture.* New York: A & W.

Martinotti, Guido. 1994. The new social morphology of cities. Discussion paper series no. 16, UNESCO/MOST meeting, Vienna, Austria. February.

Mauman, Laura. 2002. Joan W. and Irving B. Harris commit $39 million to music and dance theater Chicago. Millennium Park Project press release.

Mayer, Harold M., and Richard Wade. 1969. *Chicago: Growth of a metropolis.* Chicago: University of Chicago Press.

Metropolis Magazine. 2000. Going to towns: New York. <metropolismag.com/html/content_0100/ny.html>. Available.

Midway Airport. 2002a. <chase.com/midway/about/about _midway.shtm_midwayexhibits.shtm>, September 23.

————. 2002b. A new midway has arrived. *Midway Airport Report,* no. 9 (Summer): 1–2.

————. 2002–2005. <ohare.com/midway/terminals/maps_fac ilities.shtm>. Available.

Millennium Park Project. 1999–2000. *Millennium Park News.* Newsletter. Winter.

————. 2002. Millennium Park Plan. Internal report.

Miller, Donald L. 1996. *City of the century: The epic of Chicago and the making of America.* New York: Simon and Schuster.

Miller, Ross. 1993. City Hall and the architecture of power: The rise and fall of the Dearborn Corridor. In Zukowsky 1993, 247–63.

————. 1996. *Here's the Deal.* New York: Knopf.

Mollenkopf, John H., and Manuel Castells, eds. 1991. *Dual city: Restructuring New York.* New York: Russell Sage Foundation.

Mumford, Lewis. 1952. *Roots of contemporary American architecture.* New York: Reinhold.

Muschamp, Herbert. 2000. It's history now, so shouldn't modernism be preserved, too? *New York Times,* December 17. Arts and Leisure, section 2, p. 1.

————. 2003. The scrimmage of old and new. *New York Times,* September 30. Arts section, p. E1.

NEGSC. See *A new economy growth strategy for Chicagoland.*

Newbart, Dave. 2001. State Street side of Sears. *Chicago Sun-Times,* May 23. News section, p. 4.

Newbart, Dave, and Lynn Sweet. 2005. FAA OKs O'Hare expansion, court grounds it. *Chicago Sun-Times,* October 1.

A new economy growth strategy for Chicagoland. 2001 Report. *City of Chicago:* Mayor's Council of Technology Advisors (Chicago Technology Today).

Newman, M. N. 1998. A former flapper roars to life. *Chicago Tribune,* October 15.

Nute, Kevin. 1999. "Ma" and the Japanese sense of place revisited by way of cyberspace. Paper presented at the Third

East-West Architectural Symposium, University of Hawaii at Manoa. April.

Office of the Mayor. *See* City of Chicago, Office of the Mayor.

O'Hare Airport. 2002. <ohare.com/ohare/terminals/terminal.shtm>, accessed September 23.

———. 2002–2005. <ohare.com/dba/about/statistics.shtm>.

———. 2004. <modernization.ohare.com/program.html>, accessed July 25.

108 North State Street. 2005. <108northstatestreet.com>.

O'Neill, Bob. 2002. S. Michigan landmark status welcome. Letter to *Chicago Sun-Times*, March 3.

One River Place. 2001. Real estate promotion. *Chicago Tribune*, October 28. Real Estate, section 16, p. 5L.

Oudolf, Piet. 1999. *Designing with plants*. Portland, OR: Timber Press.

———. 2002a. Phone interview, October 4 (also October 26).

———. 2002b. E-mail questionnaire, November 14.

Park, Robert Ezra. [1925] 1967. *The city*. Midway reprint, with Ernest W. Burgess and Roderick D. McKenzie. Chicago: University of Chicago Press.

———. 1974. *The collected papers of Robert E. Park*. Vols. 1–4. Edited by Robert K. Merton and Aron Halberstam. New York: Arno Press.

Piano, Renzo. 2002. Interview with Charlie Rose. PBS: WNET, NYC. First aired, August 27.

Pierce, Andy. 1999. Camera. *Skyline*, April 8, p. 1.

Polshek, James Stewart. 2000. Interview with Leonard Lopate. New York and Company. WNYC, New York, first aired: 3 December.

Pridmore, Jay. 2000. *A view from the river*. San Francisco: Pomegranate.

Ragon, Michel. 1986. *Goldberg: On the city*. Paris: Paris Art Center.

Rau, Deborah Fulton. 1993. The making of the merchandise mart, 1927–1931: Air rights and the plan of Chicago. In Zukowsky 1993, 99–117.

Revive Wacker Drive Project. 2001–2002. [a]. <w15.cityofchicago.org/trans/wacker/pages.html>.

———. [b]. <w15.cityofchicago.org/trans/Wacker/pages/overview.html>.

———. [c].<w15.cityofchicago.org/trans/Wacker/pages/achievements.html>.

Ritzer, George. 1992. *The McDonaldization of society*. 3rd ed. New York: McGraw-Hill.

The River Reporter. 2003. Friends of the River newsletter. Vol. 17, no. 2.

Roeder, David. 2001a. Challenges face plan for Block 37. *Chicago Sun-Times*, January 26.

———. 2001b. Developer building south and north. *Chicago Sun-Times*, March 21.

———. 2001c. Condo sales called slower at two sides. *Chicago Sun-Times*, April 4.

———. 2001d. Condo sales slowing. *Chicago Sun-Times*, April 26.

———. 2001e. Printer's Row condos planned. *Chicago Sun-Times*, May 21.

———. 2001f. New York firm to attend meeting on Block 37. *Chicago Sun-Times*, September 5.

———. 2001g. "World's tallest" plan lost in September 11 ruins. *Chicago Sun-Times*, December 19.

———. 2002a. Outlook good for downtown condos. *Chicago Sun-Times*, February 15. Business section.

———. 2002b. Block 37 attracts developers. *Chicago Sun-Times*, March 25.

———. 2002c. Condo slowdown hits home at Habitat Co. *Chicago Sun-Times*, July 31.

Roeder, David, and Fran Spielman. 2001. Bad timing, bad planning, bad vibes over the years. *Chicago Sun-Times*, June 21. Metro section, p. 8.

Rowe, Colin. 1956. Chicago frame. *Architectural Review* 120 (November): 285–89.

Ruda, Mark. 2001. One-mil SF East Loop mixed-use project gets nod. <Globest.com>, June 15. <heritagecondo.com/press_061501b.html>, accessed December 12.

———. 2002. Developer search begins anew for Block 37. January 14. <globest.com/RM1GN2154WC.html>, accessed March 29.

Ryan, George H. 2001. Governor Ryan, Mayor Daley welcomes Boeing home. Governor's press release, September 5.

Sachs, Lloyd. 2001. Film center's big break. *Chicago Sun-Times*, May 30. Showcase, Arts and Leisure, p. 41.

Salingaros, Nikos. 2001. Interview with Leon Krier, on Plantizen Web site. Accessed November 6.

Sassen, Saskia. 1996. Analytic borderlands: Race, gender and representation in the new city. In *Re-presenting the city*, ed. Anthony D. King, 183–201. New York: New York University Press.

———. 1998a. *Globalization and its discontents*. New York: New Press.

———. 1998b. Urban economics and fading distances. Second Mega Cities Lecture. November. <conflicts.org>.

———. 1999. Globalization and telecommunications: Impacts on the future of urban centrality. Conference paper.

———. 2000. *Cities in a world economy*. 2nd ed. Thousand Oaks, CA: Pine Forge.

———. 2001a. The city: Strategic site/new frontier. <conflicts.org/Numeros/33sassangl.html>, accessed November 6.

———. 2001b. *The Global City: New York, London, Tokyo*. Princeton, NJ: Princeton University Press.

———. 2003. The locational and institutional embeddedness of electronic markets: The case of the global capital markets. Manuscript draft.

Satler, Gail. 1999–2005. Personal Chicago journals. In author's possession.

Schlosser, Eric. 2001. *Fast food nation*. New York: Houghton Mifflin.

Schnell, Lisa. 2002. A brief history of Chicago. IEANEA <ieanea.org/features/chicago/chihist.html>, accessed September 3.

Schulze, Franz, and Kevin Harrington, eds. 1993. *Chicago's famous buildings*. 4th ed. Chicago: University of Chicago Press.

Schwartz, Chris. 1999. *The first comprehensive report on the state of tax increment financing in Chicago*. Chicago: Neighborhood Capital Budget Group. August.

Scott, Allen J., and Edward Soja, eds. 1996. *The city: Los Angeles and urban theory at the end of the twentieth century*. Berkeley and Los Angeles: University of California Press.

Scully, Vincent. 1991. *Architecture: The natural and the man-made*. New York: St. Martin's Press.

Sharoff, Robert. 2000. Two major projects for a once seedy Chicago area. *New York Times*, November 12. Real Estate, section 11.

———. 2001. Midway Airport is undergoing a major expansion. *New York Times,* February 25. Real Estate, section 11, p. 9.

Shevsky, Eshrev, and Wendell Bell. 1955. *Social area analysis.* Stanford: Stanford University Press.

Shinn, Marybeth, and Colleen Gillespie. 1994. The roles of housing and poverty in the origins of homelessness. *American Behavioral Scientist* 37, no. 4 (February): 505–21.

Sirefman, Susanna. 1996. *Chicago.* London: Artemis London.

Skertic, Mark. 2001. Tough times for renters. *Chicago Sun-Times,* May 28.

———. 2002. All racial groups took a piece of the pie. *Chicago Sun-Times,* August 20.

Skertic, Mark, and Scott Fornek. 2002. Lincoln Park becomes wealthiest community. *Chicago Sun-Times,* August 20.

Skertic, Mark, Lucio Guerrero, and Robert C. Herguth. 2002. Same neighborhood, different worlds. *Chicago Sun-Times,* August 27.

Skertic, Mark, and Andrew Hermann. 2002. Chicago area economy hummed in the 1990s. *Chicago Sun-Times,* May 15.

Smith, Adrian, and Phil Enquist. 1996. State Street: Reviving the heartbeat of the Loop. *Urban Land* (February): 14–19.

Smoron, Paige. 2001. McCafe is the anti-Starbucks. *Chicago Sun-Times,* May 3.

Sneed, Michael. 2001. The Donald is coming. *Chicago Sun-Times,* July 18.

Soja, Edward. 1989. *Post modern geographies: The reassertion of space in critical social theory.* London: Verso.

Soja, Edward, and Allen J. Scott, eds. 1996. *The city: Los Angeles and urban theory at the end of the twentieth century.* Berkeley and Los Angeles: University of California Press.

Solomon Cordwell Buenz & Associates. 2001a. Crate and Barrell.

———. 2001b. Heritage at Millennium Park.

———. 2001c. Sheraton Chicago and Hotel Towers.

———. 2001d. 100 N. State Street.

Sorkin, Michael, ed. 1992. *Variations on a theme park: The new American city and the end of public space.* New York: Hill and Wang.

Southwick, Richard (for Beyer Blinder Belle, Architects). 2001. Correspondence concerning the Merchandise Mart Project, August 13.

Spaeth, David. 1981. The Chicago School: Architecture series. Bibliography A581. Monticello, IL: Vance Bibliographies. October.

Spear, William. 1995. *Feng shui made easy.* New York: Harper-Collins.

Spielman, Fran. 1999a. Proposal to extend deck over river is criticized. *Chicago Sun-Times,* March 18. Metro section, p. 12.

———. 1999b. Developments bank on boom near the Loop. *Chicago Sun-Times,* December 1.

———. 2001a. Daley's dream of 24-hour Loop takes a hit. *Chicago Sun-Times,* April 8.

———. 2001b. Daley refuses to raise Block 37 subsidy. *Chicago Sun-Times,* May 9.

———. 2001c. Plan commission OKs luxury condos. *Chicago Sun-Times,* May 18, p. N62.

———. 2001d. Plan commission OKs luxury condos: Developers to link project to theater district. *Chicago Sun-Times,* June 15.

———. 2001e. City Hall wants Block 37 back. *Chicago Sun-Times,* June 21. Metro section, p. 8.

———. 2001f. Daley: Trump's got chance at world's tallest. *Chicago Sun-Times,* July 19.

———. 2001g. Millennium Park bailout continues. *Chicago Sun-Times,* August 7. Metro section, p. 10.

———. 200lh. Make Block 37 a "destination," city told. *Chicago Sun-Times,* September 8.

———. 2001i. Harrod's, city meet on Block 37. *Chicago Sun-Times,* December 20.

———. 2002a. City to seek Block 37 chief. *Chicago Sun-Times,* January 9.

———. 2002b. O'Hare plans change on the fly. *Chicago Sun-Times,* April 9.

———. 2002c. Yellow Cab seeks to bring Chicago London-style taxis. *Chicago Sun-Times,* September 19.

———. 2003a. City eyes smaller stores on Block 37 after Harrods talks fail. *Chicago Sun-Times,* March 27.

———. 2003b. New cab firm operating here: Yellow Cab awaiting city OK on London taxis. *Chicago Sun-Times,* June 19.

———. 2005. Mayor Daley grudgingly stands behind change. *Chicago Sun-Times,* September 21.

Spielman, Fran, and Robert Herguth. 2001. Plan aims to speed up Loop buses. *Chicago Sun-Times,* January 24. Metro section, p. 8.

Spielman, Fran, and David Roeder. 2001a. Projects don't pause for cooling economy. *Chicago Sun-Times,* March 12.

———. 2001b. Another Block 37 snag. *Chicago Sun-Times,* May 4. Business section, p. 59.

———. 2001c. Block 37 proposal rejected as city seeks open plan. *Chicago Sun-Times,* July 6.

———. 2002. Mills Corp. wins Block 37 rights. *Chicago Sun-Times,* June 25.

———. 2003. Chamber head files Block 37 as casino site. *Chicago Sun-Times,* May 22.

Stamper, John W. 1991. *Chicago's North Michigan Avenue.* Chicago: University of Chicago Press.

Steele, Jeffrey. 2000. A second life: Making architectural past serve the new century. *Chicago Tribune,* September 20.

Stoner, Madeline R. The globalization of urban homelessness. In Dear 2002a, 217–34.

Tabing, Ty. 2000. Personal interview, November 6.

———. 2001. Personal interview, January 5.

———. 2004. Personal interview, July 14.

———. 2000–2005. E-mail correspondence.

Talaske Group. 2002. Millennium Park Music Pavilion. <talaske.com/lfm.html>, accessed October 4.

Tamarkin, Bob. 1993. *The Merc: The emergence of a global financial powerhouse.* New York: HarperCollins.

Terkel, Studs. 1967. *Division Street: America.* New York: Pantheon.

———. 1985. *Chicago.* New York: Pantheon.

———. 1988. *The Great Divide.* New York: Pantheon.

Thomas, Jim, ed. 1983. The tradition and the legacy. *Urban Life* 11, no. 4. Special issue on the Chicago School. Beverly Hills, CA: Sage.

Thomas, William I., and Florian Znaniecki. 1918–1920. *The Polish peasant in Europe and America.* 5 vols. Chicago: University of Chiago Press.

Tigerman, Stanley. 2004. A critique of Soldier Field (after the fact). *Architectural Record,* May issue, 118.

Tita, Bob. 2002. Playing hardball at O'Hare. *Crain's Chicago Business* 25, no. 29 (July 22): 4.

Uhlir, Edward. 2000. Park it here. *Urban Land,* September, 36–37.

———. 2001. *Constructing Millennium Park.* Internal report for the Millennium Park Project.

———. 2002. Personal interview, January 9.

Van Vechten, Peter (for Skidmore, Owings & Merrill, Chicago). 2001. Personal interview, January 8.

———. 2000–2002. E-mail correspondence.

Venkatesh, Sudhir Alladi. 2000. *American project: The rise and fall of a modern ghetto.* Cambridge, Mass.: Harvard University Press.

Vision plan. *See* Greater State Street Council. *Vision for the future of Greater State Street.*

von Klan, Laurene. 1999. Letter written to Albert Friedman of Friedman Properties, February 23.

Waldheim, Charles. 2001. *Constructed ground: The Millennium Garden design competition.* Urbana/Chicago: University of Illinois Press.

Washburn, Gary. 2001a. Daley defends delay on Block 37 project, cites design changes. *Chicago Tribune,* January 24. Metro section.

———. 2001b. No financial clouds for Block 37 project, developer tells city. *Chicago Tribune,* January 26.

———. 2005. City giving the green light to Block 37 project—for real. *Chicago Tribune,* May 12.

Washburn, Gary, and Jim Kirk. 2003. WWBM-Ch. 2 eyes Block 37. *Chicago Tribune,* May 17.

Wendt, Lloyd, and Herman Kogan. 1952. *Give the lady what she wants.* South Bend: And Books.

Whyte, William Foote. 1988. *City: Rediscovering the center.* New York: Doubleday.

Willis, Carol. 1995. *Form follows finance.* New York: Princeton Architectural Press.

Wirth, Louis. 1928. *The ghetto.* Chicago: University of Chicago Press.

———. 1964. *On cities and social life: Selected papers.* Midway reprint, Chicago: University of Chicago Press.

Wolff, Jane. 2002–2003. Constructed ground: The Millennium Park competition. Book review. *Harvard Design Magazine* 17 (Fall/Winter): 79–81.

Wolinsky, Howard. 2001. How Chicago can seize the new economy future. *Chicago Sun-Times,* July 19.

World Gateway Program. 2002. <ohare.com/ohare/about_world _gateway_faq.shtm>, accessed September 25.

Wozniak, John. 2002. Personal interview, February 25.

Wright, Frank Lloyd. 1931. The tyranny of the skyscraper. *Modern Architecture: Published Lectures.* Princeton: Princeton University Press.

———. 1960. The destruction of the box. In Kaufmann and Raeburn 1960, 284–89.

Zorbaugh, Harvey W. 1929. *The Gold Coast and the slum.* Chicago: University of Chicago Press.

Zoti, Ed. 1985. River City. *The Reader,* August 23, 1–8.

Zukowsky, John, ed. 1984. *Chicago and New York: Architectural interactions.* Exhibition catalog. Chicago: Art Institute of Chicago.

———. 1993. *Chicago architecture and design, 1923–1993.* Chicago: Art Institute of Chicago; Munich, Germany: Prestel-Verlag.

INDEX

DeStefano, James, 84
DeStefano & Partners: Donnelley Building, 109–11, *110;* RiverBend, *104*–5; RiverView, 139–40
dialogue, 12
digital age aesthetics, 140
Dinkeloo & Associates: Burnett Building, 109–11, *110*
display windows, 28
diversity, 157
Donnellcy Building, 109–11, *110;* materials, 109; sculptures, 110
dormitories, 63
Downtown Lighting Master Plan, 29
Driehaus Foundation. *See* Richard H. Driehaus Foundation
dual city, 9–13, 78, 82, 83, 102, 212, 227; architecture design, 84–86; bascule bridges, 134; fractal forms, 200–202

e-port (Montgomery Ward warehouse), 106–8; landmarking, 106; symbolism of, 108; tenants, 107
easements, 39
Eckstorm, Christian: North Pier Terminal, 143–44
Economic Base and Sector Analysis, Central Area, Chicago, IL, 2000-2020 Report, 197
economic issues: class, 202–4; economic growth, 202–3, 222; employment, 204; income, 203; manufacturing, 85; relocating business headquarters, 102; service economy *vs.* manufacturing economy, 6; service sector, 218–20; street as marketplace, 67–72; tax bases, 6. *See also* class issues; demographics; globalization; TIF financing
EDGE tax credit, 102
elevated train. *See* Chicago Union Loop Elevated Railway
Energy Star rating, 212
Enquist, Phil, 12
Entenza, John, 36
Environdyne Engineers, 224
environmental issues, 212, 229. *See also* landscaping and landscape architecture
Ethington, Philip J., 25
ethnography, 25; life histories, 24; *vs.* historiography, 9–10

family: concept of, for cities, 95
Fannie Mae, 207

Federal Aviation Administration (FAA), 225
Federal Congestion Mitigation Air Quality Program, 229
Federal Highway Administration, 229
Federal Housing Authority (FHA), 95, 207
Federal Transit Administration, 229
Federal Urban Mass Transportation funding, 21
Festenstein, Mary, 107
Field, Marshall, 213. *See also* Marshall Field's and Company
FJV Venture, 232
Flesch, Donald, and family, 52–54
Flicker, Russell, 132
Ford Oriental Theater, 61; TIF benefits, 39
Forever 21, 66
fractal forms, 200–202
frame analysis, 26, 237; applied to river, 82–84, 87; applied to State Street, 26–35; asymmetry, 241; center and periphery, 82–84, 187; globalization, 90; Millennium Park, 157
Freddie Mac, 207
Friedman, Albert, 129
Friends of the River, 130, 132, 133
Frost, Charles: Navy Pier, *144*–46
Fujikawa, Johnson, Associates: Chicago Mercantile Exchange, 10, *11,* 87, 88–91, *89*
Fulton House, 105–6; walkways, 105
Fusco, Anthony, 209

Gallery 37 Storefront Theater, 63
Garden & Martin, 107
Garland Court, 195
Gateway Center IV (300 South Riverside Plaza), 100–101
Gehry, Frank, x, 154, 185, 208
Gehry Partners, LLP: BP Pedestrian Bridge, 162–65; Great Lawn, 158–59; Jay Pritzker Music Pavilion, 159–62; Walt Disney Concert Hall, 185
Gene Siskel Film Theater, 61
Gensler, 107; e-port, 106–8
gentrification, 68–69, 73, 96, 200, 201
Ghetto, The (Wirth), 25
Giampetro, Bob, 46
Giaver & Dinkenberge: Jewel-

ers Building, 135
glass, 84
glass-reinforced concrete (GRFC) panels, 61
Gleacher Center, *137*–38; educational facility, 137; style, 137
global cities. *See* dual city; globalization
globalization, 83, 156; class issues, 202–4; effect on central city, 187; effect on Chicago River, 77; frame analysis, 90; markets, 70; polarization, 202–4; service sector, 218–20
GLOBEX, 88
Goettsch, James, 84
Goffman, Erving, 26, 169
Gold Coast, 199
Gold Coast and the Slum, The (Zorbaugh), 25
Gold Coast Dogs, 223
Goldberg, Bertrand, 29, 86, 90, 181, 240; "city within city," 95; Marina City, 5–6, 91–92; Raymond Hilliard Center, 211; River City, 6–7, 92–95; sociology joined with architecture, 211; vision, 4–7
Goodman Theater extension, 38, 61; seating, 62; TIF benefits, 39
Gospel of Freedom, The (Herrick), 35
Graham, Anderson, Probst & White, 29, 189; Merchandise Mart, 111–12, 129; Reliance Building, 56–58; Wrigley Building, 134–35
Graham, Ernest, 36
Grant Park, x, 154, 192; buildings framing park, 196–97. *See also* Millennium Park
Grant Park Conservancy, 196–97
Great Chicago Flood (1992), 22
Great Fire of 1871, 19
Great Lawn, *122*–*23,* 158–59
Greater State Street Council (GSSC), 15, 23, 237. *See also* Chicago Loop Alliance
green developments, 212
greenspace, 33–35
grid, 98–99, 172; public housing, 210
Griggs, Eric, 223
Gustafson Guthrie Nichols: Lurie Garden, 176–84

Haller, Benet, 84, 111, 132, 143, 204
Hammond, Beeby and Babka, 66

Hancock Building, 87
Hanson, Booth, 55
Harold Washington College, 63–65
Harold Washington Library, 38, 66–67, *117*
Harris Theater (Joan and Irving), 63, 165–67, *166;* lighting, 165; mid-sized groups, 167; nonprofit groups, 165; space of flows, 167; space of place, 167
Harris Theatre (Goodman), 61
Harrod's, 234
Harry Caray's, *128,* 223
Hartray, Jack, 96
Harvard, 25
Hayden, Dolores, 31, 174
Haymarket Riot, 218
Helmick, Ralph, 223
Here's the Deal (Miller), 236
Heritage at Millennium Park condominium tower, x, 194–96, *195;* design, 195; grid, 195; influences, 195; materials, 195
Herrick, Robert, 35
heteropolis, 157, 229
high-tech corridors, 100–101, 107
Hill, Christopher, 68, 129
historiography. *See* ethnography
HNTB Architects and Engineers, 222
Hobo, The (Anderson), 25
Holabird, William, 36, 66
Holabird and Roche, 66, 189; McCormick Building, 192; Palmer House Hilton Hotel, 54–55
Holabird and Root, 47; Soldier Field, 230–32, *231*
Holophane Corporation, 30
Home Suite Home exhibit, *128*
homelessness, 10, 72–74; federal policy, 207; housing issues, 206–7; panhandlers, 22
Homestart Program, 209
Hope VI Revitalization Plan, 210
Horan, Jim, 215
Hot Tix, 63
Hotel Burnham (Reliance Building), 37, 38, 56–58, *57;* archives, 11; Atwood Café, 56, 57; TIF benefits, 39
housing, 73, 201; affordable, 205–11, 234; homelessness, 206–7; households with children, 202; middle-class, 192; mixed-income, 207, 209, 210; mixed-use residencies, 90, 197, 200; prices, 200;